AI MASTERY

FOR FINANCE PROFESSIONALS

Foundations, Techniques, and Applications

Leaders
Press

by GLENN HOPPER

PRAISE

"Glenn Hopper is my most trusted source on AI in finance. *AI Mastery for Finance Professionals*, filled with practical wisdom and real-world examples, is an essential resource for anyone looking to navigate the AI revolution."

~ Conor Grennan, CEO, AI Mindset
& Best-Selling Author of *Little Princes*

"AI is transforming corporate finance, and Glenn Hopper is the perfect guide to this revolution. As the host of FP&A Today, Glenn has his finger on the pulse of the changes AI is bringing to finance departments. With this book, he expertly translates complex AI concepts into practical guidance for CFOs. It's not just about understanding AI – it's about harnessing its power to model budgets on the fly, surface hidden insights, and make data-driven decisions that propel your business forward. Glenn's insights are a must-read for any CFO ready to embrace the AI-powered future of finance."

~ Didi Gurfinkel, CEO and Co-Founder, Datarails

"The AI era is here, and it will usher in unmatched levels of efficiency and performance for businesses around the globe. Glenn Hopper's AI Mastery for Finance Professionals is essential for any finance professional looking to gain a better understanding of AI to drive innovation and strategic decision-making in their organization."

~ Stephen DeWitt, CEO, MindBridge Analytics

"Glenn is my go-to resource when it comes to AI's impact on finance professionals and institutions, and his new book does not disappoint. It's a brilliant guide that demystifies AI, packed with real-world applications and hands-on strategies that are sure to make an impact — both today and in the future. Highly recommend!"

~ Anna Talerico, CEO, Corporate Finance Institute

"A must-read for finance professionals, this book demystifies AI, equipping readers with the tools to engage confidently in AI projects within their organizations."

~ George Mount, Founder, Stringfest Analytics
& Author of *Modern Data Analytics in Excel* and *Advancing into Analytics*

"Glenn Hopper didn't just write the book on artificial intelligence — he wrote it twice! First, with *Deep Finance: Corporate Finance in the Information Age*, he transformed our understanding of how AI and automation are revolutionizing finance. Now, with *AI Mastery for Finance Professionals*, Glenn provides actionable, expert guidance on embracing AI to drive real impact in the finance world. With his forward-thinking insights, he has become a visionary in this field. If you want to stay ahead in the rapidly evolving landscape of finance, this book is an essential read!"

~ Don Tomoff, Founder, Invenio Advisors LLC

"With AI set to transform the finance function, finance professionals have several questions on how it works and its applications. With his deep, expert understanding of both finance and technology, Glenn Hopper is uniquely qualified to explain this. The book demystifies how AI/ML works. By providing readers a systematic understanding of AI, it will help them leverage it more effectively across functions and tasks. In fact, the book will be useful in explaining AI to all professionals, not just finance."

~ R. Ravikumar, Author of *The CFO Lens* and Ex-CFO of IBM India

"This book is for anyone in the finance industry looking to move beyond a surface-level understanding of AI. Glenn Hopper's expertise in both AI and finance shines through, providing readers with practical applications and real-world examples that demonstrate the transformative power of AI in finance. This book is not just about theory – it's about truly understanding AI at a deep level so you can harness its full potential."

~ Julio Martínez, Co-Founder & CEO, Abacum

"*AI Mastery for Finance Professionals* is an invaluable resource for any finance professional looking to dig deep into the foundations of AI. The book covers how AI and ML models work, how they can be applied to finance, and can be used to solve complex problems in areas such as fraud detection, customer analytics, and risk management. A must-read for anyone looking to truly level up their understanding of this powerful technology."

~ Damon Fletcher, Founder & CEO, Caliper

"Glenn Hopper has an extraordinary ability to make the complex seem simple. While many of his contemporaries focus heavily on technology and innovation in their space, Glenn's super power is doing this while never losing sight of mapping emergent capabilities back to pain points, use cases, and ultimately, outcomes. He has an exhaustive understanding of not only finance and operations, but equally important, he possesses a deep empathy for and understanding of the people involved in execution. He never loses sight of the 'why', and never stops asking 'what can be improved?'. Any finance leader would be well-served by his counsel."

~ Andrew Zwerner, CEO, Chassi

"Companies must learn to live with AI, or they will die without it. Glenn has command of the subject matter and understands its practicalities. This primer takes a daunting subject and makes it knowable for the reader. While you may not be an AI expert upon completion, you will know certainly more than nearly everyone else, and you will position yourself and your company to lead rather than lag. Thank you, Professor Hopper!"

~ David Waddell, President & CEO, Chief Investment Strategist, Waddell & Associates

"This book is an essential resource for finance professionals who recognize the growing impact of AI, but struggle to see how it fits into their daily work. Glenn Hopper expertly demystifies complex AI concepts and presents them in a way that is both practical and accessible."

~ Nicolas Boucher, Founder, AI Finance Club

"Glenn Hopper is a thought leader in how Artificial Intelligence works and can transform the finance function. He has laid out a practical foundation for CFOs and financial professionals to understand AI, lead its adoption, and leverage it to drive growth and efficiency. It's an essential guide for CFOs."

~ Michael Bayer, CFO, Wasabi

"Glenn Hopper is the right person to write a book on AI and finance. I appreciate that his book is about much more than just generative AI. Glenn has always been my go to resource when it comes to finance and technology and this book is a must read for finance professionals looking to better understand the benefits of AI."

~ Paul Barnhusrt, Founder, The FP&A Guy

"Bluntly, this book isn't for everyone. But if you want to develop a deep understanding of how AI works and how it can be applied in finance, *AI Mastery for Finance Professionals* is a single source for all you need to know. Glenn has been forward-thinking on AI in finance from early days, and has written a foundational resource for finance professionals and students who want to dive deep into ML, how it works, and how it can be applied to finance."

~ Mitchell Troyanovsky, Co-Founder, Basis.ai

"Glenn Hopper is a visionary leader at the intersection of finance and technology, and is one of the most trusted voices on the integration of AI and finance. This book showcases his profound expertise and foresight. *AI Mastery for Finance Professionals* dives deep into AI theory and practical applications – from foundational AI concepts to the intricate details of machine learning, deep learning, and specific AI techniques tailored for finance."

~ Tom Hood, EVP of Business Engagement & Growth, AICPA-CIMA

"Glenn Hopper has uniquely captured the intersection of finance and artificial intelligence in a way that every modern CFO must understand. His deep expertise shines through in this comprehensive guide, making complex AI concepts accessible and directly applicable to the financial profession. As the role of the CFO evolves, driven by technological advancements, Glenn's insights will be invaluable for those looking to harness AI to drive strategic decision-making and operational excellence. This book is an essential read for finance professionals eager to stay ahead in the rapidly transforming landscape of finance."

~ Jack McCullough, President & Founder, CFO Leadership Council

"Glenn's ability to blend technical know-how with real-life applications and examples is unmatched. This is the most complete source of information on AI and finance I've ever seen."

~ Adam Shilton, Founder - Shilton Digital / Technologist, TEDx Speaker, Consultant

"As a long time CFO and executive for large public, small private and PE backed organizations, AI is something that boards expect us to have some direction on. Similarly being in the technology services industry currently, our customers are looking to us to help understand when is the right time to make investments and where should those investments be made. Glenn's book gives clear direction on where we as financial leaders should focus our energy and dollars and is a must read for anyone, especially finance executives, to ensure you stay ahead of the competition."

~ Chris Caprio, CEO, Focus Technology

Leaders
Press

ISBN 978-1-63735-353-0 (hcv)
ISBN 978-1-63735-352-3 (pbk)
ISBN 978-1-63735-351-6 (e-book)

Library of Congress Control Number: 2024919958

AI MASTERY
FOR FINANCE PROFESSIONALS
Foundations, Techniques, and Applications

Leaders
Press

by GLENN HOPPER

CONTENTS

Contents

FOREWORD

Brian Chess
Senior Vice President, Technology and AI
Oracle NetSuite Global Business Unit
September, 2024

Since the beginning of recorded history, accounting has been at the forefront of many of the most critical breakthroughs in technology. Big breakthroughs like written language. And math.

Accounting has played this influential role by providing purpose and a proving ground for new technology. And today, AI is the latest gee-whiz technology for which accounting can provide a powerful sense of purpose and value. In fact, we need accounting — and accountants — to step up and help AI reach its potential.

But I'm getting ahead of myself. Before we jump into AI, I'll offer up some proof points for how accounting has led the way.

Let's start with written language. The earliest known writing system, created in Mesopotamia somewhere between 8000 and 3500 BC, used shaped clay tokens for accounting. It wasn't until thousands of years later that we started to see writing that matched the spoken word, to capture ideas beyond bookkeeping. (We then needed a few millennia more for pictograms to come back into fashion 😊).

Then consider math. Archeological records of simple counting techniques, like tally marks on the famed "Ishango bone," date back to earliest civilizations. But it wasn't until Sumerian and Babylonian societies needed to do large-scale accounting-ish tasks such as trading and taxing that what we recognize as modern math really took root.

Computing, one could argue, began with the abacus, a tool needed once activities such as trading required more than our 10 fingers to track. And while we can't really say the first computers as we know them today were built purely for accounting, certainly the widespread adoption of modern computer hardware and software was driven to support accounting and related business functions.

That takes us back to AI. As I was saying, accounting, it's time for you to step up once again. AI needs your sense of purpose. And your ironclad demand for trust.

The Demands of Finance Make Tech Better

With AI, we're at that key point of asking where and how much we can trust it. Applying AI to accounting will help deepen our understanding of where we are on the AI trust spectrum, and it could help AI to earn our trust.

Trust is the essential trick that all those historical technologies had to earn. "Don't worry, I scratched these marks into this clay tablet, and that really does mean you own these sheep now." How did people get comfortable with an idea like that? At the time, it was a significant leap. Or, how did people start trusting an IBM computer to make a company's payroll calculations rather than using the tried-and-true, see-it-on-paper way of doing it?

In every technology shift, people using it for accounting tasks had to come to believe in the new way of doing things. First, they had to conclude that the new method was superior, so the leap was worth taking, and then they had to trust the result.

Accounting is so important in this leap of technology adoption because it demands a right answer. If we just want to know *about* how many sheep you own, well, I can look over the field, eyeball it, and say, "Seems like about three dozen." You don't need accounting for that. You need accounting to get the correct answer. So accounting isn't going to accept technology that sometimes gets roughly the right answer.

Accountants, We Need You Again

Accountants aren't just casual observers in this process of assessing trust. They set standards, they demand verification, they demand visibility. Meeting those demands forces technology to get better.

In my day job, I think about these demands every day. I work with a team of software developers at NetSuite, where we're adding AI capabilities into business software that more than 40,000 companies run on. Essentially, we make those same two "clay tablet" calculations: Will this AI feature make life better? And can we trust the outcome? We think about whether AI in our software will make work easier for business professionals—from finance professionals counting cash to warehouse workers moving boxes—and whether the resulting data will be accurate. We know that in business, accountants will ultimately be the judge of that accuracy standard.

Trust comes from accepted norms and standards. If there is an error in a financial statement, everybody's going to be alarmed, and one key question will be, "Were we calculating that number using traditionally accepted practices, and an unusual problem just snuck in? Or did we attempt some newfangled approach that nobody's ever tried before?" Accountants aren't really looking for that latter experimental approach.

This cycle for establishing norms and building trust explain why Glenn Hopper's ideas in this book are so important right now. Accountants might hear about ideas like AI "hallucination"— where AI models simply make things up — and decide AI isn't ready for accounting. Instead, Glenn urges accountants and other financial professionals to push up their sleeves and get to work understanding AI. He lays out a process for digging into the models, risks, ethics, uses, and implementation approaches for AI.

As a finance professional, you'll benefit from doing that work and gaining that insight into AI. It will help you take control of your career as AI reshapes what people in accounting and other finance roles do. Your companies also will gain because you can guide them into using AI well, to save time, lower costs, and find new ways to use data.

And all the rest of us will also win, because you will force AI to get better. You will demand trust, transparency, and accuracy. You will expect consistency and verifiable outcomes. We're at a "clay tablets" moment for AI technology, where we're asking, "Can we trust it?" Accounting pros, we're looking to you to help us find the answer.

INTRODUCTION

Generative AI tools like ChatGPT and Claude have captured global attention in recent years by making the transformative power of artificial intelligence accessible to everyone; but the foundations of this technology run deep – stretching back much further.

For decades, AI has quietly powered a range of applications we use every day – from spam filters and product recommendation systems to advanced clustering algorithms. Machine learning, in particular, has been successfully deployed at scale across fields from marketing to finance for over a decade. We've seen AI embedded in everything from smart devices and homes to self-driving cars, often operating behind the scenes without most of us even noticing.

As someone who's spent the bulk of my career at the intersection of finance and technology, I've witnessed firsthand the immense potential of technology to revolutionize the way we work. This has never been more true than it is today with the rapid acceleration of AI capabilities.

But there's a significant gap in understanding AI among finance professionals, particularly those in non-technical roles. This is understandable; our education and careers have been focused on mastering our specific fields, not on becoming technologists. But the reality is that finance, like every other profession, is undergoing a transformation as AI capabilities rapidly evolve.

This book, *AI Mastery for Finance Professionals*, is my effort to bridge that gap. It's designed to be comprehensive and detailed, yet accessible to those without a background in AI or computer science. My goal is to elevate you from an AI novice to an informed user, no matter your current level of technical expertise.

Think back to when we first learned to use financial calculators — bulky, archaic devices that required manual input for complex calculations like Net Present Value (NPV) or the Capital Asset Pricing Model (CAPM). Even when spreadsheets made those calculations easier, understanding the underlying principles was still important to our larger understanding of the work we're doing. It wasn't enough to just punch in numbers; we needed to understand the formulas to make informed decisions.

The same principle applies to AI today.

It's not just about using AI and blindly trusting its outputs; it's about understanding the algorithms that power it, the data it relies on, and the assumptions it makes. Without this understanding, we risk making decisions based on blind faith, which is akin to trading complex financial instruments without fully grasping their mechanics, risks, and rewards.

It's a recipe for disaster!

As finance professionals, we've always valued our ability to analyze, question, and understand the tools we use. AI should be no different. By explaining and unraveling the mysteries of AI, we can move from passively accepting its outputs to actively shaping its applications, which will help us mitigate risks, drive innovation, create more precise tools, and find new ways to integrate this technology into our daily workflows.

The more we understand AI, the more we can innovate and enhance the value we bring to our profession. Whether you're an analyst looking to integrate AI into your investment strategies, a risk manager seeking more precise predictive tools, or an advisor aiming to deliver AI-powered personalized recommendations, this book will equip you with the insights and knowledge you need.

Throughout this book, we'll explore different types of AI, break down the algorithms that drive it, and examine how these technologies can be applied to various financial tasks. The focus will always be on you, the finance professional, with practical, real-world examples you can apply directly to your work.

Let's empower ourselves with a deep understanding of AI, and in doing so, shape a future where finance and AI work together to drive innovation, efficiency, and success.

ABOUT THIS BOOK

AI Mastery for Finance Professionals covers the fundamentals of AI, specific AI techniques used in finance, real-world applications of AI in various financial domains, practical guidance on implementing AI in financial institutions, and an outlook on the future of AI in finance.

Part 1: AI Fundamentals

The first part of the book lays the foundation by introducing the key concepts and techniques of AI, with a focus on machine learning and deep learning.

- **What is AI?** Defines AI and its levels, from ANI for specific tasks to the potential of AGI and ASI to match or exceed human intelligence. Discusses AI's learning and data processing capabilities.
- **Introduction to Machine Learning**: Covers the basics of machine learning, including supervised, unsupervised, and reinforcement learning, and explains key concepts like features, labels, training data, and model evaluation.
- **The Building Blocks of Deep Learning**: Dives into the fundamentals of deep learning, including artificial neural networks, activation functions, loss functions, and optimization algorithms. Introduces types of neural networks like convolutional and recurrent neural networks.
- **Training Deep Learning Models**: Explores the practical aspects of training deep learning models, including data preparation, model selection, hyperparameter tuning, and regularization techniques.
- **Deep Learning Applications in Finance**: Provides an overview of deep learning applications in finance, such as financial time series forecasting, algorithmic trading, fraud detection, and customer analytics.
- **Challenges and Future Directions**: Discusses current challenges in applying deep learning in finance, such as interpretability, data limitations, and computational requirements, and explores future directions like federated learning and quantum machine learning.

Part 2: AI Techniques in Finance

The second part of the book focuses on specific AI techniques that are particularly relevant to finance.

- **Computer Vision in Finance**: Explores applications of computer vision in finance, such as analyzing satellite imagery for economic forecasting, reading financial documents, and customer identification.
- **Natural Language Processing in Finance**: Covers how natural language processing is used in finance for sentiment analysis, news analytics, chatbots, and document processing.
- **Reinforcement Learning in Finance**: Introduces reinforcement learning and its applications in finance, particularly in algorithmic trading and portfolio optimization.
- **Generative Models in Finance**: Discusses generative models, like GANs, and their potential uses in finance, such as generating synthetic financial data and creating new financial products.
- **Graph Neural Networks in Finance**: Introduces graph neural networks and their applications in finance, such as fraud detection in transaction networks and modeling interconnections in financial systems.

Part 3: AI Applications in Finance

The third part of the book dives into specific applications of AI in different areas of finance.

- **AI in Trading and Investment Management**: Covers AI usage in algorithmic trading, portfolio optimization, asset pricing, and risk management.
- **AI in Risk Management and Fraud Detection**: Explores AI techniques used to identify and prevent fraudulent activities and manage various financial risks.
- **AI in Customer Service and Personalization**: Discusses how AI is transforming customer interactions through chatbots, robo-advisors, and personalized financial services.
- **AI in Lending and Credit Assessment**: Covers AI's role in automating and improving the accuracy of credit scoring and lending decisions.
- **AI in Regulatory Compliance**: Explores AI's contribution to compliance with regulations, such as AML and KYC requirements.
- **AI in Corporate Finance**: Examines how AI optimizes financial planning, forecasting, scenario analysis, and metrics tracking, enabling more accurate and strategic corporate decision-making.
- **AI in Investment Banking, Venture Capital, and Private Equity**: Uncovers AI-driven innovation in deal origination, due diligence, and portfolio management within these sectors.

Part 4: Implementing AI in Financial Institutions

The fourth part of the book provides practical guidance on how financial institutions can implement AI.

- **Developing an AI Strategy**: Discusses how to align a comprehensive AI strategy with the overall business strategy of a financial institution.
- **Building AI Capabilities**: Covers building AI capabilities, including data infrastructure, talent acquisition and development, and AI governance.
- **Partnering with AI Vendors**: Provides guidance on selecting and working with AI vendors and partners.
- **Measuring the Value of AI**: Discusses measuring the business value and ROI of AI initiatives.
- **AI Governance and Risk Management**: Covers establishing effective governance and risk management frameworks for AI.
- **Step by Step Guide to Implementing AI**: Provides a summary guide to AI deployment.

Part 5: The Future of AI in Finance

The final part of the book looks ahead to the future of AI in finance.

- **Emerging AI Technologies**: Explores emerging AI technologies, such as explainable AI, federated learning, and quantum machine learning, and their potential applications in finance.
- **The Impact of AI on Financial Jobs**: Discusses AI's likely impact on jobs in the financial sector, including roles most likely to be automated and potential new roles.
- **Ethical Considerations in Financial AI**: Covers ethical considerations in applying AI in finance, such as fairness, transparency, and accountability.
- **Regulatory Outlook for AI in Finance**: Discusses the current and future regulatory environment for AI in finance, including existing regulations and expected developments.
- **AI and the Transformation of Finance**: Provides a forward-looking perspective on how AI is likely to transform the financial industry, impacting business models, customer experiences, and the competitive landscape.

By the end of this book, readers will have a deep understanding of AI in finance, from the fundamental techniques to the practical applications, and will be equipped with the knowledge and insights needed to navigate the AI-driven future of finance.

Chapter One

WHAT IS ARTIFICIAL INTELLIGENCE?

Throughout human history, very few technological advancements have held the power to reshape industries, redefine the nature of work, and challenge the very foundations of our economic systems. We stand now in the early stages of a technology that is poised to rival the invention of the wheel, the printing press, and the Internet ... combined. Artificial intelligence has the potential to upend not only the world of finance, but our very lives as we know them.

It is important as potential users and beneficiaries of this technology that we develop a core understanding of how it works.

Let's start with a simple explanation:

Artificial Intelligence (AI) is a branch of computer science that aspires to mimic human thought. It accomplishes this through an array of technologies and approaches ranging from rule-based systems to advanced algorithms that can learn from data through experience, adapt to new inputs, and perform human-like tasks by processing inputs and recognizing the patterns within them. This might include recognizing images of objects and faces, making decisions, understanding and communicating in natural language, or even creating original art and music.

AI engineers have made tremendous strides toward this goal in recent years, with AI systems now capable of performing tasks that were once thought to be the exclusive domain of human intellect.

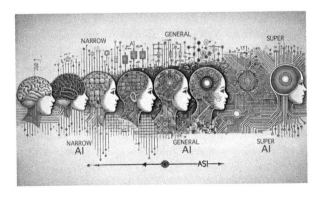

Levels of AI

To better understand the current state and future potential of AI, it's useful to categorize AI systems based on the scope and complexity of the tasks they can perform.

AI researchers often distinguish between three levels of AI:

Artificial Narrow Intelligence

Artificial Narrow Intelligence (ANI), also known as Weak AI, represents the current state of AI technology, where systems are engineered to perform specific tasks exceptionally well within a narrowly defined scope. Unlike human intelligence, which is versatile and capable of adapting to a wide range of activities, ANI is specialized and limited. These systems are designed to excel in particular functions such as voice recognition, image classification, or recommendation generation. In these focused areas, ANI often performs with remarkable efficiency and accuracy, sometimes even surpassing human abilities in specific tasks.

AI-powered virtual assistants like Siri, Alexa, and Google Assistant process spoken language, respond to queries, and execute commands with a level of speed and precision that can be difficult for humans to consistently match ... well except for Siri (depending on when you're reading this). Similarly, recommendation systems on platforms like Netflix and Amazon analyze user behavior and preferences to deliver personalized content suggestions, tailoring recommendations to individual tastes. This reflects the nature of AI systems we are dealing with today: focused, efficient, and highly specialized in their respective domains.

While ANI programs may excel in their designated areas, these systems lack the general intelligence, adaptability, and self-awareness that characterize human cognition. They don't understand context beyond their programmed functions and can't transfer knowledge from one domain to another. For example, a virtual assistant that is excellent at scheduling meetings or playing music can't suddenly learn to perform a completely different task, such as driving a car or diagnosing a medical condition, without being explicitly reprogrammed and retrained for that new purpose. This narrow focus distinguishes ANI from more advanced forms of AI, such as Artificial General Intelligence (AGI), which remains a theoretical concept. Despite their limitations, ANI systems are highly effective within their domains and have been integrated into many aspects of modern life, from personalized shopping experiences to customer service automation, marking significant progress in the field of artificial intelligence.

Artificial General Intelligence

Artificial General Intelligence (also referred to as Strong AI) is the ambitious and *currently* theoretical frontier of artificial intelligence — where machines would possess the ability to perform *any* intellectual task that a human being can. Unlike ANI, which excels in specific, well-defined tasks, AGI would exhibit a broad, adaptable intelligence, capable of reasoning, planning, solving complex problems, thinking abstractly, and learning quickly from experience across a wide array of domains. An AGI system would move beyond programmed instructions, possessing the capacity to understand context, draw from huge knowledge bases, and apply its intelligence creatively to new, unforeseen challenges. This level of intelligence would essentially mirror the cognitive abilities of a human mind, potentially even exceeding human capabilities in processing speed and access to information.

While exciting, AGI remains a largely theoretical concept; there are significant scientific, technical, and philosophical challenges to overcome along the way. Tasks such as replicating the nuances of human cognition (e.g. consciousness, self-awareness, emotional understanding, and ethical decision-making) are well outside the capabilities of current AI systems. With the recent meteoric rise of AI capabilities, the timeline for achieving AGI has become an ongoing debate. Some experts predict it could emerge within a few years, others suggest decades, and others argue it may never be realized. If achieved, AGI would completely transform human life in ways most of us can't yet imagine. This raises a litany of ethical concerns, particularly around the control, safety, and alignment of such powerful systems with human capabilities.

Artificial Super Intelligence

Artificial Super Intelligence is the next hypothetical advancement beyond AGI. A super intelligent system would surpass human cognitive abilities in virtually every domain. While AGI aims to replicate the broad intellectual capacities of the human mind, ASI would vastly exceed it as the machines would be able to learn and grow without human intervention. The implications of such a system are profound. Imagine how such a system might be applied to scientific discovery, mathematical formulas, and creative problem-solving. ASI systems would have the ability to learn, adapt, and innovate at a pace and scale far beyond human capabilities, potentially leading to breakthroughs in fields ranging from medicine and engineering to ethics and governance.

While such prospects are amazing to consider, they come with their own set of potential dangers and reasons for concern. On one hand, ASI could unlock unprecedented technological possibilities, solving some of the world's most intractable problems, such as curing diseases, addressing climate change, and even advancing human knowledge and civilization. But such a system would also bring ethical and existential risks. The power of an ASI system could be so great that it might pose a threat to humanity if not properly controlled and aligned with human values. There are concerns about whether humans would be able to retain control over such a superintelligent entity and whether its goals would necessarily align with ours. The potential for unintended consequences or malicious use of ASI technology adds to the gravity of these concerns. Despite the intense interest and debate surrounding ASI, it remains a speculative concept, deeply rooted in science fiction ... for now. The path from AGI to ASI certainly fuels much imagination and discourse, but the actual realization of ASI is still far beyond our current technological horizon.

Key Characteristics of AI Systems

Despite the diversity of AI systems, they tend to share some key characteristics:

Ability to Learn and Adapt

Perhaps the most distinctive capability of AI systems is their ability to learn and improve their performance over time. Unlike traditional software programs that are rule-based and designed to execute predefined instructions, AI systems adapt their behavior based on new inputs. Once the core model is trained, it is able to use what it has learned when exposed to new data.

AI learning could be supervised (where the system is trained on labeled data), unsupervised (finding patterns in unlabeled data), or reinforcement-based (where the system learns through trial-and-error interactions with its environment). This learning ability allows AI systems to improve their performance on tasks over time, discover new patterns and insights, and even perform new, emergent tasks they weren't originally designed for.

Ability to Process Large Amounts of Data

AI systems are able to process and analyze data much faster and more efficiently than humans. This is extremely valuable in a big data environment, where data is being generated at an unprecedented scale. AI systems could help us make sense of this data deluge by quickly identifying patterns, correlations, and anomalies in large datasets. AI systems can provide valuable insights and predictions that would be difficult or impossible for humans to discern.

Ability to Recognize Patterns and Make Predictions

AI systems can recognize complex patterns in data and use those patterns to make predictions or decisions. By learning from data, machine learning models are able to make predictions on new, unseen data, which has applications in a wide range of business processes – from predicting consumer behavior for targeted advertising to forecasting stock prices.

Common Misconceptions about AI

Despite the rising influence and visibility of AI, several misconceptions persist around its nature and capabilities, making it essential to clarify these misunderstandings for informed discourse about AI's role in society.

It is important to understand that AI is not a singular, unified technology. It is an ever-expanding collection of tools and programs that includes a variety of technologies, techniques, and approaches, including machine learning, natural language processing, computer vision, and robotics. Another common misunderstanding is the conflation of AI with automation. While AI can be used for automation, not all automation requires AI. Traditional automation like the mechanical processes used in manufacturing or, more recently, simple rule-based systems in software, does not necessarily involve AI. The difference between traditional automation and AI-driven automation is that AI is capable of learning and adapting over time; not just executing a fixed set of instructions.

One of the most common concerns since the advent of generative AI and the proliferation of large language models is the widespread fear that AI will eliminate huge swaths of human jobs and professions. While AI will certainly automate many tasks and alter the nature of work, it is unlikely to lead to the complete replacement of human employment in the foreseeable future. It is more likely that AI will generate new types of jobs, such as AI ethicists, trainers, and explainability specialists, who will be crucial in guiding and interpreting AI systems. Much of human work will continue to require complex social, emotional, and creative skills that AI is not yet capable of replicating. Just as every preceding technological revolution has driven socio-economic shifts, the AI-driven future will undoubtedly change the nature of work. But it is yet unclear how these changes will manifest themselves.

Looking Ahead

The field of AI has made remarkable progress in recent years, and is poised to have an even more transformative impact in the coming decades. From self-driving cars to personalized medicine to intelligent financial forecasting, the potential applications of AI are broad and exciting.

The development of this new technology also brings with it a host of important questions.

- How can we ensure that AI systems are fair, transparent, and accountable?
- How do we prepare for the economic disruptions that AI may cause?
- How do we ensure that the benefits of AI are widely shared and not just concentrated in the hands of a few tech giants?

Answering these questions will require ongoing collaboration and dialogue between AI researchers, policymakers, ethicists, and the academics. It will also require a commitment to developing AI in a responsible and human-centered way, with a focus on augmenting and empowering human capabilities rather than replacing them.

Artificial Intelligence is already transforming many aspects of our lives and has the potential to significantly reshape our world in the very near future. Whether you're a business leader looking to leverage AI for competitive advantage, a policymaker grappling with the societal implications of AI, or simply a curious individual fascinated by this transformative technology, a solid grasp of the fundamentals of AI is essential.

The Evolution of AI

From its early origins in the 1950s to the current era of deep learning and big data, AI development has had a bit of a jagged road marked by periods of intense optimism and progress, followed by times of disappointment and reduced funding, often referred to as "AI winters." Despite these fluctuations, AI has persistently advanced, and stands even in its nascent stages as one of the most transformative and influential technologies of all time.

Early Origins: 1950s - 1970s

The field of AI began in the 1950s – a decade that saw the birth of the modern computer and the first attempts to create "thinking machines."

Alan Turing, often referred to as the "father of computer science," proposed his famous Turing Test in 1950 as a way to evaluate a machine's ability to exhibit intelligent behavior. The test involves a human operator engaging in natural language conversations with both a human and a machine programmed to generate "human-like responses." If the evaluator can't reliably distinguish the machine from the human, the machine is said to have passed the test.

The term "Artificial Intelligence" was introduced in 1956 during the Dartmouth Conference, which marked the official birth of AI as a field. The early AI researchers who attended the conference were optimistic in their belief that any aspect of learning or intelligence could be precisely defined and replicated by a machine within a matter of years. While the attendees vastly underestimated the time it would take to create true artificial intelligence, their vision sparked an area of research that has persisted for decades and culminated in recent years in an explosion of artificially intelligent machines integrated across our personal and professional lives.

During the early years of AI research, scientists focused largely on problem-solving and symbolic methods. They developed algorithms for playing chess, proving mathematical theorems, and understanding simple English sentences. Allen Newell and Herbert A. Simon developed The General Problem Solver (GPS) in 1957 as a first attempt at a universal problem-solving machine. While the machine fell short of its creators goals, it was a key part of the foundation of the field along with the Perceptron and other early inventions. These early efforts ultimately did not achieve the desired results, as computers at the time were not powerful enough to handle the complexity of real-world problems. Many of the early successes were limited to toy examples in controlled environments.

The AI Winters: 1970s - 1990s

Funding and interest in AI research faltered during the 70s and 80s in a period known as the "AI Winter." The limitations of computer hardware at the time, combined with the realization that many AI problems were much more complex than initially thought, led to a period of disillusionment, but AI research continued – albeit at a slower pace.

There was a bit of an emergence in the field in the 1980s, when we saw the rise of "expert systems," which used rule-based reasoning to mimic the decision-making ability of a human expert. These systems were widely used in industries like finance, medicine, and manufacturing. Later in the decade and into the 1990s, there was a resurgence of interest in AI, driven by the success of these expert systems and the introduction of new techniques like machine learning and neural networks. This resurgence was short-lived, however, and another AI winter followed in the mid-1990s, again due to AI researchers and companies overpromising and under-delivering.

One bright spot for AI occurred as the millennium drew to a close. In 1997, IBM's Deep Blue, a powerful chess-playing computer, defeated the reigning world chess champion, Garry Kasparov, in a highly publicized match. This victory marked the first time a computer had ever beaten a world champion in a match under standard chess tournament time controls. The heavyweight bout between man and machine was seen as a landmark achievement for AI, showcasing the ability of machines to perform tasks that require complex decision-making and strategic thinking.

Deep Blue's victory over the greatest human player in the world sparked widespread debate about the potential of AI and the future of human-machine interaction, foreshadowing the significant advances in AI that would follow in the years to come.

Deep Blue was a world apart from "The Turk," the chess-playing machine created by Wolfgang von Kempelen in 1770. While Deep Blue was a genuine technological achievement, The Turk turned out to be an elaborate hoax. Though it appeared to be an automaton playing chess against human opponents, the machine was secretly operated by a hidden human chess master. The Turk toured Europe and America, defeating notable figures like Napoleon Bonaparte and Benjamin Franklin, before eventually being exposed as a fraud.

While The Turk was a clever hoax, it highlighted the fascination and skepticism that surrounded the idea of machine intelligence, a theme that would continue to play out in the centuries to come, culminating in real AI breakthroughs like Deep Blue's victory over Kasparov.

The Modern Era: 2000s - Present

The modern era of AI began in the early 2000s, driven by several factors, including the exponential growth in available data, computing power, and storage capacity, which enabled the training of much larger and more complex AI models. The explosion of data that accompanied the digital age kicked off the new era of "Big Data." When combined with increased computing power, this wealth of new data led to AI systems that were able to learn and improve in remarkable ways, which enabled researchers and engineers to create more effective machine-learning algorithms. "Deep Learning" was one of the biggest breakthroughs of this era, and has continued to gain in ability and prominence throughout.

As these models became increasingly powerful, the public at large started to witness their remarkable abilities.

In 2011, IBM's Watson computer defeated the reigning human champions on the TV quiz show *Jeopardy*, showcasing AI's ability to understand natural language and reason over massive knowledge bases. The following year, a deep learning system achieved human-level performance in the ImageNet challenge (a benchmark for object recognition in images), marking the beginning of the deep learning revolution that has since transformed the field, driving many of the advancements we see today.

A few years later, in 2016, when Google DeepMind's AlphaGo program defeated Lee Sedol, the world champion in the complex game of Go, there was a sense that the genie was out of the bottle. WIth its ability to display both qualitative and quantitative thinking, this application's abilities far exceeded those of even Watson and Deep Blue.

By 2020, OpenAI's GPT-3 language model using the transformer architecture demonstrated a remarkable ability to generate human-like text, sparking intense interest and debate about the future of AI in language and writing.

But beyond gaming and publicity stunts, AI has become a practical technology applied across various industries for the last decade or more. From self-driving cars and personalized medicine to intelligent financial forecasting and automated customer service, AI is transforming the way we live and work, impacting nearly every aspect of modern life.

The Future of AI

There are as many questions as there are opportunities regarding the future of AI. On one hand, the rapid progress in AI capabilities opens up immense possibilities: We can envision a future where AI helps solve seemingly intractable global challenges like climate change, disease outbreaks, and poverty; and is harnessed to augment human capabilities, making us smarter, more productive, and more creative. On the other hand, the increasing power and pervasiveness of AI also surfaces significant challenges and risks: Concerns include AI's impact on jobs and the economy, its potential to be used for surveillance and control, and the existential risk posed by the possibility of artificial superintelligence.

There are also important questions and concerns about the ethics and governance of AI:

- How can we ensure that AI systems are fair, transparent, and accountable?
- How do we align AI systems with human values and ensure they are used for beneficial purposes?

The concern of many today is that we are barreling forward with the advancement of this technology without putting the necessary guard rails and safety systems in place to control it.

Why AI Matters in Finance

AI's ability to process data, identify patterns, and make complex decisions is already impacting a wide range of financial activities in areas ranging from trading and risk management to customer service and regulatory compliance.

For years, financial services have grown increasingly digitized with customers interacting with financial institutions via mobile apps, online platforms, and digital assistants – generating a ton of data in the process. With AI, companies can make sense of this data and derive valuable insights from it. In this landscape, we have seen the rise of financial technology (fintech) companies and digital-native firms disrupting traditional financial services. These companies are leveraging AI to offer innovative, personalized services that are challenging the old guard of the industry. Traditional financial institutions must adopt AI to stay competitive in this shifting terrain. Due to the changes in recent years, customer expectations are evolving. Accustomed to the personalized, on-demand services offered by big tech companies, they now expect the same level of service from their financial providers. AI enables financial institutions to meet these expectations by providing personalized recommendations, 24/7 customer support, and seamless user experiences.

In addition to these industry-wide changes, there are several specific factors driving the adoption of AI in finance:

Explosion of Financial Data

Financial institutions now have unprecedented access to huge amounts of information, ranging from transaction records and market data to online sentiment and news articles. This influx, often termed "Big Data," offers the potential for deeper insights into market trends, customer behavior, and economic conditions. But the sheer volume and complexity of this data make manual analysis nearly impossible. By harnessing advanced algorithms, machine learning models, and natural language processing techniques, AI can process and analyze these massive datasets at scale. These sophisticated algorithms allow financial institutions to uncover patterns, correlations, and insights that traditional methods could never achieve.

Examples of AI in action include real-time analysis of millions of transactions to detect fraud, monitoring social media sentiment to predict stock market movements, and analyzing news articles to evaluate the impact of global events on financial markets. Through these applications, AI is already transforming raw data into actionable intelligence, empowering institutions to make more informed decisions.

Need for Real-Time Decision-Making

Financial markets can change in an instant, with prices, interest rates, and other key indicators fluctuating rapidly. Delays in decision-making in this fast-paced environment can lead to missed opportunities or significant losses, and traditional methods of data analysis, which have historically relied on batch processing and human intervention, are simply too slow to keep up with these demands.

AI addresses this need for speed by enabling near-instantaneous data processing and analysis. Machine learning algorithms can continuously monitor financial data streams, identify trends, and generate insights in real-time. The relatively new field of high-frequency trading arose when investors realized how AI-driven systems could execute trades within milliseconds to capitalize on minute price discrepancies before they disappear.

Pressure to Improve Efficiency and Reduce Costs

Financial institutions are under relentless pressure to improve operational efficiency and reduce costs. This drive for efficiency is fueled by the need to maintain profitability in a volatile and increasingly competitive market. Traditionally, many financial operations have been labor-intensive, involving manual data entry, compliance checks, and customer service tasks. These processes are not only time-consuming but also prone to human error.

With AI, companies are able to automate many of these routine tasks, freeing up human workers to focus on higher-value activities that require critical thinking and creativity. For instance, AI-powered chatbots can handle a large volume of customer inquiries, reducing the need for human agents. Automated data processing tools can quickly and accurately manage vast amounts of financial data, from transaction records to regulatory filings. By reducing the reliance on manual processes, AI helps institutions lower operational costs while improving accuracy and efficiency.

Intensifying Competition

The financial sector is facing intensifying competition, driven by the rise of fintech startups and the encroachment of tech giants into traditional financial services. These new entrants are leveraging advanced technologies, including AI, to offer innovative products and services that challenge established firms by using AI to provide personalized financial advice, automate lending decisions, and offer seamless digital banking experiences. In response to this competitive pressure, traditional financial institutions are increasingly turning to AI as a means of differentiation and innovation. By adopting AI, these institutions can enhance their product offerings, improve customer experiences, and streamline operations. AI can be applied to develop personalized investment strategies for clients, detect fraudulent transactions more effectively, and optimize their trading strategies.

Given these drivers, it's not surprising that AI is being applied across a wide range of financial domains. It is being used in trading and investment management to analyze market data, make trading decisions, and optimize portfolio allocations. In risk management and fraud detection, AI algorithms are identifying potential risks and suspicious activities far more efficiently than human analysts ever could.

In customer-facing applications, AI is powering chatbots and virtual assistants that provide 24/7 customer support. It's also enabling personalized financial advice and product recommendations tailored to each customer's unique needs and circumstances. Even in back-office functions like credit assessment and regulatory compliance, AI is changing the nature of how we work. Machine learning models are making credit decisions more accurate and less biased, while natural language processing algorithms are helping firms stay on top of constantly evolving regulations.

Wealthfront (www.wealthfront.com), a pioneer in the robo-advisory space, exemplifies how AI is revolutionizing personal finance. The platform uses sophisticated algorithms to create and manage personalized investment portfolios, automatically rebalancing them to optimize returns while minimizing risk. By leveraging AI, Wealthfront offers a level of customization and efficiency that was once only available from traditional financial advisors, but at a fraction of the cost. Additionally, the platform's AI-driven features, such as tax-loss harvesting and financial planning tools, provide clients with tailored advice and strategies that adapt to their individual financial goals and changing circumstances. Wealthfront's use of AI is not only democratizing access to high-quality financial advice but also setting a new standard for the industry.

For financial institutions, the adoption of AI is becoming a strategic imperative. Firms that successfully leverage it can gain a significant competitive edge, offering more innovative products, making better decisions, and adapting more quickly to market changes. Conversely, firms that fail to adopt AI risk falling behind and losing market share to more technologically advanced competitors.

The adoption of AI brings significant challenges, including data privacy, algorithmic bias, job displacement, and technological dependence. Financial institutions must address these issues with strategic care and strong governance.

As AI advances, its impact will become increasingly significant. To thrive in this new era, institutions will have to not only understand AI, but actively embrace and harness its power.

Chapter Two

INTRODUCTION TO MACHINE LEARNING

What is Machine Learning?

Machine Learning (ML) is a subset of Artificial Intelligence focused on developing algorithms capable of learning from data, identifying patterns, and making decisions with minimal human intervention. Unlike traditional programming, where a developer writes explicit instructions for every possible scenario, ML models are designed to learn and improve their performance based on the data they process. This means that instead of being programmed for specific tasks, they learn from examples and use that experience to make predictions or decisions. As these algorithms are exposed to more data over time, they can refine their algorithms, leading to increasingly more accurate outcomes.

The core strength of ML lies in its ability to generalize from the data it has seen to new, unseen data. A machine learning model trained to recognize images of cats and dogs, for instance, will not just memorize the images it was trained on. It additionally will learn to identify features such as shapes, colors, and textures that distinguish one from the other. When presented with a new image, the model will use what it has learned to make an educated guess about whether the image contains a cat or a dog. This ability to generalize makes ML powerful in a broad range of applications, enabling it to be used in a wide range of problems, from spam detection in emails to recommendation systems in e-commerce.

However, the effectiveness of an ML model heavily depends on the quality and quantity of data it is trained on. If the data is biased, incomplete, or unrepresentative, the model's predictions will likely be flawed, reflecting those biases or gaps. Further, building a successful ML model requires careful consideration of factors like selecting the right algorithms, fine-tuning hyperparameters, and evaluating the model's performance using appropriate metrics. By understanding these nuances, we will be better able to deploy ML effectively in real-world applications.

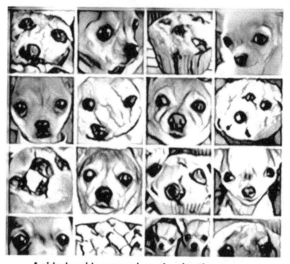

A side-by-side comparison showing the uncanny resemblance between a chihuahua's face and a blueberry muffin, highlighting how machine learning models (and also human brains) can find unexpected visual similarities between unrelated objects.

Definition and key concepts

Learning from Data

The ability for ML systems to evolve and improve by learning from data is fundamental to the value of the technology. Instead of relying on explicit programming, ML models are able to identify patterns within vast datasets, then use what they've learned to make informed decisions. The beauty of ML is its ability to function with minimal human intervention once the initial model is trained. By continuously ingesting new data, these systems refine their predictions and decisions over time, becoming more accurate and efficient as they encounter new scenarios, enabling them to tackle complex problems that would be difficult or impossible to solve with traditional programming approaches.

Models

Machine learning models are mathematical representations of real-world processes. These models are the core tools that allow ML systems to make predictions or decisions based on input data. The model's structure is determined by the specific ML algorithm chosen (e.g. linear regression, decision trees, neural networks, or support vector machines). During the training phase, these models are "taught" by adjusting their parameters to minimize errors in predictions, enabling them to generalize from the training data to new, unseen inputs. The accuracy and effectiveness of an ML model depend on its ability to capture the underlying patterns in the data without overfitting to the noise or specificities of the training set.

Training and Testing

Developing an effective machine learning model involves training and testing phases. Datasets are divided into subcategories and applied to the training, testing, and validation of the models. Initially, the model is trained using a subset of the available data, known as the training data. This data includes input-output pairs (in supervised learning) that allow the model to learn the relationships between variables. Once trained, the model's performance is evaluated using a separate set of data, known as testing data, which it has not seen before. This testing phase assesses the model's generalization ability—its capacity to apply learned patterns to new data accurately. A successful model will perform well on both the training and testing data, indicating it has learned the underlying patterns without overfitting to the specifics of the training set. In some applications, the data is also validated in a third step with a previously unseen subset of the original data.

Difference between traditional programming and Machine Learning

In traditional programming, developers explicitly define the rules and logic that a computer must follow, crafting specific instructions for every possible scenario it may encounter. This approach requires a deep understanding of the problem domain – the developer needs to anticipate all potential inputs and prescribe the correct responses. Conversely, machine learning shifts the paradigm by allowing systems to learn the rules directly from the data by analyzing it to identify patterns and relationships. These models are effectively teaching themselves the rules needed to make decisions or predictions, which is particularly powerful for complex problems where defining explicit rules would be impractical or impossible.

Traditional programs are static and deterministic, meaning they produce the same output for a given input every time. This predictability is beneficial in environments where consistency is key, but it limits the program's ability to adapt to new information. Machine learning models, on the other hand, are dynamic: they evolve as they are exposed to more data, continuously improving their accuracy and effectiveness. This adaptability, combined with ML's ability to automatically scale to handle large and complex datasets, allows machine learning to tackle problems that are beyond the reach of traditional programming approaches. ML can identify and leverage subtle patterns in big data, providing insights and solutions that would be impossible to achieve through explicit programming alone.

The Machine Learning process

Machine Learning Process Flow

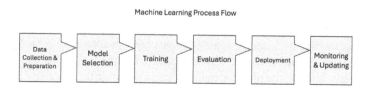

Data Collection and Preparation

The first step in any machine learning project is data collection and preparation. This step involves gathering relevant data that will be used to train the model. Once collected, the data needs to be preprocessed, which includes cleaning to remove any noise or irrelevant information, formatting to ensure consistency across datasets, and transforming it into a format suitable for the ML algorithm. Preprocessing may also involve feature selection and engineering, as well as data normalization, where data is scaled to a uniform range.

Model Selection

Next, it's time to select the appropriate model. In this phase, a suitable ML algorithm is chosen based on the nature of the problem being solved and the characteristics of the data. Models include decision trees, neural networks, and support vector machines, all of which have different strengths. Neural networks, for example, are often used for complex tasks like image recognition, while decision trees might be preferred for more interpretable models. The selection process may involve trying out multiple algorithms and comparing their performance on the specific dataset to identify the most effective one.

Training

The training process involves optimizing the model's weights (parameters that determine the importance of different input features) and biases, which adjust the output independently of the input, through techniques like gradient descent to minimize error, which enables the model to accurately capture patterns in the data and make reliable predictions or decisions on new inputs.

While this process is essential for building an effective model, it also highlights a critical aspect of model training: the balance between bias and overfitting. Bias and overfitting are interconnected through the bias-variance tradeoff in model training. High bias leads to underfitting, where a model is too simplistic and fails to capture underlying patterns, which results in poor performance on both training and new data. On the other hand, low bias can lead to overfitting, where a model becomes overly complex and captures noise in the training data, causing it to perform well on training data but poorly on unseen data. The challenge is to balance bias and variance to create a model that accurately captures patterns without overfitting, ensuring it generalizes well to new data.

Evaluation

After the model is trained, its performance has to be evaluated to ensure it generalizes well to unseen data. This is done by testing the model on a separate dataset, known as testing data, which was not used during the training phase. The evaluation process typically involves calculating metrics such as accuracy, precision, recall, and F1-score. The model's generalization ability is assessed by how well it performs on the testing data compared to the training data. If the model performs well, it is considered ready for deployment.

Deployment

When a model passes the evaluation phase, it is deployed into a production environment, where it is able to make predictions or decisions based on real-world data. Deployment involves setting up the necessary infrastructure of servers, Application Programming Interfaces (APIs), and various interfaces that connect the model to the data streams it will process. This phase also includes monitoring the model's performance in the live environment to ensure it continues to operate as expected.

Monitoring and Updating

Post-deployment, the model is continually monitored and updated to ensure it remains effective over time. As new data becomes available or as the environment changes, the model's performance may degrade. To ensure the model continues to improve as expected or, ideally, improve performance over time, the model may need to be retrained on new data, or continued fine-tuning of its parameters. If significant changes in the data or problem domain occur, the model may need to be replaced. Continuous monitoring ensures that the model remains accurate and relevant, and delivers consistent value.

Types of Machine Learning

Machine learning, the workhorse of modern AI, comes in three main flavors: supervised learning, unsupervised learning, and reinforcement learning. Each type has its own unique characteristics, strengths, and common algorithms.

Each type of machine learning has its strengths and weaknesses. The choice of which to use depends on the nature of the data and the problem. In many real-world applications, these approaches are often combined to build powerful AI systems. For example, an AI system for stock trading might use supervised learning to predict future prices, unsupervised learning to identify market regimes, and reinforcement learning to optimize trading decisions.

Supervised Learning

Supervised learning involves feeding an algorithm a set of input-output pairs, allowing it to learn a mapping function that can predict the output for any given input. The primary objective of supervised learning is to develop a model that can generalize well to new, unseen data, meaning it can accurately predict the output when presented with novel inputs outside the training dataset.

The term "supervised" is used because this method of learning is similar to a teacher guiding students in the human learning process. During training, the algorithm makes predictions based on the input data, and these predictions are then compared to the actual, correct outputs provided in the labeled dataset. The difference between the predicted and actual outputs is used to adjust the model's parameters, with the aim of reducing errors in future predictions. This process is repeated iteratively, with the algorithm gradually improving its accuracy as it learns from its mistakes, much like a student receiving feedback and improving their understanding over time.

Supervised learning can be applied to a wide variety of tasks, including classification, where the goal is to categorize inputs into distinct classes (such as determining whether an email is spam or not), and regression, where the aim is to predict a continuous output (such as estimating house prices based on various features). The performance of a supervised learning model is typically measured using metrics like accuracy, precision, recall, or mean squared error, depending on the specific task at hand. Achieving high performance requires not only a well-designed algorithm but also a well-curated training dataset that is representative of the real-world scenarios the model will encounter. Supervised learning is a structured and highly effective way to train models for a wide range of predictive tasks.

Some popular supervised learning algorithms include:

- Linear Regression for predicting continuous values
- Logistic Regression for binary classification
- Decision Trees and Random Forests for both classification and regression
- Support Vector Machines (SVMs) for classification
- Neural Networks for learning complex non-linear relationships

Applications of Supervised Learning in Finance

Supervised learning is the most commonly used type of machine learning in finance. It's particularly useful for prediction and classification tasks where there is historical data with known outcomes.

Supervised learning is used heavily in credit scoring and loan approval to help financial institutions make more accurate lending decisions and manage their risk exposure. By training on historical data about borrowers' characteristics and their repayment behaviors, supervised learning models can learn to predict the likelihood that a new applicant will default on a loan..

Supervised learning is also widely used for fraud detection, where it is trained on historical patterns of fraudulent and legitimate transactions. Once the models are trained, they are able to flag new transactions that show signs of potential fraud in real-time – something that was not possible with human effort alone. This is particularly valuable in an era where financial fraud is becoming increasingly sophisticated and hard to detect manually.

Another area where supervised learning has been used successfully is in predictive analytics for financial markets. By training models on historical market data, firms are able to better predict future price movements, volatility, or the likelihood of certain events like company defaults or mergers. While financial markets are notoriously difficult to predict with high accuracy, machine learning is helping to uncover complex patterns and improve the quality of financial forecasting.

Unsupervised Learning

Unsupervised learning operates without the guidance of labeled data. Its goal is to uncover the underlying structure, patterns, and relationships within the data on its own. The algorithm is provided with input data, but isn't given any corresponding outputs or labels. Instead, the algorithm must identify and learn from the inherent features of the data to identify clusters, associations, or anomalies, which makes it particularly useful for tasks where the goal is to explore and understand the data rather than make specific predictions.

One popular use case for unsupervised learning is to identify customer segments in marketing data, where the algorithm groups customers based on similarities in purchasing behavior, demographics, or other features. These discovered patterns can then inform targeted marketing strategies for each segment or customer type.

Unsupervised learning is also frequently used as a precursor to more complex tasks in ML engineering, such as in feature learning, where the algorithm identifies important attributes that can be used to improve the performance of supervised learning models.

It is used heavily in exploratory data analysis (EDA), where the goal is to uncover insights from the data without any preconceived notions. Techniques like clustering (e.g., k-means clustering) help group data points with similar characteristics, while dimensionality reduction methods (e.g., Principal Component Analysis or PCA) simplify datasets by reducing the number of variables while retaining most of the original information. Unsupervised learning is also used in data compression, where it helps reduce the amount of data storage needed by identifying and eliminating redundancy.

In finance, unsupervised learning is used for tasks such as:

Customer Segmentation

Using unsupervised learning, it is possible to analyze a dataset of customers with various attributes to identify distinct groups that share similar characteristics and group them into clusters or segments. The customer segments can then be targeted with customized marketing strategies. For instance, a financial institution might segment its customers based on attributes like income level, spending habits, and product preferences, which could be used to tailor specific products, offers, or communication strategies

for each group. This approach enhances marketing effectiveness and improves customer satisfaction by addressing the unique needs and preferences of each group.

Anomaly Detection

Anomaly detection is used to identify unusual transactions or activities that deviate from the norm within a dataset. This inherent ability is incredibly useful in fraud detection, as computers are much better at identifying anomalies than humans. By training a model on a dataset of normal financial transactions, the system can learn what constitutes typical behavior. Then when a new transaction is processed, the model assesses whether it fits the established pattern or if it exhibits anomalies that might indicate fraud.

Portfolio Diversification

Investment managers work to diversify their portfolios to manage risk by spreading investments across various assets or groups of assets that behave differently under the same market conditions. The goal is to minimize exposure to any single asset or risk factor, thereby reducing the overall volatility of the portfolio. Machine learning algorithms can help in this diversification by identifying groups of investments that tend to move together (i.e., have high correlations), which could give insights that help build a diversified portfolio that balances risk and return. This technique is fundamental in creating resilient investment strategies that can withstand market fluctuations.

Some common unsupervised learning algorithms include:

- K-Means for clustering data into groups
- Hierarchical Clustering for creating a hierarchy of clusters
- Principal Component Analysis (PCA) for reducing the number of variables while retaining most of the information
- t-SNE for visualizing high-dimensional data in a low-dimensional space

Applications of Unsupervised Learning in Finance

One key use case is customer segmentation. By clustering customers based on their financial behaviors, demographics, or other attributes, unsupervised learning can help financial institutions identify distinct customer groups and tailor their services accordingly. This can improve customer satisfaction, loyalty, and ultimately, profitability.

Unsupervised learning is also useful for anomaly detection in financial data. By modeling the normal behavior of a financial system, unsupervised learning algorithms can identify unusual patterns that may indicate errors, fraud, or impending financial distress. This can serve as an early warning system for financial institutions, allowing them to investigate and intervene before problems escalate.

In investment management, unsupervised learning can be used to identify hidden correlations and structures in financial markets, which can help investors construct more resilient portfolios that are less vulnerable to market shock to assist in portfolio diversification and risk management.

Reinforcement Learning

Reinforcement learning (RL) is similar to how humans are taught in schools. The students in RL are AI agents that learn by engaging directly with their environment. Unlike supervised or unsupervised learning, where the model is provided with data and outcomes, the RL agents must make decisions, take actions, and then learn from the consequences of those actions. The agent's objective is to maximize cumulative rewards over time by making choices that lead to desirable outcomes and avoid those that result in penalties.

This trial-and-error exploration is how the algorithm learns. The agent is not given explicit instructions on how to achieve its goals; instead, it must discover the best strategies through continuous interaction with its environment. After each action, the agent receives feedback in the form of rewards for actions that bring the agent closer to achieving its goals or penalties for actions that move it further away. Over time, the agent adjusts its behavior to maximize the total rewards and learns the optimal policy or strategy for navigating its environment.

Reinforcement learning is particularly well-suited for complex decision-making tasks where the consequences of actions unfold over time, such as in robotics, gaming, or autonomous systems. For example, in a game like chess, the agent must decide on moves without knowing the final outcome until the game ends. By learning which moves lead to winning positions, the agent gradually improves its strategy. This approach is used in robotics in exercises where an agent might learn to navigate a maze by receiving rewards for moving closer to the exit and penalties for hitting walls.

This training method allows the agent to develop sophisticated behaviors that would be difficult to program manually, making reinforcement learning a powerful tool for developing intelligent systems capable of adapting to dynamic and complex environments.

Reinforcement learning is well-suited for problems where decision-making is sequential and the goal is long-term, such as game-playing and robotics.

In finance, it's used for tasks like:

- **Algorithmic trading:** An AI agent learns to make trading decisions by maximizing profit over many trades.
- **Portfolio management:** An AI agent learns to adjust portfolio allocations by maximizing return and minimizing risk over time.
- **Financial chatbots:** An AI agent learns to provide personalized financial advice through conversations with users.

Reinforcement learning is built on several key concepts. At the center is the agent: the learner and decision-maker. The agent might be a person, a robot, or software. The agent functions within an environment (the world it interacts with). The state represents the agent's current situation in this environment, while an action is a decision the agent makes that affects the environment. As the agent takes actions, it receives a reward — feedback from the environment that indicates its performance. The policy is the strategy guiding the agent's decisions, mapping states to actions to maximize the reward over time.

Applications of Reinforcement Learning in Finance

Reinforcement learning is the least mature, but perhaps most promising type of machine learning for finance. It's particularly well-suited for problems that involve sequential decision-making under uncertainty, which is a core characteristic of many financial applications.

The most prominent application of reinforcement learning in finance is in algorithmic trading. By modeling the financial market as an environment and defining reward functions based on trading objectives, reinforcement learning agents can learn to make trading decisions in real-time based on market conditions. This can lead to more profitable and adaptive trading strategies compared to traditional rule-based approaches.

Reinforcement learning is also being explored for portfolio management. By learning to adjust portfolio weights based on changing market conditions and risk-reward tradeoffs, reinforcement learning agents could potentially outperform traditional portfolio optimization methods. However, this application is still in its early stages and faces challenges related to the high dimensionality and nonstationarity of financial markets.

Another promising application is in financial chatbots and robo-advisors. By using reinforcement learning to guide the conversation and provide personalized recommendations based on the user's responses and financial situation, these AI-powered agents could provide more engaging and effective financial advice compared to scripted or rule-based approaches.

Use Case	Description
Credit Scoring	Given a dataset of individuals' financial histories and whether they defaulted on a loan, learn a model to predict the risk of default for new applicants.
Fraud Detection	Given a dataset of fraudulent and non-fraudulent transactions, learn a model to identify potential fraud in real-time.
Stock Price Prediction	Given historical stock price data and related indicators, learn a model to predict future stock prices.

Key Machine Learning Concepts

To effectively apply machine learning, it's important to understand several key concepts that are common across different types of learning and algorithms. These concepts form the foundation upon which more advanced techniques, such as deep learning, are built.

Let's dive into each of these crucial concepts in more detail.

Features and Labels

Features, also known as input variables or attributes, are the individual measurable properties or characteristics of the phenomena being observed. Think of features as the columns in a spreadsheet that could be email addresses, dates, product IDs or any other variable data you've collected. The rows in this case would be the examples or observances. Consider a dataset of houses. The features might include the size of the house (measured in square feet), the number of bedrooms, and the location (represented as a zip code). These are the variables that we believe have some influence or predictive power over the outcome we're interested in.

Labels, on the other hand, are the output variables or target values that we're trying to predict. In supervised learning tasks, each label corresponds to a specific instance of the input data. Continuing with our house price prediction example, the label would be the actual price of each house. The goal of the machine learning model is to learn the relationship between the features (house size, number of bedrooms, location) and the label (price), so that it can predict the price of a new, unseen house based on its features.

We use features to make our predictions, but there is a science to selecting the right ones. Feature engineering is the process of selecting, manipulating, and transforming raw data into features that can be used to make predictions. This might involve scaling the features to a consistent range, handling missing values, or creating new features based on domain knowledge. For instance, instead of using the raw house size, we might create a new feature by dividing the size by the number of bedrooms to get the average room size. The quality of the features can have a significant impact on the performance of the machine learning model.

In a financial context, features might include financial ratios (e.g. price-to-earnings ratio or debt-to-equity ratio), market indicators (such as stock prices or trading volumes), or economic variables like interest rates or GDP growth. Labels might be future stock prices, credit risk categories, or fraud indicators.

Training and Testing Data

Once we have our features and labels, the next step is to split our data into training and testing sets. The training data is the subset of the data used to train the machine learning model. This is the data that the model learns from, identifying patterns and relationships between the features and the labels (in supervised learning) or just the features (in unsupervised learning). It's important that the training data is representative of the overall data distribution to avoid biased models.

The testing data, on the other hand, is the subset of the data used to evaluate the performance of the trained model. This data is kept separate from the training data to assess how well the model generalizes to unseen data. By evaluating the model on data it hasn't seen before, we get an unbiased estimate of its real-world performance.

In some cases, especially when the amount of data is limited, we might also use a validation set. The validation data is used for model selection and hyperparameter tuning. It helps prevent overfitting to the test data during model development. A common technique when data is scarce is cross-validation, where the data is partitioned into subsets, the model is trained on some subsets and validated on others, and the results are averaged.

Model Selection and Evaluation

With our data prepared, we're ready to select and train our machine learning model. The type of model used is important to maximize results. To select the appropriate model, ML engineers and data scientists consider factors like the type of problem (e.g., classification vs. regression), the size and structure of the data, and the interpretability and computational requirements of the model. Different models have different strengths and weaknesses, and the choice of model can have a significant impact on the results.

Once we've trained our model, we need to evaluate its performance by using evaluation metrics. Evaluation metrics are quantitative measures used to assess the performance of a machine learning model. Different metrics are used for different types of problems:

- For classification problems, common metrics include accuracy (the proportion of correct predictions), precision (the proportion of true positive predictions among all positive predictions), recall (the proportion of true positive predictions among all actual positives), and the F1 score (the harmonic mean of precision and recall).
- For regression problems, common metrics include mean squared error (MSE), root mean squared error (RMSE), mean absolute error (MAE), and R-squared (the proportion of the variance in the dependent variable that is predictable from the independent variables).
- For clustering problems, common metrics include silhouette score (a measure of how similar an object is to its own cluster compared to other clusters), Davies-Bouldin index (the ratio of within-cluster distances to between-cluster distances), and Calinski-Harabasz index (the ratio of the between-clusters dispersion mean and the within-cluster dispersion).

Given the high stakes and potential consequences of financial decisions, careful model selection and evaluation is crucial. A model that performs well on historical data, but fails to generalize to new market conditions can lead to significant financial losses. It's key, therefore, to rigorously test the model on out-of-sample data and continuously monitor its performance.

Overfitting and Underfitting

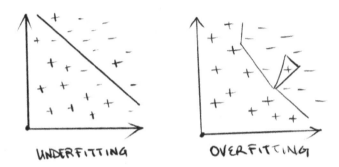

UNDERFITTING   OVERFITTING

Two common pitfalls in machine learning are overfitting and underfitting. Overfitting occurs when a model learns the noise in the training data to the extent that it negatively impacts the performance of the model on new data. Overfitting occurs when the model is too complex and has essentially memorized the training data rather than learning the underlying patterns. An overfit model will perform very well on the training data but will fail to generalize to new, unseen data.

Underfitting, on the other hand, occurs when a model is too simple to learn the underlying data structure. An underfit model will perform poorly on both the training data and new data.

> *"All models are wrong. Some are useful."*
>
> *~ George Box*

The challenge is to find the right balance between overfitting and underfitting. This is known as the bias-variance tradeoff. Models with high bias are too simple and tend to underfit, while models with high variance are too complex and tend to overfit. The goal is to find the sweet spot where the model is complex enough to learn the important patterns in the data, but not so complex that it learns the noise.

There are several strategies for avoiding overfitting. Tools like regularization (adding a penalty term to the model's loss function to discourage complexity), dropout (randomly dropping out nodes in a neural network during training), and early stopping (stopping the training process before the model starts to overfit) can all be effective.

Underfitting, on the other hand, can usually be addressed by increasing the model complexity, adding more informative features, or increasing the number of training epochs.

Overfitting is a particularly serious concern in financial modeling. Financial data is often noisy and non-stationary, meaning that patterns that held in the past may not hold in the future. A model that is overfit to historical data may fail catastrophically when market conditions change. Therefore, techniques for mitigating overfitting, such as regularization and cross-validation, are commonly used in financial machine learning applications.

Chapter Three

FUNDAMENTALS OF DEEP LEARNING

From Machine Learning to Deep Learning

As we've seen with machine learning, the ability for algorithms to learn from data opens an incredible world of possibility in fields ranging from data analysis and prediction to image recognition and natural language processing. But as the complexity and volume of data have grown, traditional ML techniques have begun to hit a peak in their ability to provide meaningful outcomes.

Limitations of Traditional Machine Learning

Traditional ML algorithms (decision trees, support vector machines, logistic regression) are great at a lot of data analysis, but they struggle when faced with more complex problems.

Some of the limitations of traditional machine learning include:

Feature Engineering

In traditional ML, human engineers are heavily involved in designing and selecting input features. They have to transform raw data into a format the algorithm can use, which involves selecting the relevant variables, identifying appropriate features, and usually creating new ones to get the best results from the models (i.e. they have to get the data into a format the algorithms can use and sometimes add new data to the set). This is because ML algorithms can't always identify the underlying patterns in the data. When datasets become larger, more complex, and high dimensional, this process becomes increasingly challenging and time consuming. In addition to being time consuming, feature engineering requires deep domain knowledge and expertise to identify the most relevant features, and even then, key information could be overlooked or misrepresented.

Handling Unstructured Data

Machine learning works really well with structured, tabular data, where information is organized into rows and columns. But they often fall short when dealing with unstructured data types like images, audio, and text, which don't fit neatly into a tabular format. Extracting meaningful features from unstructured data is a non-trivial task that requires sophisticated techniques and, often a combination of methods, which makes it difficult to effectively use unstructured data in the models.

Scalability

When dealing with big data, traditional ML becomes increasingly computationally expensive. These algorithms require a significant amount of processing power and memory (compute) to handle larger datasets. This limitation around scalability means that as data grows, the resources needed to train and deploy models grow exponentially, which makes it difficult for traditional ML to keep pace with modern data demands.

Capturing Complex Patterns

Traditional algorithms can also struggle to capture intricate, hierarchical patterns in data. These algorithms may miss out on subtle dependencies and interactions between variables, leading them to make inaccurate predictions. While ML models excel when dealing with linear relationships where there is a direct, linear relationship between input features and the target variable, they don't perform as well on complex tasks that involve non-linear relationships or interactions between multiple variables. This makes them overly simplistic in many real-world scenarios.

Enter Deep Learning ...

As AI researchers sought solutions to these more complex problems, they shifted their focus to a new type of model architecture.

Artificial Neural Networks

The concept of Deep Learning is built on the idea of constructing Artificial Neural Networks (ANNs) that were designed to mimic the structure and function of biological neural networks (i.e. the human brain). They are designed to recognize patterns and learn from experience, much like their biological counterparts.

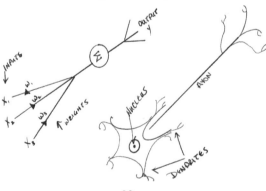

Biological Inspiration

While current ANNs are orders of magnitude smaller than the human brain – one of the most complex and efficient systems known to science – they have proven incredibly effective in deep learning models. The human brain has around 86 billion neurons and trillions of connections, while even the largest ANNs (such as those employed by cutting-edge frontier models like OpenAI's GPT) pale in comparison. Further, while the brain consumes just 20 watts of power, ANNs require significant computational resources and struggle to generalize beyond specific tasks.

In the human brain, neurons are specialized cells that receive, process, and transmit data through electrochemical signals. These signals are passed between neurons via connections (synapses) through intricate organic networks that enable us to think, perceive, feel, learn, and adapt to our environment. These connections are what give us the ability to learn due to the dynamic nature of these connections, which change and strengthen based on experiences through a process called plasticity.

Artificial Neural Networks are designed to mimic this biological structure. The basic unit of an ANN is called an artificial neuron or node, which is designed to function similarly to a biological neuron. These nodes are organized into layers that include an input layer, hidden layer(s), and an output layer. Each node receives input from nodes in the preceding layer. The receiving neuron then processes this input using a mathematical function, and transmits it to the output to nodes in the following layer. This layered structure allows ANNs to model complex relationships in data, much like the layers of neurons in the brain contribute to different levels of processing and abstraction.

ANNs learn in much the same way as human brains. In biological systems, the connections between neurons are strengthened or weakened based on the "experience," or input received. This process allows the brain to adapt and optimize its responses over time. ANNs' learning occurs when weights are adjusted between the connections. Before training, the weights are set to random values, which are iteratively adjusted as the network is trained on new data. The goal of these adjustments is to minimize the error between the ANN's predictions and the actual outcomes using calculus-driven tools like backpropagation, which uses gradient descent to find the minimum error, based on feedback received during training.

Key to the effectiveness of these models is the way information processing is distributed. In the human brain, no single or small group of neurons is responsible for a specific function; rather, cognitive processes emerge from the collective activity of large networks of neurons. ANNs replicate this process by distributing knowledge and functionality across the entire network, which allows them to generalize the data they've seen. Using this ability, the models are able to recognize patterns, make decisions, and even perform creative tasks that they weren't explicitly programmed to do.

ANNs have also been designed to handle noise and incomplete information in the same way the human brain does. The brain is incredibly resilient, and is capable of making sense of incomplete or ambiguous data through processes like pattern recognition and inference of context. ANNs were designed to be similarly robust when faced with noisy or incomplete data. They learn the underlying patterns or structures in the training data, which enables them to make predictions and decisions, even when the input data is not perfect. This ability to infer and generalize from imperfect information is a critical feature that makes ANNs effective in a wide range of applications.

New insights are continually being discovered and translated into more sophisticated neural network models, which continues to advance areas like deep learning, reinforcement learning, and neuromorphic computing. These developments are pushing the boundaries of what artificial intelligence can achieve, while bringing us closer to creating machines that can learn, adapt, and think in ways that are increasingly similar to human cognition.

Structure of an ANN

A typical ANN consists of three types of layers:

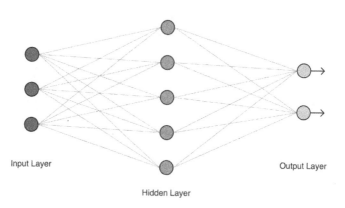

Artificial Neural Network

Input Layer

Hidden Layer

Output Layer

Input Layer

The Input Layer is the first component of an Artificial Neural Network and serves as the point of entry for the input data. Each node in this layer captures a single feature from the input data. This could be a pixel in an image or a numerical value in a dataset. In tasks like image recognition, the input layer could have thousands of nodes, each corresponding to an individual pixel in the image being analyzed. The input layer is the interface between the external data and the neural network – passing this raw data to the subsequent layers without any transformation.

Hidden Layers

Hidden Layers are the intermediate layers between the input and output layers. Each node within the hidden layers receives weighted inputs from the input layer or the previous hidden layer, and processes the input using an activation function, which generates the output that is transmitted to the next layer. These layers are called "hidden" because their operations and outputs are not visible or directly interpretable from outside the network. This hidden processing is what leads to the "black box" problem, which we will discuss later in the text. It is these hidden layers, however, that enable the network to extract hierarchical features from the data, making them essential for tasks that require understanding intricate, non-linear relationships in tasks ranging from image recognition to natural language processing.

Output Layer

The final layer of an ANN is called the Output Layer, which (as you might expect) is responsible for producing the network's output. The output layer takes the processed data from the hidden layers and converts it into a format that can be interpreted as the final prediction or classification result. Its structure varies based on the specific task required. For instance, in a binary classification task, the output layer might consist of a single node that generates a probability score that indicates the likelihood that an input belongs to a particular class (as in a classification problem). In a multi-class classification task, the output layer might have multiple nodes, each representing a different class.

The number of hidden layers determines the depth of the network. This is where the term "Deep Learning" comes from - it refers to the learning done by ANNs with many hidden layers.

How ANNs Learn

Let's take a deeper look at how ANNs learn.

Like humans, deep learning algorithms learn through a process called training. As in machine learning, ANNs are fed with labeled examples. As the network processes the training data, it adjusts the weights of the connections to minimize the difference between the network's output and the desired output. This process is typically done using an algorithm called backpropagation.

Forward Propagation

In the forward step, the input data is fed into the network, and each node in the first hidden layer calculates its activation (output) by applying an activation function to the weighted sum of its inputs. This process is repeated for each subsequent layer with the output of each layer serving as the input for the next until the final output is produced (via the output layer).

Backpropagation

Once the data has passed through its forward pass, the output is compared to the desired output and an error is calculated. This error is then "propagated" backwards through the network. Using a technique called gradient descent, the weights of the connections are adjusted in a way that minimizes the error. This process is repeated for many iterations (known as epochs) until the network's output is satisfactorily close to the desired output.

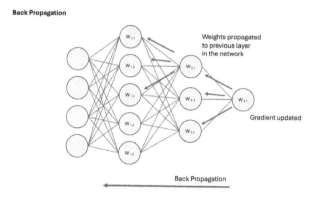

Through this process of forward propagation and backpropagation, the ANN learns to recognize patterns in the input data and map these to the correct outputs.

The Rise of Deep Learning

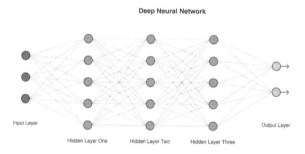

Deep Learning refers to Artificial Neural Networks with multiple layers — hence the term "deep." These multi-layered networks are designed to mimic the way the human brain processes information, enabling them to automatically learn complex patterns and representations from raw data. Unlike earlier machine learning techniques, which often required extensive manual feature engineering to identify the most relevant attributes of the data, deep learning networks are able to identify and extract these attributes without human intervention.

With deep learning, there is no need for extensive feature engineering, which can be both labor-intensive and prone to bias, as it relies heavily on the assumptions and expertise of the individuals designing the features. Deep learning can automatically discover and learn hierarchical representations of the data, which means the model itself identifies and extracts the features that are most relevant, and optimizes the learning process to uncover patterns that human engineers might miss.

This ability to learn hierarchical representations in data is particularly powerful. In a deep neural network, the early (hidden) layers are responsible for learning low-level features, such as edges or simple textures in the case of image data. As the data is passed through subsequent layers, these low-level features are combined and transformed into more abstract, higher-level representations. For example, in an image recognition task, the first layers of a Deep Learning model might focus on detecting basic elements like edges and corners. These features are then used by the middle layers to identify more complex shapes or parts of objects, such as circles or rectangles. Finally, the deeper layers combine these shapes to recognize whole objects, such as faces, cars, or animals. This hierarchical learning process is what enables deep learning models to understand and represent data at multiple levels of abstraction.

This is particularly useful when working with unstructured data that doesn't fit neatly into traditional tables or predefined formats. Unstructured data might include images, audio, text, and video, which are all increasingly prevalent in an evermore digital world. Deep Learning models have achieved remarkable success in image recognition, for example, by learning to identify objects and scenes with a high degree of accuracy. These same principles also apply to natural language processing, where they can understand and generate human language by learning from a huge corpora of text. In these cases, the models don't just identify simple features, they also "understand" the context and relationships between different elements of the data. This contextual understanding enables them to perform complex tasks like translation, sentiment analysis, and even creative writing.

Deep Learning models are not only more flexible and scalable than traditional ML models; they are also capable of tackling a broader range of problems, particularly those involving large, complex datasets that would be challenging or impossible to handle with manual feature engineering. This flexibility has led to widespread adoption of Deep Learning across myriad tasks in various industries – from healthcare, where it is used for tasks like medical image analysis and drug discovery, to finance, where it is applied in areas such as fraud detection and algorithmic trading.

Key Advantages of Deep Learning

Deep Learning offers several key advantages over traditional Machine Learning approaches:

Automated Feature Learning

As we've discussed, one of the most significant advantages of deep learning models vs. traditional machine learning is their ability to automatically learn the most relevant features directly from raw data without human guidance. This automatic learning reduces the need for human intervention in the feature engineering process and allows models to capture intricate patterns that might be missed by manual methods.

Handling Unstructured Data

Deep learning models excel at extracting meaningful features from unstructured data, making them indispensable in modern AI applications. Convolutional Neural Networks (CNNs), in particular, have revolutionized image recognition by automatically learning spatial hierarchies in images. Similarly, Recurrent Neural Networks and their variants, such as Long Short-Term Memory (LSTM) networks, have driven significant advancements in natural language processing (NLP), enabling breakthroughs in tasks like language translation, sentiment analysis, and speech recognition. It is worth noting, however, that the NLP algorithms we used just a few years ago have now been blown away by the power of transformers and the rapid advancement of generative AI.

Scalability

Deep learning is immensely scalable, meaning it can effectively handle massive volumes of data. In fact, deep learning algorithms actually perform better in many cases as the size of the training dataset increases. This characteristic makes deep learning particularly well-suited for applications in big data environments, where the ability to process and learn from huge datasets is crucial for generating accurate predictions and insights.

Capturing Complex Patterns

The hierarchical structure of deep learning models allows them to capture complex patterns and dependencies within data. By design, each layer the model can learn progressively more abstract features, which enables it to understand intricate relationships that simpler models might not identify. This capability has led to state-of-the-art performance on many data science challenges that traditional machine learning algorithms can't handle. Deep learning's ability to model complex, non-linear interactions between variables makes it applicable across a wide range of domains.

But deep learning is not a silver bullet. It requires significant amounts of training data and can be computationally expensive. It also lacks the interpretability of some traditional methods, leading to the "black box" problem.

Key Concepts in Deep Learning

To better understand how deep learning models work, it's important to understand the building blocks of these models. These include activation functions, loss functions, optimizers, and hyperparameters.

Activation Functions

We talked previously about how each node of a neural network receives inputs from a previous layer, processes it, and passes it on to the next layer. In this process, the inputs are received from the nodes of the previous layer and combined into a weighted sum that reflects the cumulative influence of these inputs. But without an activation function, this weighted sum would just pass through the network unchanged, resulting in a linear model, regardless of the complexity or depth of the network. Without an activation function, this weighted sum would simply pass through the network unchanged, resulting in a linear model regardless of the network's complexity or depth. This would undermine the effectiveness of deep networks, as they wouldn't be able to capture the intricate, non-linear patterns present in more complex data structures.

Activation functions transform the outputs by applying a non-linear transformation to the weighted sum of inputs at each node. This nonlinearity is what enables neural networks to learn and approximate complex functions. Without non-linear activation functions, a deep neural network would essentially be equivalent to a single-layer linear model, no matter how many layers it had. The activation functions allow each layer to build upon the transformations performed by the previous layers, enabling the network to represent complex, hierarchical structures within the data.

There are several types of activation functions, each with its own properties and applications. Some of the most commonly used activation functions include the Sigmoid function, the Hyperbolic Tangent (Tanh) function, and the Rectified Linear Unit (ReLU).

The Sigmoid and Tanh functions are smooth and bounded, meaning they map inputs to a range between 0 and 1 or -1 and 1, respectively. These functions were among the earliest used in neural networks and are particularly useful in cases where output values need to be interpreted as probabilities. But these functions have their limitations in areas like vanishing gradients, which is where the gradients become too small during backpropagation. Vanishing gradients impact the model by significantly slowing the learning process. One way AI engineers have addressed this problem is by using the ReLU function, which introduces non-linearity by setting all negative input values to zero, while leaving positive values unchanged. This simplified approach helps to mitigate the vanishing gradient problem and allows for faster and more effective training of deep networks.

The choice of activation function can significantly impact the performance of a neural network, influencing its ability to learn and generalize from data, and is therefore a critical consideration in the design of ANNs.

Some common activation functions include:

1. **Sigmoid:** This function squashes the input to a value between 0 and 1. It was commonly used in the past but has fallen out of favor due to the vanishing gradient problem.
2. **Tanh:** Similar to the sigmoid, but squashes the input to a value between -1 and 1. It often performs better than the sigmoid but still suffers from the vanishing gradient problem.
3. **ReLU (Rectified Linear Unit):** This function outputs the input directly if it is positive, otherwise, it outputs zero. ReLU has become very popular in recent years because it helps alleviate the vanishing gradient problem.

4. **Leaky ReLU:** A variant of ReLU that allows a small, non-zero gradient when the input is negative. This can help prevent "dead" neurons that always output zero.

5. **Softmax:** This function is often used in the output layer for multi-class classification tasks. It squashes the outputs so that they sum to 1, giving a probability distribution over the classes.

Vanishing Gradients

The vanishing gradient problem occurs during the training of deep neural networks, particularly when using activation functions like Sigmoid or Tanh. "Vanishing" gradients of the loss function become very small in relation to the weights as they propagate back through the layers of the network during backpropagation. This leads to extremely slow updates of the weights in the earlier layers, effectively preventing the network from learning. The result is that the network may fail to converge at the global minimum or learn meaningful patterns – especially in very deep networks.

Loss Functions

Loss functions represent the delta between what an ANN predicts vs. the true or desired output, expressed in numerical terms. This difference is called the model's loss or error, which signifies how well or poorly the model is performing on a given task. This is the guiding mechanism by which the network learns to make accurate predictions. The objective of training an ANN is to minimize this loss, thereby improving the network's predictions and overall performance.

The loss function directly influences how the ANN's parameters (weights and biases, specifically) are adjusted through training. The network uses the gradients of the loss function with respect to each parameter to update the weights in a way that reduces the loss throughout the iterative process of backpropagation. The goal of the training is to find the set of parameters that minimizes the loss function across all training examples, effectively enabling the network to generalize well to new, unseen data. Optimization algorithms, such as SGD or Adam (see p. 38), work hand-in-hand with the loss function to guide the network towards this minimum.

Loss functions are not a one-size-fits-all solution. The choice of loss function is important to model training because it directly impacts how the network learns. A poorly chosen loss function can lead to suboptimal training and, consequently, poor performance. Selecting the appropriate loss function depends on the problem the model is trying to solve, as different types of tasks require different approaches to quantifying error.

In regression tasks, where the goal is to predict continuous values, the Mean Squared Error (MSE) is commonly used. MSE calculates the average squared difference between the predicted values and the actual values. Squares are used because they penalize larger errors more severely and thus encourage the network to make predictions that are as close as possible to the true values.

For classification tasks, where the goal is to categorize inputs into discrete classes, loss functions like Cross-Entropy Loss or Binary Cross-Entropy are more effective. These functions measure the difference between the predicted probability distribution and the actual distribution. This approach effectively penalizes the model when it assigns high probabilities to incorrect classes.

More complex scenarios might require custom solutions beyond the standard loss functions. These loss functions might incorporate specific domain knowledge or address particular challenges of the task. For example, in imbalanced classification problems where one class is significantly underrepresented in the data, a weighted loss function would be used to give more importance to the minority class, ensuring that the network learns to identify it correctly. In tasks like image segmentation, for example, where the model is tasked with classifying each pixel in an image, loss functions might be designed to account for spatial coherence, ensuring that neighboring pixels are classified consistently.

The loss function is a fundamental element of the training process in ANNs, providing the metrics by which the model's predictions are evaluated and improved. Careful selection of an appropriate loss function tailored to the specific task is essential for successful model training, as it determines how well the network learns from the data and how effectively it can perform in real-world applications.

Common Loss Functions

Loss Function	Task	Explanation
Mean Squared Error (MSE)	Regression	MSE is commonly used for regression tasks, where the goal is to predict continuous values. It calculates the average squared difference between the predicted values and the actual target values, penalizing larger errors more heavily. A lower MSE indicates better model performance.
Binary Cross-Entropy	Binary Classification	Binary Cross-Entropy is used for binary classification tasks, where the objective is to distinguish between two classes. It measures the difference between the predicted probabilities (ranging from 0 to 1) and the true binary labels (0 or 1). A lower binary cross-entropy indicates more accurate predictions.

Categorical Cross-Entropy	Multi-Class Classification	Categorical Cross-Entropy is used for multi-class classification tasks involving more than two classes. Similar to binary cross-entropy, it calculates the difference between the predicted probability distribution and the true class labels but extends it to multiple classes. A lower categorical cross-entropy indicates better alignment between the predicted probabilities and the actual classes.

Optimizers

In artificial neural networks, optimizers are used to adjust network parameters (again, primarily the weights and biases) in a way that minimizes the loss function. The optimizer's job is to find the optimal set of parameters that reduces this loss (as determined by the loss function) as much as possible. Optimizers navigate the "loss landscape," which is a metaphorical representation of how the loss function changes in relation to different configurations of the network's parameters. Picture the landscape as a multidimensional surface with peaks, valleys, and plateaus that all correspond to various levels of error. The optimizer is the sherpa that guides the network through this landscape, seeking the lowest point — or the global minimum — where the loss is minimized.

There are various types of optimizers, each with its own approach to adjusting the network's parameters. Some of the most commonly used optimizers include Stochastic Gradient Descent (SGD), Adam, RMSprop, and AdaGrad. These optimizers differ in how they calculate the direction and magnitude of parameter updates. For instance, SGD updates the weights by moving in the direction of the steepest descent of the loss function, using a fixed learning rate to determine the step size. One negative of SGD is that it can sometimes be inefficient – especially in complex loss landscapes with many local minima or saddle points. More advanced optimizers like Adam combine the benefits of both momentum (which helps the optimizer move faster along flat regions) and adaptive learning rates (which adjust the step size based on the history of gradients). This makes Adam particularly effective in navigating difficult loss landscapes and often leads to faster and more stable convergence.

The choice of optimizer can significantly impact the efficiency and success of the training process, as it influences how quickly and effectively the network can learn from the data and reach an optimal set of parameters.

The Descent Is Right

Fans of the long-running game show *The Price is Right* may be familiar with the mountain climber, "Hans Gudegast," from the Cliffhanger game on the show. Let's use Hans as a way to visualize the gradient descent algorithm in machine learning.

In the context of machine learning, the mountain represents the error or "loss" landscape, where the height of the mountain at each point corresponds to the error in the model's predictions. The goal is to minimize this error and find the lowest point on the mountain, which represents the optimal parameters for the model.

The mountain climber represents the current position in the parameter space, and our goal is to guide him to the lowest point on the mountain (the bottom of the valley).

Gradient descent is an optimization algorithm that helps the mountain climber find the path of least resistance (steepest descent) to reach the bottom of the mountain. In each step, the mountain climber looks around and determines the direction with the steepest slope downhill.

He then takes a small step in that direction. This process is repeated until the mountain climber reaches a point where he can no longer move downhill or the change in the position becomes too small (meaning that he has found the minimum point, or very close to it).

In the context of machine learning, the "direction" the mountain climber looks for is determined by the gradient of the loss function (the mathematical representation of the error).

The size of the steps taken is determined by a parameter called the "learning rate," which controls how fast the algorithm converges towards the minimum point. If the learning rate is too large, the mountain climber may overshoot the minimum point and end up oscillating back and forth. If the learning rate is too small, the convergence will be slow, and it might take a long time for the mountain climber to reach the bottom of the mountain, potentially making the learning process inefficient.

Hyperparameters

Hyperparameters define both the architecture of the network and the training process itself. Unlike the weights and biases (parameters that are learned during training through optimization) hyperparameters are set *before* the training begins, and are not adjusted by the training process. Hyperparameters dictate the structure of the network (e.g. the number of hidden layers, the number of nodes or neurons in each layer) and the type of activation functions used. Additionally, hyperparameters also govern how the network learns, including the learning rate, which determines the step size for each update during optimization, the number of epochs (or training runs), and the batch size (number of training examples used to calculate the gradient at each step).

The process of choosing optimal hyperparameters is known as hyperparameter tuning, and it is often one of the most difficult aspects of machine learning model development. Hyperparameter tuning typically involves experimenting with different combinations of hyperparameters to identify the configuration that yields the best performance on the testing or validation set. Techniques for hyperparameter tuning include a simple grid search, where all possible combinations of a predefined set of hyperparameters are tested, and more advanced methods like random search, Bayesian optimization, or automated machine learning (AutoML) frameworks that explore the hyperparameter space more efficiently.

The goal of hyperparameter tuning is to find a balance between underfitting, where the model is too simple to capture the underlying patterns in the data, and overfitting, where the model is too complex and performs well on training data but poorly on unseen data.

Types of Neural Networks

There is a wide variety of neural network architectures designed to address a broad range of data science problems. It is important to understand the characteristics and use cases of these different architectures in order to apply Deep Learning models effectively.

Feedforward Neural Networks

Feedforward Neural Networks, also known as Multi-Layer Perceptrons (MLPs), are characterized by a straightforward, unidirectional flow of information, where data is passed forward from the input layer, through one or more hidden layers, and finally to the output layer. Each node, or neuron, in a given layer is connected to every node in the subsequent layer, forming a fully connected network. The primary function of these connections is to transform the input data by applying weights and biases, followed by a nonlinear activation function and passing it to the next layer.

In a typical feedforward network, the input layer receives the raw data and passes it through the hidden layers, where the network learns to extract and refine features that are relevant to the task at hand. Remember, each hidden layer then progressively refines the input data, capturing more abstract and higher-level representations as it moves deeper into the network. The final output layer produces the network's prediction or decision, which could be a classification label, a continuous value, or some other form of output, depending on the application.

The defining characteristic of feedforward neural networks is the absence of cycles or loops in their structure. Unlike recurrent neural networks (see p. 43), where information can loop back to previous layers or neurons, feedforward networks maintain a strict one-way progression from input to output. This simplicity makes feedforward networks easier to analyze and train, as the flow of information is linear and predictable. However, it also means that feedforward networks are limited to tasks where the data does not have temporal dependencies, such as image recognition or basic pattern classification. Despite their simplicity, feedforward neural networks remain a foundational building block in deep learning, serving as the basis for more complex architectures with applications in a wide range of use cases.

Classification

Multilayer Perceptrons are frequently used for classification tasks, where the goal is to assign an input to one of several discrete categories. For example, an MLP can be trained to determine whether an email is spam or not by analyzing various features such as the presence of certain keywords, the sender's reputation, and the email's structure. In this case, the MLP would take these features as input, process them through multiple layers of neurons, and output a probability distribution over the possible classes (e.g. spam or not spam). The class with the highest probability would be the model's final prediction.

Beyond spam detection, MLPs are also widely used in other classification tasks like image recognition, sentiment analysis, and medical diagnosis. MLPs are used in image recognition, for example, to classify images of handwritten digits into discrete categories. Each pixel in the image would be treated as an input feature, and the MLP would learn to recognize patterns in the pixel arrangements that correspond to different digits.

Regression

MLPs are also used for regression tasks, where the objective is to predict a continuous value based on input features. In this case, an MLP could be trained to predict the price of a house based on various factors like the size of the house, the number of bedrooms, the location, and the year it was built. In this scenario, the MLP would process these input features through its layers and output a single continuous value representing the predicted price of the house. In finance, MLPs can be used to predict stock prices based on historical data and market indicators.

MLPs are versatile but may struggle with complex, hierarchical patterns in data.

Convolutional Neural Networks (CNNs)

Convolutional Neural Networks (CNNs) are a specialized class of neural networks specifically designed to process data with a grid-like topology, making them particularly well-suited for tasks such as image and video recognition. Unlike traditional feedforward neural networks, which treat each input independently, CNNs take advantage of the spatial structure of the data. This means that CNNs are capable of recognizing patterns such as edges, textures, and shapes by preserving the spatial relationships between pixels in an image. This ability to capture local dependencies and hierarchical patterns is what makes CNNs so powerful for visual tasks.

The name "Convolutional Neural Networks" is derived from the mathematical operation of convolution, which is central to their architecture. Convolution is a type of linear operation that involves sliding a filter, also known as a kernel, over the input data (such as an image) to produce a feature map. Each filter is designed to detect specific features in the input, such as edges, corners, or textures. As the filter moves across the image, it performs a dot product between the filter's weights and the input pixels within the filter's receptive field, effectively extracting features that are then passed on to subsequent layers. This process allows CNNs to automatically and efficiently learn to recognize complex patterns in the data, even when those patterns are shifted or distorted.

CNNs typically consist of multiple layers, each responsible for different stages of feature extraction and processing. The early layers in a CNN might detect simple features such as edges and corners, while deeper layers combine these simple features to recognize more complex structures, like parts of objects or entire objects themselves. After the convolutional layers, the network usually includes pooling layers, which reduce the spatial dimensions of the feature maps, making the network more computationally efficient and less sensitive to the precise location of features. This combination of convolutional and pooling layers allows CNNs to achieve a high level of performance in tasks like image classification, object detection, and facial recognition, where understanding the spatial hierarchy of features is critical.

Convolutional Neural Network (CNN)

Convolutional Layers

Convolutional layers apply filters to input data to create feature maps that detect patterns such as edges, textures, and shapes. As the filter slides across the input, it performs element-wise multiplication and sums to capture the presence of these features at different locations. This hierarchical learning process allows CNNs to identify simple patterns in early layers and more complex structures in deeper layers, making them particularly effective for tasks like image recognition.

Pooling Layers

Pooling layers reduce the spatial dimensions of feature maps by downsampling, commonly using max pooling, which retains the most significant feature within each patch. This operation decreases computational complexity and enhances the network's ability to generalize by focusing on the presence of features rather than their exact positions, making the model more robust to variations like shifts or distortions in the input data.

Fully-Connected Layers

Fully-connected layers in CNNs function similarly to those in traditional neural networks, connecting every neuron in one layer to every neuron in the next. Positioned after the convolutional and pooling layers, they take the high-level features learned throughout the network and use them to perform the final classification or regression task, outputting probabilities or predictions based on the detected patterns.

CNNs have achieved breakthrough results in image recognition, video analysis, and recommender systems.

Recurrent Neural Networks (RNNs)

Recurrent Neural Networks (RNNs) are a specialized type of neural network architecture designed to effectively handle and process sequential data, making them particularly well-suited for tasks such as time series analysis, natural language processing, and speech recognition. Unlike feedforward neural networks, which assume that all inputs are independent of each other, RNNs are explicitly designed to capture dependencies and relationships across different time steps or sequence elements. This is achieved through their unique structure, which allows them to maintain a form of memory by considering not only the current input but also the context provided by previous inputs.

The term "recurrent" in Recurrent Neural Networks refers to the network's ability to perform the same operation on each element of the sequence, while carrying forward information from one step to the next. In an RNN, the output at any given time step is influenced not only by the current input but also by the outputs from the previous time steps via the network's internal or hidden state state, which is updated at each step. This internal state acts as a memory that captures relevant information from earlier in the sequence, allowing the RNN to make decisions that are informed by past inputs, thereby creating a feedback loop where information cycles through the network.

This looping mechanism enables RNNs to exhibit dynamic temporal behavior. This allows them to understand context, sequential dependencies, and temporal patterns within the data. In natural language processing, for example, an RNN can keep track of the words previously encountered in a sentence, allowing it to predict the next word more accurately based on the context. Similarly, in time series forecasting, an RNN can analyze past trends to predict future values. One downside of standard RNNs, however, is that they can struggle with long-term dependencies due to issues like vanishing gradients. In recent years, advanced variants such as Long Short-Term Memory (LSTM) networks and Gated Recurrent Units (GRUs) have been developed to better handle long-range dependencies.

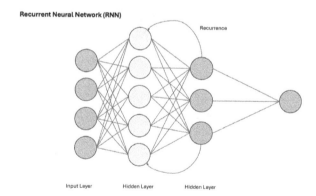

RNNs come in several variations:

One-to-One

Traditional RNNs follow a one-to-one structure, where the network processes a single input to produce a single output. This type of RNN is useful for tasks like image classification where the input and output have a direct correlation. One-to-one networks retain a memory of previous inputs, allowing them to consider context, which makes them "pretty good" at tasks like predicting the next word in a sequence.

One-to-Many

In a One-to-Many RNN, a single input leads to a sequence of outputs. This is commonly used in tasks like image captioning, where the input is an image, and the output is a sentence that describes the image. One-to-many RNNs generate a sequence by progressively decoding the input and producing a word at each step, allowing them to build coherent sentences that accurately describe the image.

Many-to-One

Many-to-One RNNs process a sequence of inputs to produce a single output. This type of network is particularly effective for tasks such as sentiment analysis, where the input is a sequence of words (a sentence or paragraph), and the output is a single sentiment label (positive, negative, or neutral). The network considers the entire sequence before making its prediction, capturing the overall context.

Many-to-Many

Many-to-Many RNNs take a sequence of inputs and produce a sequence of outputs. This variation is used widely in tasks like machine translation, where the input is a sentence in one language, and the output is the translated sentence in another language. The network handles the entire sequence, translating word by word while maintaining the correct syntax and meaning throughout the process.

RNNs can struggle with long-term dependencies due to the vanishing gradient problem, which can lead to inaccurate predictions.

Long Short-Term Memory (LSTM) Networks

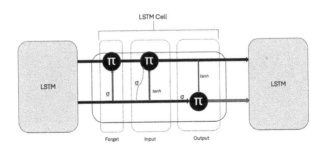

Long Short-Term Memory (LSTM) networks are a specialized variant of Recurrent Neural Networks (RNNs) designed to overcome the limitations of standard RNNs, particularly in learning long-term dependencies. Introduced by Hochreiter and Schmidhuber in

1997, LSTMs were developed to address the challenge of vanishing gradients, which can hinder the ability of traditional RNNs to capture and retain information over long sequences. LSTMs have been refined and popularized by numerous researchers in recent years, leading to their widespread adoption in various applications that require sequential data processing.

At their core, LSTMs retain the chain-like structure typical of RNNs, but with a crucial difference: the repeating module in an LSTM is far more complex. While a standard RNN module typically consists of a single neural network layer, an LSTM module is composed of four interacting layers, each playing a distinct role in managing the flow of information through the network. This intricate design allows LSTMs to selectively retain or discard information as it propagates through the sequence, making them particularly adept at handling long-term dependencies in data.

The key innovation in LSTMs is the concept of the cell state, which acts as a form of long-term memory for the network. The cell state runs through the entire chain of the LSTM, allowing information to flow along it relatively unchanged, much like a conveyor belt. This design enables LSTMs to preserve important information across many time steps while mitigating the risk of information loss that can occur in traditional RNNs. The ability to maintain and manipulate the cell state is what gives LSTMs their unique advantage in learning complex patterns over long sequences.

LSTMs rely on structures known as gates, which regulate the flow of information into, out of, and within each cell state. These gates act as filters that decide what information should be kept, added, or removed at each step in the sequence. By carefully controlling the information that passes through the network, LSTMs can effectively balance the retention of long-term context with the introduction of new, relevant data. This ability has made LSTMs much more effective in areas like natural language processing, where they have been successfully used in translation and speech recognition.

Generative Adversarial Networks (GANs)

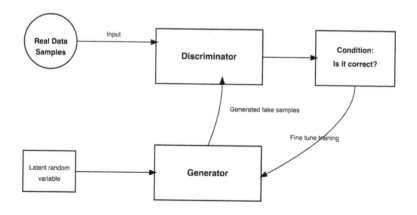

Generative Adversarial Networks, commonly known as GANs, are the popular new kids in the world of deep learning algorithms.

Introduced by Ian Goodfellow and his colleagues in 2014, GANs are unique in that they consist of two neural networks that work in opposition to each other: a generator and a discriminator. This adversarial relationship forms the basis of GANs' ability to generate highly realistic data, making them one of the most innovative techniques in the field of artificial intelligence.

The generator network creates new data samples that mimic the characteristics of the training data. This generation starts with a random noise input, which it transforms into samples that resemble the real data. On the other side, the discriminator network acts as a critic that tries to differentiate between the genuine data samples from the training set and the synthetic samples generated by the generator. The discriminator is essentially a binary classifier, tasked with assigning probabilities to determine whether a given sample is real or fake.

The training process of GANs is highly iterative and competitive and is reminiscent of reinforcement learning techniques. The generator and discriminator engage in a continuous game where each network is trying to outsmart the other. Initially, the generator produces crude, unrealistic samples, but as the discriminator improves its ability to detect these fakes, the generator is forced to enhance its output, learning to produce more and more realistic data. Conversely, as the generator's outputs improve, the discriminator must become more adept at distinguishing between real and fake samples. This push-and-pull dynamic continues until an equilibrium is reached, where the generator is so proficient at creating realistic samples that the discriminator is left guessing with 50% confidence — essentially indicating that it can no longer distinguish between real and generated data.

GANs have been applied across a wide range of domains, most notably in generating human-like text and highly realistic images. In image processing, GANs have been utilized to improve the resolution of images through a process known as super-resolution, where low-resolution images are enhanced to a higher quality. GANs have also shown promise in the field of drug discovery, where they are used to generate novel molecular structures that could serve as the basis for new pharmaceuticals.

In the finance sector, GANs can be used to generate realistic synthetic financial time series data that mimics the statistical properties of real market data, such as stock prices or market indexes, which is beneficial to financial analysts as real data is often limited and highly sensitive, making it difficult acquire enough data to adequately train machine learning models. This synthetic data can be invaluable for stress testing financial models, developing trading strategies, or training predictive models without exposing sensitive or proprietary data. For instance, a GAN might be trained on historical stock price data and then used to generate new sequences of price movements that are indistinguishable from the real data, allowing traders or analysts to explore potential market scenarios or test algorithms under a variety of conditions.

Each of these applications showcases the versatility and power of GANs, but they also highlight the complexities and challenges associated with this technology. The dual-network architecture of GANs means that training them can be particularly difficult and sensitive to hyperparameters, often requiring careful tuning and substantial computational resources. Additionally, the equilibrium reached during training is delicate, and issues such as mode collapse — where the generator produces a limited variety of samples — can arise.

Chapter Four

TRAINING DEEP LEARNING MODELS

The Deep Learning Process

Deep Learning is a powerful tool, but it's not a magic wand. Successful application of Deep Learning requires a systematic, iterative process. This process typically involves four main stages: collecting and preparing data, choosing a network architecture, training the model, and evaluating and tuning the model.

> *"It is a capital mistake to theorize before one has data."*
> *~ Sherlock Holmes in*
>
> *"A Study in Scarlet" by Arthur Conan Doyle*

Collecting and Preparing Data

Data is the fuel that powers Deep Learning. The quality and quantity of data directly impact the performance of Deep Learning models. Therefore, the first step in any Deep Learning project is to collect and prepare the data.

This involves several sub-steps:

1. **Data Collection:** This could involve scraping data from websites, accessing public datasets, or generating synthetic data. The goal is to gather a large, diverse dataset that is representative of the problem domain.
2. **Data Cleaning:** Raw data is often noisy and inconsistent. It may contain missing values, outliers, or incorrect labels. Data cleaning involves identifying and correcting these issues to ensure the data is accurate and reliable.
3. **Data Preprocessing:** This step involves transforming the data into a format suitable for the Deep Learning model. This could include scaling the features,

encoding categorical variables, or splitting the data into training, validation, and test sets.

4. **Data Augmentation:** In some cases, particularly in image-related tasks, the dataset can be artificially expanded by applying transformations such as rotations, flips, or shifts to the existing images. This helps the model learn to be invariant to these transformations.

Choosing a Network Architecture

The next step is to choose a suitable neural network architecture for the problem at hand. This choice is influenced by several factors:

The Type of Problem
Different types of problems demand different neural network architectures. For instance, CNNs are specifically designed for image-related tasks, where they excel at identifying spatial hierarchies in visual data, while RNNs are better suited for sequence data, such as text or time series, where understanding temporal dependencies is crucial.

The Size and Nature of the Data
The complexity of the network should align with the complexity of the data being processed. If the network is too simple, it may underfit, but if the network is too complex, it may overfit, capturing noise in the data rather than the actual signal.

Computational Resources
Training deeper and more complex networks requires significant computational resources. Therefore, the choice of architecture must strike a balance between the desired performance and the available resources. In practice, this means choosing a model that can be trained effectively within the constraints of the available hardware and time, without compromising too much on accuracy or efficiency.

There are many standard architectures that have been proven effective for various tasks, such as ResNet for image classification, BERT for natural language processing, or U-Net for image segmentation. These can serve as good starting points.

Training the Model

With the data prepared and the architecture selected, the next step is to train the model. This involves several key decisions, each of which we'll explain in more detail in an upcoming section:

1. **Loss Function:** The loss function quantifies how well the model is performing. It provides a feedback signal for the model to learn from. Common choices include

Mean Squared Error for regression tasks and Cross-Entropy for classification tasks.

2. **Optimizer:** The optimizer determines how the model's parameters are updated based on the loss function. Popular choices include Stochastic Gradient Descent (SGD), Adam, and RMSprop.

3. **Hyperparameters:** These are the settings that control the training process, such as the learning rate, the number of epochs, or the batch size. They need to be carefully tuned for optimal performance.

During training, the model is exposed to the training data, and its parameters are updated to minimize the loss function. This process is repeated for a fixed number of epochs or until a certain performance threshold is reached.

Evaluating and Tuning the Model

After training, the model's performance is typically evaluated on a separate testing set, which provides an unbiased estimate of how well the model generalizes to new, unseen data. If a validation set is used, it helps in tuning the model's hyperparameters, ensuring it generalizes well. (Validation sets are sometimes omitted in simpler models or when data is limited.) If the model's performance is unsatisfactory, adjustments may be necessary, such as tuning hyperparameters, modifying the architecture, or revisiting the data preparation steps to optimize the model.

The outputs must be monitored and compared on both the training and validation sets. A model that performs well on the training set but poorly on the validation set is likely overfitting (i.e. it has learned to memorize the training data rather than generalize from it). In these cases, the model may need to be simplified or regularized to improve its ability to generalize. Once the model's performance on the validation set is satisfactory, it can be tested on a final, held-out test set to confirm its generalization ability. This iterative process of training, evaluating, and tuning is at the core of deep learning.

Key Concepts in Deep Learning

Understanding the inner workings of Deep Learning models can seem daunting at first, but by focusing on a few key concepts we can better understand how these models work – in general. The specific activities of deep learning are generally opaque and impossible to fully understand in many cases. We'll get into that below.

Activation Functions: Bringing Non-Linearity to the Party

Picture a neural network as a series of workers in an assembly line. Each worker takes in an input, performs a simple operation on it, and passes the result to the next worker. In this analogy, the activation function is the tool each worker uses to transform their input.

The most basic activation function is a linear function, where the output is simply a scaled version of the input. But if we only used linear functions, our network would just be a series of linear transformations - no matter how many layers we add.

This is where nonlinear activation functions come in. They allow the network to learn complex, non-linear patterns in the data. Some common activation functions include:

- **Sigmoid:** Squashes the input to a value between 0 and 1, often used for binary classification.
- **Tanh:** Similar to sigmoid, but outputs values between -1 and 1.
- **ReLU (Rectified Linear Unit):** Outputs the input directly if it's positive, otherwise outputs zero. It has become very popular in recent years due to its simplicity and effectiveness.

Loss Functions: Guiding the Learning Process

For a neural network to learn, it needs a way to measure how wrong it is. It has to have a way to quantify the difference between its predictions and the true values. This is the role of the loss function.

For example, if we're training a network to classify images of cats and dogs, the loss function might compare the network's predicted probabilities to the true labels (1 for cat, 0 for dog) and calculate the average difference. The network's goal, then, is to minimize that loss.

Different types of problems require different loss functions. Some common ones include:

- **Mean Squared Error:** Often used for regression problems, it calculates the average squared difference between the predicted and true values.
- **Binary Cross-Entropy:** Used for binary classification, it quantifies the difference between predicted probabilities and true labels.
- **Categorical Cross-Entropy:** An extension of binary cross-entropy for multi-class classification.

Optimizers: Navigating the Loss Landscape

Once we've quantified how wrong our network is with the loss function, we need a way to systematically adjust its parameters to reduce this loss. This is the job of the optimizer.

Think of the optimizer as a hiker trying to reach the bottom of a valley (the minimum loss). The loss function provides the elevation map, and the optimizer decides which direction to take a step in.

The most basic optimizer is Gradient Descent. It calculates the gradient (the direction of steepest ascent) of the loss function with respect to the network's parameters, and takes a step in the opposite direction.

However, there are many more advanced optimizers that adapt the step size based on various factors to converge faster and avoid getting stuck in suboptimal solutions. Some popular ones include:

- **Stochastic Gradient Descent (SGD):** A variation of Gradient Descent that calculates the gradient based on a single random sample at a time, rather than the entire dataset.
- **Adam (Adaptive Moment Estimation):** Adapts the learning rate for each parameter based on the historical gradients.
- **RMSprop:** Adjusts the learning rate based on a moving average of the magnitude of recent gradients.

Hyperparameters: The Dials and Knobs of Deep Learning

Finally, hyperparameters are the settings that we choose before training the network. They include things like the number of layers, the number of units in each layer, the learning rate of the optimizer, and the type of activation and loss functions to use.

You can think of hyperparameters as the dials and knobs on a complex machine. The right settings will make the machine run smoothly and efficiently, while the wrong settings can cause it to underperform or even break down entirely.

Choosing the right hyperparameters is more of an art than a science, and often involves a lot of trial and error. However, there are some systematic approaches like grid search and random search that can automate the process of finding good hyperparameter combinations.

Techniques for Improving Model Performance

Imagine deep learning as an athlete training for a big competition. The athlete, in this case, is your model, and the training routine is the data it's learning from. If the athlete just practices the same routine over and over without variation, they might get really good at that specific routine, but struggle when in live game situations. This is similar to overfitting in deep learning, where the model becomes too specialized in the training data and fails to perform well on new data. Just as a well-rounded training regimen that includes different drills, rest periods, and varying exercises prepares an athlete for the competition, deep learning models can benefit from a variety of techniques to improve their adaptability and generalization.

Fortunately, several techniques have been developed to help address these challenges and improve the performance of deep learning models.

Regularization Techniques

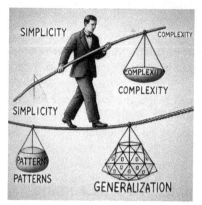

Regularization is a set of techniques in machine learning designed to help models avoid overfitting. Regularization works by intentionally imposing constraints on the learning process, encouraging the model to find a balance between capturing the important patterns in the data and avoiding unnecessary complexity.

Two popular forms of regularization are L1 and L2 regularization, also known as Lasso and Ridge regularization, respectively. These techniques modify the model's loss function, which you'll remember is the measure of how well the model's predictions match the actual data. In L1 and L2 regularization, a penalty is added to this loss function based on the size of the model's weights. In simpler terms, these techniques work by discouraging the model from assigning too much importance to any one feature, thereby keeping the model simpler and reducing the risk of overfitting. The degree to which the weights are penalized is controlled by a hyperparameter, which is like a dial that adjusts the balance between fitting the training data well and keeping the model straightforward and generalizable.

Another effective regularization technique is Dropout, which takes a different approach by randomly "dropping out" or turning off a percentage of neurons (the units in a neural network that process information) during the training process. This means that during each training step, some of the neurons don't contribute to the model's predictions. By doing this, Dropout prevents any single neuron from becoming too dominant or relying too heavily on specific inputs, which can lead to overfitting. When the model is used for making predictions on new data, all the neurons are active again, but their outputs are scaled down slightly to account for the fact that they were sometimes turned off during training. This results in a model that is more robust and better able to generalize to new data.

In essence, regularization techniques like L1, L2, and Dropout help create models that are not just good at making predictions on the data they were trained on, but also on new, unseen data. By keeping the model from becoming overly complex or overly reliant on specific details in the training data, regularization improves the model's ability to perform well in real-world scenarios, where the data it encounters may be different from what it has seen before. This makes regularization an essential tool in building reliable and effective machine learning models.

Batch Normalization

Batch normalization is a widely used technique in deep learning that helps to improve the stability and performance of neural networks. It works by standardizing the inputs to each layer of the network, ensuring that they have a consistent range of values. Specifically, batch normalization normalizes the activations (or outputs) of the previous layer within each batch of data, keeping the mean activation close to 0 and the standard deviation close to 1. This consistent scaling of the inputs makes it easier for the network to learn and adjust its parameters effectively.

The benefits of batch normalization are significant. First, it stabilizes the learning process, making it less sensitive to the initial conditions of the model. When training a deep learning model, the weights and biases (the parameters that the model adjusts to make accurate predictions) are usually initialized randomly. Without batch normalization, small changes in these initial values can lead to large variations in the activations, causing the training process to become unstable or slow. By standardizing the inputs to each layer, batch normalization reduces this sensitivity, allowing the model to use higher learning rates—essentially letting the model learn faster and reach its optimal performance more quickly.

Additionally, batch normalization acts as a form of regularization, which helps prevent overfitting. Overfitting occurs when a model becomes too tailored to the training data, performing well on that data but poorly on new, unseen data. By maintaining a consistent range of activations, batch normalization reduces the likelihood that the model will become overly reliant on any specific feature or pattern in the training data. This regularizing effect, combined with the stabilization of the learning process, results in models that are not only faster to train but also more robust and capable of generalizing well to new data.

Batch normalization is a powerful technique that enhances the training of deep learning models by ensuring that each layer receives inputs that are standardized across batches. This standardization leads to faster learning, greater stability, and improved model performance, making batch normalization a key component in modern deep learning architectures. Whether you're building a simple neural network or a complex deep learning model, incorporating batch normalization can help you achieve better, more reliable results.

Transfer Learning

Transfer learning is a powerful approach in machine learning that allows models trained on one task to be repurposed for different, but related, tasks. This method is particularly advantageous in scenarios where you have access to a large amount of data for one task (known as the "source" task), but only a limited amount of data for the task you are primarily interested in (referred to as the "target" task). By transferring knowledge from the source task to the target task, transfer learning enables the creation of effective models even when data is scarce for the specific task at hand.

In deep learning, transfer learning typically involves using a pre-trained neural network — one that has already been trained on a large and diverse dataset, such as ImageNet, which contains millions of images labeled for object recognition. The idea behind this approach is that the early layers of the pre-trained network have learned to detect general features, such as edges, textures, and shapes, that are common across a wide range of images. These general features are not specific to the original task and can be valuable for many different tasks. The later layers of the network, however, are more specialized and tailored to the specific details of the original task.

To apply transfer learning to a new task, you typically keep the early layers of the pre-trained network intact and only fine-tune the later layers or add new layers that are specific to the target task. This fine-tuning process involves training the network on the limited data available for the target task, but since the early layers have already learned useful representations from the source task, the network can quickly adapt to the new task with relatively little data. This approach not only accelerates the training process but also often results in a model that performs significantly better than one trained from scratch on the small target dataset.

Transfer learning is used all of the time in fields like computer vision, natural language processing, and even reinforcement learning, where large amounts of labeled data are often hard to come by. By leveraging the knowledge embedded in pre-trained models, researchers and practitioners can build high-performance models for specialized tasks – without the need for extensive data collection and training resources. This makes transfer learning a practical and efficient strategy for tackling a wide range of machine learning problems, particularly in situations where data is limited or expensive to obtain.

Data Augmentation

As the name suggests, data augmentation is expanding the size of a training dataset by creating modified versions of the existing data. This is another approach that is frequently used in image classification, where variations in the dataset can significantly improve the model's performance. By applying random but realistic transformations to the original data (e.g. image rotations, shifts, shears, flips, zooms, etc.) data augmentation effectively increases the diversity of the training data without the need for collecting new data.

This technique is also widely used in computer vision, where a model might be trained on images of objects in various orientations, lighting conditions, or positions; but it can also be applied to other types of data, such as text or audio, where similar transformations can be used to create varied training examples.

By augmenting the dataset with these kinds of variations, the model learns to recognize the essential features of the objects, regardless of the specific conditions in which they appear. By augmenting data in situations where the amount of training data is limited, engineers can build more robust models that can accurately classify images in real-world situations where the conditions may differ from those in the original training set. When obtaining data is not possible or is prohibitively difficult or expensive, data augmentation can be used to effectively increase the size and variability of a dataset, which can lead to better model performance without the need for more "actual" data.

Pro Tip for Finance Folks

Techniques like regularization, batch normalization, transfer learning, and data augmentation are particularly valuable in the finance industry due to three key factors:

- Financial data can be sensitive and difficult to obtain in large quantities, but these techniques help models learn effectively even with smaller datasets.
- Privacy is a major concern in finance, and these techniques can improve model performance without requiring access to sensitive information.
- In the highly-regulated financial industry, the cost of errors can be significant. These techniques help create more robust and reliable models, reducing the risk of costly mistakes.

These techniques are powerful tools in the deep learning practitioner's toolkit. By understanding and applying them appropriately, it is possible to train models that are more robust, generalize better to new data, and require less training data.

Tools and Frameworks for Deep Learning

"If I have seen further, it is by standing on the shoulders of giants."

~ Isaac Newton

For non-engineers and programmers, it might seem like every one of these models is built by scratch every time a data scientist has a wild hair to solve a data problem; but the truth is that there are many tools and applications that can be replicated and applied to novel problems. These tools make it easier to build, train, and deploy deep learning models, allowing researchers and practitioners to focus on the high-level design of their models rather than low-level implementation details.

In this section, we'll explore some of the most popular tools and frameworks for deep learning, including open-source libraries, cloud platforms, and hardware considerations.

Open-Source Libraries

Open-source libraries provide high-level APIs for building and training deep learning models, abstracting away much of the complexity and allowing developers to work more efficiently.

Google's TensorFlow is a powerful and versatile deep learning library that has become a cornerstone in the machine learning community. Launched in 2015, TensorFlow has evolved into a complete and comprehensive ecosystem that caters to both researchers and industry professionals. Its flexibility, scalability, and extensive support for various machine learning tasks make it a go-to choice for building and deploying sophisticated models across a wide range of applications.

TensorFlow is a one-stop shop that covers the entire machine learning workflow from model development to deployment. It offers a full range of tools for building neural networks – offering support for both high-level APIs like Keras (an open-source software library that provides a Python interface for artificial neural networks) and low-level operations for those who need fine-grained control over their model architecture. Further, TensorFlow's computational graph model allows for efficient execution on the full spectrum of processors: CPUs, GPUs, and TPUs (Tensor Processing Units). This versatility makes it highly scalable and suitable for both small-scale experiments and large-scale production environments.

Hardware Considerations

Deep learning models, particularly large ones, can be computationally intensive to train and run. Therefore, the choice of hardware is a crucial consideration in any deep learning project.

Central Processing Units (CPUs) are the traditional workhorses of computing and can be used for deep learning, particularly for smaller models or inference tasks. However, for training large models, CPUs can be prohibitively slow.

Graphics Processing Units (GPUs) have become the standard for deep learning due to their ability to perform massive parallel computations. GPUs were originally designed for graphics tasks but have proven to be exceptionally well-suited for the matrix operations that form the core of deep learning algorithms. NVIDIA's GPUs, in particular, have become synonymous with deep learning, with many libraries and frameworks offering strong support for NVIDIA's CUDA parallel computing platform.

Tensor Processing Units (TPUs) are specialized application-specific integrated circuits (ASICs) developed by Google specifically for machine learning workloads. TPUs offer significant performance advantages over GPUs for certain types of models and have been used by Google to achieve state-of-the-art results on several benchmarks. However, they are less flexible than GPUs and are primarily available through Google's Cloud Platform.

The choice of hardware will depend on the specific requirements of your project, including the size and complexity of your models, your performance needs, and your budget. For many applications, a combination of CPUs for data preprocessing and model deployment, and GPUs for model training, offers the best balance of performance and cost.

TensorFlow's ecosystem is designed to support every stage of the machine learning pipeline.

TensorFlow Extended (TFX) facilitates the creation of production-ready machine learning pipelines. It includes components for data validation, feature engineering, model training, evaluation, and serving, all within a unified environment. This makes it easier for teams to standardize their workflows and ensure that models move seamlessly from research to deployment, while maintaining reproducibility and reliability.

TensorFlow Serving is a flexible and high-performance serving system designed to make it easy to deploy ML models. It's optimized for production environments and provides out-of-the-box integration with TensorFlow models, which facilitates efficient model serving at scale. Serving supports versioning (i.e. allowing multiple versions of a model to be served simultaneously,) which is crucial for A/B testing and gradual rollouts. TensorFlow Serving also integrates with monitoring tools, which make it easier to track model performance in real-time and detect issues early.

Another tool, TensorFlow Lite (a lightweight version of TensorFlow designed for mobile and embedded devices) lets developers to deploy machine learning models on the edge (e.g. smartphones, IoT devices, and microcontrollers), which brings AI capabilities directly to users without the need for constant cloud connectivity. TensorFlow Lite is optimized for low-latency and low-power inference, making it ideal for applications like image recognition, speech processing, and on-device predictive analytics. TensorFlow's versatility extends to specialized domains through its suite of dedicated libraries.

Arguably the most popular library, TensorFlow.js, allows machine learning models to be run directly in the browser using JavaScript, which is ideal for web-based AI applications. Another library, TensorFlow Federated, facilitates privacy-preserving ML by enabling decentralized training across multiple devices while preserving data locally on those devices. TensorFlow also supports TensorFlow Probability for probabilistic reasoning and uncertainty quantification, and TensorFlow Graphics for advanced computer graphics and 3D modeling.

TensorFlow is enhanced by TensorFlow Hub, a vibrant community and rich ecosystem of third-party tools and resources, which provides access to an extensive collection of pre-trained models that can be easily integrated into new projects. This is significant because it reduces the need for large datasets and accelerates development time. This community is integral to TensorFlow because it creates an application and environment that continuously expands its capabilities.

Another framework that has proven incredibly valuable for the AI community is Meta's PyTorch. Since its release, PyTorch has distinguished itself with a number of features that cater to the needs of researchers and developers alike, making it an ideal choice for a wide range of machine learning tasks. One of PyTorch's most notable characteristics is its dynamic computational graph, which offers a level of flexibility and ease of use that is particularly appealing for those who prioritize rapid prototyping, experimentation, and iterative development.

The dynamic nature of PyTorch's computational graph, also known as "define-by-run," allows users to construct the computation graph on-the-fly as operations are executed. This contrasts with the static graph approach used by frameworks like TensorFlow, where the computation graph is defined once and can't be changed during runtime. PyTorch's dynamic graph is highly intuitive and aligns closely with the native Python programming language, allowing for more "pythonic" code that is easier to write, debug, and modify. This makes PyTorch exceptionally well-suited for exploratory research, where the ability to quickly iterate on models and experiment with different architectures is crucial.

In addition to its dynamic graph, PyTorch offers seamless integration with Python's extensive ecosystem of libraries, such as NumPy, SciPy, and Pandas, further enhancing its appeal for researchers and developers. This integration allows for smooth interoperability between PyTorch and other tools commonly used in the scientific and machine learning communities. The framework's support for GPU acceleration through CUDA also enables efficient training of deep learning models, making it suitable for both academic research and industrial applications.

Another strength of PyTorch is its focus on simplicity and transparency. The framework's simple API design ensures that users can focus on the core aspects of model development without getting bogged down by unnecessary complexity. PyTorch's straightforward approach to defining and training neural networks has made it a favorite among those who value a clean and readable codebase, which is particularly important in collaborative environments where multiple researchers may be working on the same project.

PyTorch's flexibility extends to its support for a wide variety of deep learning tasks. The framework's modular design allows users to easily customize and extend its functionality to suit their specific needs. PyTorch's TorchText, TorchVision, and TorchAudio libraries provide pre-built modules and utilities for handling text, image, and audio data, respectively, making it easier to develop models for these domains.

The research community's preference for PyTorch is also bolstered by its active development and strong community support. Facebook AI Research and other contributors continuously update and enhance the framework, ensuring it stays at the cutting edge of deep learning technology. PyTorch's ecosystem is rich with tutorials, documentation, and open-source projects that help users get started and deepen their understanding of the framework. Additionally, many state-of-the-art research papers and models are implemented in PyTorch, providing a wealth of resources for those looking to learn from the latest advancements in the field.

PyTorch's adoption has expanded beyond academia and into industry, where its flexibility and ease of use have proven valuable in production environments. The introduction of tools like PyTorch Lightning and Fastai has further streamlined the process of training and deploying models, making PyTorch an increasingly popular choice for both research and real-world applications.

We mentioned Keras above, but it's worth expanding on its functionality here.

Keras is a high-level neural network API designed to simplify the development of deep learning models, making it accessible to a wide range of users, from beginners to experienced practitioners. Initially developed by François Chollet, Keras was created with the goal of enabling rapid experimentation, allowing users to go from an idea to a fully trained model with minimal effort and delay. Its focus on user-friendliness and ease of use has made Keras a popular choice for those who want to quickly prototype ideas without getting bogged down by the complexities of lower-level programming.

One of the standout features of Keras is its versatility. While it is often used as a frontend for TensorFlow, Keras can also run on top of other deep learning frameworks, including Microsoft Cognitive Toolkit (CNTK), Theano, R, and PlaidML. This ability to seamlessly integrate with multiple backends allows users to choose the underlying engine that best fits their needs, whether they prioritize speed, scalability, or compatibility with specific hardware. Keras abstracts away many of the technical details involved in building neural networks, providing a consistent and simple interface that remains the same regardless of the backend used. This makes it easier for users to experiment with different frameworks without needing to learn a new API each time.

Keras excels in making deep learning accessible to those who may not have a deep background in machine learning or programming. Its API is designed to be intuitive and straightforward, with clear and concise commands that allow users to define and train models in just a few lines of code. The architecture of Keras is modular, enabling users to build complex models by simply stacking layers or connecting them in more sophisticated ways. This simplicity does not come at the cost of flexibility—Keras still offers the ability to customize and extend models as needed, providing advanced users with the tools to tackle more complex tasks.

In addition to its ease of use, Keras has a rich set of built-in utilities that streamline the process of model development. These include functions for data preprocessing, model evaluation, and visualization, which help users prepare their data, monitor training progress, and interpret results with minimal hassle. Keras also includes pre-built layers, activation functions, loss functions, and optimizers, which can be easily configured to suit a wide variety of tasks. Whether you're working on image classification, natural language processing, or any other deep learning application, Keras provides the components needed to get up and running quickly.

Keras is also well-supported by an active community and a wealth of educational resources. The extensive documentation, tutorials, and examples available online make it easier for newcomers to learn the basics of deep learning while providing more experienced users with insights into advanced techniques. Moreover, because Keras is tightly integrated with TensorFlow, it benefits from the ongoing improvements and updates to

TensorFlow's core functionalities, ensuring that it remains a relevant and powerful tool for modern deep learning tasks.

Cloud Platforms

Cloud platforms are arguably as important to the development and rapid deployment of AI systems as the frameworks and models themselves. They offer access to the significant computational resources needed to train large models on big data. The leading cloud providers, Amazon Web Services (AWS), Google Cloud Platform (GCP), and Microsoft Azure, all offer deep learning services and tools.

Amazon Web Services

SageMaker from Amazon is a fully managed machine learning platform designed to simplify the process of building, training, and deploying ML models at scale. With SageMaker, developers and data scientists can bypass much of the complexity typically associated with machine learning workflows, allowing them to focus on creating models that deliver real business value. By providing a comprehensive set of tools and services, SageMaker enables users to take their machine learning projects from concept to production in a seamless and efficient manner.

One of the standout features of Amazon SageMaker is its integration with a wide range of pre-built algorithms and popular deep learning frameworks, including TensorFlow, PyTorch, and Apache MXNet. This flexibility allows users to choose the tools and frameworks that best suit their specific needs, whether they are working on a simple regression model or a complex deep learning application. SageMaker also supports custom algorithms, giving users the ability to bring their own models or frameworks to the platform. This adaptability makes SageMaker a versatile solution for a broad spectrum of machine learning tasks, from computer vision to natural language processing to predictive analytics.

SageMaker goes beyond just model building by offering robust tools for every stage of the machine learning lifecycle. For data preparation, SageMaker provides built-in tools for data labeling, transformation, and analysis, which help ensure that data is clean, well-structured, and ready for training. SageMaker Ground Truth, for instance, offers an efficient way to label datasets at scale, combining human input with machine learning to create high-quality training data. Once the data is prepared, SageMaker simplifies the training process with its managed infrastructure, which automatically provisions the necessary compute resources and optimizes the training environment for performance and cost. Users can easily scale their training jobs, leveraging powerful GPU instances or distributed computing to handle large datasets and complex models.

SageMaker also shines with deployment and includes a range of options that bring models into production quickly and reliably. SageMaker allows for one-click deployment, enabling users to easily deploy models as fully managed endpoints that can handle real-time predictions or batch processing. These endpoints are automatically scaled based on demand, ensuring that the model can serve predictions efficiently, regardless of the workload. SageMaker also includes features for monitoring model performance in production, such as automatic A/B testing, model versioning, and endpoint monitoring, which help maintain model accuracy and reliability over time.

Further, SageMaker's integration with the broader AWS ecosystem provides additional advantages, such as seamless data storage with Amazon S3, security and compliance features with AWS Identity and Access Management (IAM), and the ability to integrate with other AWS services like AWS Lambda for building automated machine learning workflows. This tight integration allows users to build comprehensive machine learning pipelines that are fully scalable, secure, and capable of handling the demands of enterprise applications.

Google Cloud

AI Platform from Google Cloud is a comprehensive suite of tools and services designed to facilitate the entire lifecycle of building and deploying AI models. It was engineered to meet the needs of both developers and data scientists by providing a robust set of resources that streamline the process of developing, training, and deploying machine learning models. Whether you're working on a small-scale project or deploying models in a large enterprise environment, Google Cloud's AI Platform provides the flexibility and scalability needed to bring AI solutions from concept to production efficiently.

One of AI Platform's key functionalities is its support for pre-trained models that users can use to leverage Google's state-of-the-art machine learning models. These pre-trained models can be used for a variety of tasks, such as image recognition, natural language processing, and translation, enabling users to quickly integrate advanced AI capabilities into their applications. For those who require more customization, the AI Platform also includes a workbench for experimentation and prototyping, where users can develop and fine-tune their models. This workbench provides an integrated development environment that supports popular machine learning frameworks, including TensorFlow, scikit-learn, and PyTorch, allowing users to experiment with different approaches and optimize their models before deploying them.

Google Cloud's AI Platform also offers a job submission service that simplifies the training and prediction process. This service allows users to submit their training jobs to Google's powerful cloud infrastructure, which automatically manages the compute resources required for the task. By offloading the heavy lifting of training to Google's cloud, users can significantly reduce the time and cost associated with developing complex machine learning models. Once a model is trained, the AI Platform also provides tools for deploying it as a scalable, managed service, ensuring that it can handle real-time predictions with ease.

For organizations that require enterprise-level support and reliability, Google offers TensorFlow Enterprise as part of its AI Platform. TensorFlow Enterprise provides enhanced support and services for TensorFlow, one of the most widely used machine learning frameworks in the world. This enterprise-grade offering includes long-term version support, managed services, and specialized support from Google engineers, making it an ideal choice for businesses that rely heavily on TensorFlow for their AI initiatives. TensorFlow Enterprise ensures that organizations can deploy and maintain their machine learning models with confidence, backed by the expertise and infrastructure of Google Cloud.

Microsoft Azure

Microsoft Azure offers Azure Machine Learning: a comprehensive cloud-based service designed to accelerate and manage the entire machine learning project lifecycle. Azure Machine Learning is built to support both beginners and seasoned data scientists by providing a suite of tools and services that streamline the complex processes involved in developing, training, and deploying machine learning models. Whether you're working on simple predictive models or large-scale deep learning projects, Azure Machine Learning offers the infrastructure and resources needed to bring machine learning solutions to life efficiently and effectively.

Azure Machine Learning is an automated machine learning (AutoML) that significantly simplifies the model development process. It does this by automatically selecting the best algorithms and performing hyperparameter tuning, a task that can be time-consuming and technically challenging when done manually. With AutoML, users can quickly experiment with different models and configurations to identify the most effective solution for their specific problem, making it easier to achieve high-quality results without deep expertise in machine learning, which makes it incredibly popular among ML developers.

Azure Machine Learning also includes a full host of tools for data preparation, which is a critical step in any machine learning project. The platform provides features for data cleaning, transformation, and augmentation, allowing users to prepare their datasets efficiently and ensure they are ready for training. These tools help address common data challenges, such as missing values, outliers, and inconsistent data formats, which can impact model performance if not properly handled. By simplifying data preparation, Azure Machine Learning enables users to focus more on the creative and strategic aspects of model development.

In addition to data preparation and model selection, Azure Machine Learning provides powerful resources for model training and deployment. The platform supports distributed training, allowing users to scale their training workloads across multiple compute resources, including GPUs and CPUs, to speed up the training process. Once a model is trained, Azure Machine Learning offers seamless deployment options, enabling users to deploy models as web services that can be accessed in real-time or used for batch processing. These deployment tools are fully managed, meaning that Azure takes care of scaling, monitoring, and updating the models, which simplifies the operational aspects of running machine learning models in production.

Azure Machine Learning also integrates with the broader Azure ecosystem, providing additional advantages such as secure data storage with Azure Blob Storage, data analytics with Azure Synapse Analytics, and integration with DevOps pipelines for continuous integration and continuous delivery (CI/CD). This integration allows users to build end-to-end machine learning workflows that are secure, scalable, and aligned with enterprise-grade best practices.

Chapter Five

DEEP LEARNING APPLICATIONS IN FINANCE

Deep Learning Applications in Finance

The financial industry has long been open to adopting new technologies to gain a competitive edge, and in recent years Deep Learning has been one of the most intriguing breakthrough technologies to be adopted.

In this chapter, we will explore four key areas where deep learning is being used in finance: financial time series forecasting, algorithmic trading, fraud detection, and customer analytics.

Financial Time Series Forecasting

Financial time series data, such as stock prices, exchange rates, and trading volumes, is notoriously difficult to predict, due to its non-stationary and noisy nature. Traditional statistical models often struggle to capture the complex patterns and dependencies in this data. In recent years, deep learning has shown promising results in capturing the intricate structures of financial time series, thanks to its ability to automatically learn hierarchical representations from raw data.

Challenges in Financial Time Series

Before we dive into the deep learning approaches, let's dig into why time series analysis is difficult.

Non-stationarity

The statistical properties of financial time series, including key metrics like mean and variance, are prone to fluctuations over time. Unlike stationary time series, where these properties remain constant, financial time series can experience shifts due to various factors such as economic events, market sentiment, or regulatory changes. This variability complicates the application of traditional models that rely on the assumption of a stable, unchanging distribution. For instance, models that assume a constant mean or variance may struggle to accurately predict future values when these underlying properties are actually dynamic and evolving. As a result, analysts and modelers must employ more sophisticated techniques that account for this non-stationarity, such as time-varying parameter models or methods designed to detect and adapt to structural breaks within the data. Understanding and addressing non-stationarity is crucial for making reliable inferences and predictions in the context of financial time series analysis.

Noise

Financial markets are inherently characterized by a high degree of noise, meaning that prices and other financial metrics are constantly influenced by an extensive array of factors, many of which are difficult to quantify or even observe. This noise stems from a variety of sources, such as investor sentiment, market rumors, geopolitical events, macroeconomic data releases, and random fluctuations in supply and demand. The presence of such noise can significantly obscure the underlying trends and patterns that analysts seek to identify, making it challenging to develop reliable predictive models. As a result, predictions in financial markets often come with a level of uncertainty, as the noise can lead to volatility and unexpected movements that are not easily captured by traditional modeling approaches. To address this, financial analysts may use advanced techniques such as signal processing, noise filtering, or machine learning algorithms that are designed to separate meaningful signals from the noise, thereby improving the accuracy of their predictions and decision-making processes.

High Dimensionality

Modern financial markets produce an immense volume of data, ranging from tick-level price quotes that capture every transaction in real-time, to more abstract metrics like news sentiment scores that gauge the mood of the market. This flood of information presents a substantial challenge when it comes to incorporating it all into a coherent and effective forecasting model. The sheer diversity and scale of the data mean that models must be capable of handling various data types, time frequencies, and levels of granularity, all while filtering out irrelevant noise and identifying the most predictive features. Furthermore, integrating such a wide array of data requires advanced data processing techniques and considerable computational resources, as well as the ability to update and refine models in response to new information continuously. Successfully leveraging this immense data landscape can provide a significant competitive advantage, but doing so requires sophisticated modeling approaches that can manage and synthesize the information into actionable insights.

Long-term Dependencies

Certain events or trends in financial markets can have effects that persist over extended periods, influencing prices and market behaviors long after the initial occurrence. Capturing these long-term dependencies is essential for making accurate predictions, as they often play a crucial role in shaping future market movements. However, traditional models often struggle with this task, as they are typically designed to analyze short-term patterns and may lack the capacity to account for influences that unfold over months or even years. The challenge lies in the complexity and variability of these long-term effects, which can interact with other market dynamics in unpredictable ways. To effectively model these dependencies, more advanced approaches, such as those incorporating memory-augmented neural networks or time series models specifically designed for long-range forecasting, are often required. These methods aim to recognize and leverage the ongoing impact of significant events or trends, improving the model's ability to generate reliable long-term forecasts.

Deep Learning Approaches

Several deep learning architectures have been successfully applied to financial time series forecasting, each with its own strengths and weaknesses.

Convolutional Neural Networks (CNNs) have been used to capture local patterns and correlations in financial time series. By applying convolutional filters of various sizes, CNNs can automatically extract relevant features from raw time series data. This is particularly useful when dealing with high-frequency data, such as minute-by-minute stock prices.

Long Short-Term Memory (LSTM) networks, a type of recurrent neural network (RNN), have shown great promise in modeling long-term dependencies in financial time series. LSTMs have a special memory cell that can maintain information over long sequences, allowing them to capture trends and patterns that span extended periods.

More recently, transformer models, which were originally developed for natural language processing tasks, have been adapted for time series forecasting. Transformer models rely on a self-attention mechanism to weigh the importance of different time steps, allowing them to focus on the most relevant parts of the input sequence.

Case Study: Stock Price Prediction

To illustrate the application of deep learning to financial time series forecasting, let's consider a case study of predicting stock prices.

Our goal is to build a model that can predict the future price of a stock based on its historical price data and other relevant information, such as trading volume and market sentiment.

We start by collecting and preprocessing the data. This involves downloading historical price and volume data for the stock, as well as collecting relevant news articles and other digital data. We then clean and normalize the data, and split it into training, validation, and test sets.

Next, we design our deep learning model. For this task, we choose an LSTM network, as it is well-suited for capturing long-term dependencies in the data. We feed the historical price and volume data into the LSTM, along with embeddings of the news articles and social media posts.

We train the model on the training set, using the validation set to tune the hyperparameters and prevent overfitting. Once we are satisfied with the model's performance, we evaluate it on the test set to get an unbiased estimate of its predictive power.

Finally, we can use the trained model to make predictions on new, unseen data. By feeding in the most recent price and volume data, along with current news and sentiment, the model can generate predictions for the future price of the stock.

Of course, this is a simplified example, and in practice, there are many additional factors to consider, such as the choice of loss function, the incorporation of risk metrics, and the handling of the inherent uncertainty in financial markets. Nevertheless, this case study demonstrates the potential of deep learning for financial time series forecasting.

Algorithmic Trading

Increasing demand for fast, reliable, and efficient order execution and the need for market surveillance and lower transaction costs has fueled the growth of algorithmic trading systems. These systems use automated trading strategies to execute high-speed and high-frequency orders based on pre-programmed instructions. Large financial institutions, such as investment banks and hedge funds, have widely adopted this method to optimize trade execution and reduce costs; algorithmic trading now accounts for the majority of trading volume in most financial markets.

The integration of advanced technologies, including artificial intelligence and machine learning, has further enhanced the capabilities of algorithmic trading systems. Deep learning, or in particular deep reinforcement learning (DRL), has shown promise in developing algorithmic trading strategies that can adapt to changing market conditions.

Advantages of Algorithmic Trading

Speed

Algorithmic trading systems have the remarkable ability to process and analyze data at a speed that far surpasses human capabilities. These systems are designed to scan markets, evaluate historical data, and monitor real-time information from multiple sources — all within milliseconds. This capability is made possible by sophisticated algorithms and high-performance computing infrastructure that work together to execute trades with extreme precision and speed.

In financial markets, the ability to rapidly analyze large datasets is a key advantage for traders. Algorithmic trading systems can identify and react to opportunities much faster than human traders who would need considerably more time to process the same amount of information and make decisions. For instance, an algorithm can detect slight price discrepancies between different exchanges or assets, and execute arbitrage trades to capitalize on those differences before the market corrects itself. In such scenarios, even a delay of a few milliseconds can mean the difference between a profitable trade and a missed opportunity.

These systems can continuously monitor a multitude of variables, including market prices, trading volumes, news feeds, and economic indicators. By synthesizing this data in real-time, algorithmic trading systems can make informed decisions about when to enter or exit a trade, and can do so with minimal latency. This ability to act almost instantaneously allows them to take advantage of short-lived market conditions, such as temporary mispricings or sudden news events, which might be too fleeting for human traders to capitalize on.

The speed at which algorithmic trading systems operate not only enhances the potential for profit, but also contributes to market efficiency. By rapidly executing trades in response to new information, these systems help to ensure that prices reflect all available information, thereby reducing the likelihood of prolonged mispricings. This, in turn, promotes liquidity and stability in the markets, as prices quickly adjust to reflect true market conditions.

Efficiency

By automating the entire trading process, algorithmic systems eliminate the need for manual intervention, which traditionally involves human traders analyzing data, making decisions, and executing trades by hand. This automation streamlines operations, allowing trades to be executed with previously unparalleled speed and accuracy, significantly reducing the time and resources required to manage trading activities.

One of the primary benefits of this efficiency is the minimization of human error, which can be particularly costly in the fast-paced and complex world of financial trading. Human traders are susceptible to a range of errors, from misinterpreting data to making calculation mistakes or even misclicking in a high-pressure environment. These errors can lead to substantial financial losses, especially when dealing with large volumes or high-frequency trades. Algorithmic trading systems, on the other hand, operate based on precise mathematical models and predefined rules, ensuring that trades are executed exactly as intended, without the inconsistencies or errors that can arise from human intervention.

The automation provided by algorithmic trading enables the execution of complex trading strategies that would be challenging – if not impossible – to manage manually. For instance, strategies that involve monitoring multiple markets simultaneously, executing hundreds or thousands of trades in quick succession, or reacting instantly to market events require a level of precision and speed that only automated systems can provide. This capability allows firms to capitalize on intricate market opportunities and execute trades more efficiently than ever before.

In addition to reducing errors and enabling complex strategies, the efficiency of algorithmic trading also leads to cost savings. With fewer human resources needed to manage trading operations, firms can reduce overhead costs related to staffing and training. Furthermore, the increased accuracy and speed of trade execution can lead to better pricing and reduced transaction costs, as the systems can optimize trade execution by selecting the most favorable moments to enter or exit positions.

Consistency

Algorithmic trading systems have the advantage over humans of being relentlessly consistent. In financial markets, where emotions and psychological factors can often cloud judgment, algorithmic trading provides a systematic approach to executing trades based on predefined rules and strategies. This eliminates the variability and inconsistencies that can arise when human traders are influenced by emotions such as fear, greed, or overconfidence, which can lead to impulsive decisions and erratic trading behavior.

Algorithmic trading systems operate with unwavering adherence to the rules and logic programmed into them. These rules are derived from rigorous analysis and backtesting, ensuring that each trade is executed in a manner consistent with the overall trading strategy, regardless of the market's current mood or volatility. For example, an algorithm designed to buy a stock when it dips to a certain price level will execute that trade precisely when the condition is met, without hesitation or second-guessing, which might occur if a human trader were involved. This predictability helps in maintaining a disciplined approach to trading, which is crucial for long-term success in the markets.

By removing the human element from the decision-making process, algorithmic trading systems avoid common pitfalls, such as panic selling, during market downturns or holding onto losing positions out of hope for a rebound. These emotional reactions can lead to suboptimal outcomes, but with algorithmic trading, decisions are made based purely on data and predetermined criteria. This objectivity ensures that trades are executed consistently across different market conditions, enhancing the reliability and effectiveness of the trading strategy.

Consistency in trade execution also contributes to more stable performance over time. Inconsistent trading behavior can lead to unpredictable results, making it difficult to assess the true effectiveness of a trading strategy. Algorithmic trading, by contrast, ensures that every trade aligns with the strategy's design, making it easier to evaluate performance, optimize strategies, and achieve steady returns. This reliability is particularly valuable in environments where precision and consistency are key to managing risk and maximizing profitability.

Risk Management

Algorithmic trading systems are particularly adept at incorporating advanced risk management techniques to protect against potential losses. These systems are designed to automatically implement strategies that manage and mitigate risk, ensuring that trades are executed in a manner that aligns with predefined risk tolerance levels. By embedding risk management protocols directly into the trading algorithms, these systems can react swiftly to market changes, often faster and more precisely than human traders could.

One of the most common risk management tools used in algorithmic trading is the stop-loss order. A stop-loss order is a predefined instruction to sell an asset when its price reaches a certain level, thereby limiting the loss on a position. Algorithmic trading systems can automatically trigger stop-loss orders as soon as the specified conditions are met, ensuring that losses are capped according to the trader's risk appetite. This automated approach removes the emotional element that might cause a trader to hesitate or deviate from their risk management plan, thereby providing a disciplined method to protect capital.

In addition to stop-loss orders, algorithmic trading systems often incorporate sophisticated position sizing techniques. Position sizing refers to determining the appropriate amount of capital to allocate to a particular trade or set of trades based on the level of risk involved. By carefully calculating position sizes, these systems ensure that no single trade or market event can disproportionately impact the overall portfolio. Position sizing algorithms can adjust the size of positions dynamically, taking into account factors such as market volatility, current exposure, and the trader's overall risk management strategy. This dynamic adjustment helps maintain a balanced risk profile, reducing the likelihood of significant losses.

Algorithmic trading systems can also employ other risk management strategies, such as portfolio diversification, where the system allocates investments across various assets or markets to spread risk. Additionally, some algorithms monitor market conditions in real-time and can adjust trading strategies on the fly, such as reducing exposure during periods of high volatility or increasing it when conditions are more stable. These proactive measures help manage risk more effectively, ensuring that the trading strategy adapts to changing market environments.

Despite these advantages, algorithmic trading also has its challenges. These include the potential for algorithmic errors or "flash crashes," necessitating constant monitoring and updating of the algorithms, and the regulatory scrutiny surrounding high-frequency trading practices.

Deep Reinforcement Learning for Trading

Deep Reinforcement Learning is particularly well-suited for tackling complex decision-making problems like those encountered in algorithmic trading. At its core, reinforcement learning (RL) is a method where an agent learns to make a sequence of decisions by interacting with the financial markets. The agent receives feedback in the form of rewards or penalties based on the actions it takes, with the ultimate goal of learning a policy that maximizes its cumulative reward over time.

DRL takes this concept further by incorporating deep neural networks, which are powerful tools for approximating complex functions. In DRL, these neural networks are used to approximate the optimal policy or value function, enabling the agent to make informed decisions in environments that are high-dimensional and full of uncertainty, like financial markets. The use of deep neural networks allows the DRL agent to process and interpret market data, identifying patterns and trends that might be too subtle or complex for traditional models to capture. This capability is crucial in trading, where decisions must be made based on a constantly evolving and often noisy stream of information.

A DRL agent could be trained to make trading decisions by continuously interacting with market data. The agent would be able to buy, sell, or hold a financial asset, and the rewards would be based on the financial outcomes of these actions (i.e. the profit or loss realized from a trade). Over time, the DRL agent would learn which actions are likely to yield the best returns under different market conditions, effectively developing a trading strategy that seeks to maximize long-term profitability.

Unlike traditional trading algorithms, which are otherwise rule-based and static, a DRL agent can learn and evolve its strategy as it encounters new data. This adaptability is particularly valuable in financial markets, which are characterized by non-stationarity and the influence of a multitude of unpredictable factors. A well-trained DRL agent can adjust its trading behavior in response to shifts in market conditions, such as changes in volatility, market trends, or external economic events, potentially leading to more resilient and profitable trading strategies.

DRL offers the potential to discover novel trading strategies that might not be immediately apparent to human traders or conventional algorithms. By exploring a colossal space of possible actions and strategies, DRL agents can identify and exploit inefficiencies in the market that are difficult to detect through traditional means. This exploration is guided by the reward structure defined during the training process, which encourages the agent to pursue strategies that consistently generate positive returns while avoiding those that lead to losses.

Advantages of DRL

Adaptability

Unlike static, rule-based systems that follow predefined strategies, DRL agents are capable of dynamically adjusting their strategies in response to changing market conditions. This ability to learn and adapt over time allows DRL agents to potentially outperform traditional systems, especially in volatile or unpredictable markets. As they interact with the environment, DRL agents continually refine their decision-making processes, making them well-suited for the fast-paced and ever-changing nature of financial markets.

Scalability

DRL agents leverage deep neural networks, which are highly scalable and can process vast amounts of data efficiently. This scalability enables DRL agents to consider a wide range of market variables and historical data points when making trading decisions. By analyzing these large datasets, DRL agents can identify complex patterns and relationships that might be missed by simpler, rule-based systems. The ability to handle and analyze big data is particularly advantageous in algorithmic trading, where timely and accurate decision-making is crucial.

Continuous Learning

Another key benefit of DRL in algorithmic trading is the capability for continuous learning. DRL agents are not static; they can continue to learn and improve their strategies over time by interacting with the market and receiving feedback in the form of rewards or penalties. This ongoing learning process allows DRL agents to adapt to new market trends, refine their trading strategies, and improve their overall performance. As the agents gather more data and experience from the market, they become more adept at navigating complex trading environments and maximizing returns.

But there are challenges, including the potential for overfitting to historical data, the difficulty of defining an appropriate reward function, and the computational resources required to train and deploy DRL models.

Case Study: Developing a DRL Trading Agent

To illustrate the application of DRL to algorithmic trading, let's talk about how we might create a DRL trading agent for a single stock. Our goal is to create an agent that can learn to make profitable trading decisions based on historical price and volume data.

We start by defining the environment for our DRL agent. This includes specifying the state space (the market variables the agent will observe), the action space (the trading decisions the agent can make), and the reward function (how the agent's performance will be evaluated).

For the state space, we could include variables such as the current stock price, the moving average price over various time windows, and the current volume. For the action space, we could allow the agent to choose between buying, selling, or holding the stock at each time step. For the reward function, we could use the realized profit or loss from each trade, possibly with some risk adjustment.

Next, we design the agent. To do this, we'll use a deep neural network to approximate the optimal trading policy, with the network taking the state variables as input and outputting a probability distribution over the possible actions.

We train the agent using a suitable DRL algorithm, such as Deep Q-Learning (DQN) or Proximal Policy Optimization (PPO). This involves letting the agent interact with the environment (i.e., making trades based on historical data) and updating its neural network parameters based on the observed rewards.

After training, we can evaluate the agent's performance on unseen test data, comparing its returns and risk metrics to benchmarks such as a buy-and-hold strategy or a traditional rule-based trading system.

Finally, if we are satisfied with the agent's performance, we can deploy it to make real-time trading decisions in the market. This requires integrating the DRL model with a trading platform and ensuring that it can handle the latency and throughput requirements of live trading.

Throughout this process, we need to keep in mind the practical and regulatory challenges involved in deploying a DRL trading system. These include ensuring the robustness and interpretability of the model, managing the risk of unexpected market events, and complying with applicable trading regulations.

Fraud Detection

The proliferation of fraud has only increased alongside the advancement of technology, posing significant risks to individuals, businesses, and the integrity of the global financial system. This threat manifests in various forms, ranging from common schemes like credit card fraud and identity theft to more sophisticated and high-stakes crimes such as money laundering, insider trading, and securities fraud. Each of these types of fraud has the potential to cause severe financial harm, not only through direct monetary losses but also by undermining public trust in financial institutions and markets.

The costs associated with financial fraud are staggering. On a global scale, billions of dollars are lost annually to fraudulent activities, with the impact felt by both individual victims and financial institutions. For consumers, fraud can result in stolen identities, drained bank accounts, and damaged credit scores, all of which can take years to recover from. For businesses, particularly financial institutions, the consequences include not only financial losses but also legal liabilities, regulatory fines, and reputational damage. Further, the erosion of trust caused by fraud can have long-term repercussions, leading to reduced consumer confidence in the overall financial system, increased scrutiny from regulators, and greater operational costs associated with implementing and maintaining anti-fraud measures.

In recent years, the financial industry has increasingly turned to advanced technologies to bolster its defenses against the growing sophistication and frequency of fraudulent schemes. Among these, deep learning has emerged as a powerful weapon in the fight against financial fraud. What sets deep learning apart from traditional fraud detection methods is its ability to learn and adapt over time, making it particularly effective in detecting the subtle and evolving fraud indicators.

Traditional fraud detection systems rely on rule-based approaches, where specific patterns or red flags are identified and coded into the system. While these methods can be effective in catching known types of fraud, they often struggle to adapt to new, emerging tactics used by fraudsters. In contrast, deep learning models are designed to learn from experience, continually improving their ability to detect fraud by analyzing historical data, transaction patterns, and even unstructured data such as emails or other digital activity. This ability to learn and generalize from large datasets makes deep learning particularly well-suited for identifying the complex and often subtle signals of fraudulent behavior that might go unnoticed by conventional systems.

Deep learning models have been used extensively to identify potential credit card fraud. These models can take into account not just the specifics of a single transaction, but also the broader context (customers' typical spending behavior, the geographic location of the transaction, and even the time of day) to make more accurate determinations. Similarly, in the fight against money laundering, deep learning can be employed to analyze intricate webs of financial transactions, identifying suspicious patterns that suggest illicit activity, even when those patterns are deliberately obscured by the perpetrators.

Deep learning's ability to process unstructured data (e.g. text, images, and voice recordings) adds another layer of sophistication to fraud detection efforts. For example, in cases of identity theft, deep learning algorithms could analyze voice patterns in phone calls or the content of emails and social media posts to detect inconsistencies that might indicate fraudulent activity. This multi-dimensional approach allows financial institutions to build more robust and comprehensive fraud detection systems that are better equipped to respond to the ever-evolving tactics used by fraudsters.

Types of Financial Fraud

Before diving into the deep learning techniques for fraud detection, it's important to understand the main types of financial fraud:

- **Credit Card Fraud**: This involves the unauthorized use of a credit card to make purchases or withdraw funds. It can include stolen card fraud, counterfeit card fraud, and card-not-present fraud.
- **Identity Theft**: This occurs when a fraudster uses someone else's personal information (e.g. Social Security number or bank account details), to commit fraud. This can include opening fraudulent accounts, taking out loans, or making purchases in the victim's name.
- **Money Laundering**: This is the process of disguising the proceeds of criminal activity as legitimate funds. It often involves a complex series of transactions designed to obscure the origin of the money.
- **Insurance Fraud**: This can include false or exaggerated insurance claims, or the misrepresentation of facts when applying for insurance coverage.

- **Insider Trading**: This involves the illegal use of non-public information to make profitable trades in the stock market.

Each of these types of fraud presents different challenges for detection, requiring models that can adapt to specific patterns and indicators.

Anomaly Detection with Autoencoders

Anomaly detection is based on the idea that fraudulent activities typically deviate from the normal patterns of behavior observed in a financial system. By learning what "normal" looks like (by labeling regular spending habits, typical transaction amounts, or usual geographic locations), anomaly detection systems can flag any behavior that significantly deviates from these patterns as potential fraud. For instance, if a customer's credit card is suddenly used to make large purchases in a foreign country or even another state when their usual spending is modest and local, this could be identified as an anomaly and trigger an alert for possible fraud.

Autoencoders are a specific type of deep learning model that excel in the task of anomaly detection. To visualize how they work, think of an autoencoder as a kind of data compression and reconstruction tool. Imagine you have a complex piece of information — like a detailed image or a record of financial transactions — and you want to compress it into a simpler form, capturing only the most essential details. This is what the first part of the autoencoder, known as the "encoder," does: reduces data into a more compact, lower-dimensional representation.

The second part of the autoencoder, called the "decoder," takes this compressed representation and tries to rebuild the original data from it. The goal is for the autoencoder to learn how to compress and then accurately reconstruct normal data. Through training over time, the autoencoder becomes very good at this task when the data follows the usual patterns it has seen before.

But when the autoencoder encounters data that doesn't fit the normal patterns — such as in the case of a fraudulent transaction — it struggles to reconstruct it accurately. The reason is simple: the autoencoder has learned to handle typical, everyday data, not the unusual or unexpected. As a result, when faced with something abnormal, the reconstruction it produces is often flawed or incomplete. This difference between the original data and the reconstructed version is known as the "reconstruction error."

By measuring the reconstruction error, we can identify potential anomalies. If the error is small, it suggests that the data fits within the normal patterns the autoencoder has learned, and is likely not fraudulent. But if the error is large and the data doesn't match the usual behavior, it could be an indication of fraudulent activity.

This approach is particularly powerful because it doesn't require explicit examples of fraud to be effective. Instead, it focuses on understanding normal behavior and spotting anything that deviates from it. This makes it highly adaptable and capable of detecting new types of fraud that may not have been seen before. In practical terms, this means that an autoencoder-based system can continuously monitor financial transactions, flagging unusual activity for further investigation and helping to prevent fraud before it causes significant harm.

Here's how we might apply an autoencoder for fraud detection:

1. **Data Preparation**: We start by collecting a large dataset of normal, non-fraudulent transactions. This could include data on transaction amounts, locations, times, and any other relevant features.

2. **Model Training**: We train an autoencoder on this normal data. The autoencoder learns to compress and reconstruct the normal transactions with minimal error.

3. **Anomaly Scoring**: We apply the trained autoencoder to new, unseen transactions. For each transaction, we calculate the reconstruction error. Transactions with high reconstruction errors are identified as potential anomalies.

4. **Fraud Investigation**: The transactions flagged as potential anomalies are reviewed by fraud investigators. They determine whether each flagged transaction is indeed fraudulent.

Over time, the autoencoder can be retrained on new data to adapt to evolving patterns of normal behavior. This continuous learning is important in a domain like fraud detection, where the tactics of fraudsters are constantly changing.

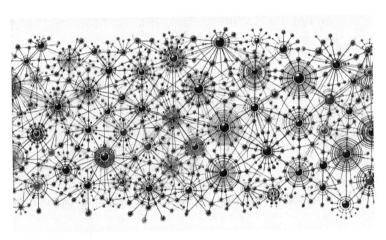

Graph Neural Networks for Fraud Detection

Graph Neural Networks (GNNs) are advanced tools designed to handle graph-structured data, where the connections between entities are as important as the entities themselves.

These networks function by passing information between nodes within a graph, enabling them to capture the intricate relationships and dependencies that characterize the data.

> **But what even is a graph structure?**
>
> A graph structure is a way of organizing and representing data in the form of nodes (or vertices) connected by edges. In this structure, nodes represent individual entities or data points, while edges represent the relationships or connections between these entities. This format allows for the analysis of both the entities and their interconnections, providing a comprehensive understanding of the system as a whole.

To fully appreciate the power of GNNs it's important to first understand what a graph is in this context. In a graph, entities (could be users, accounts, or transactions, for example) are represented as nodes (or vertices), and the connections or relationships between these entities are represented as edges (or links). For example, in a social network, the nodes might represent individuals, and the edges might represent connections or interactions between them. Similarly, in a financial network, nodes could represent individual bank accounts, and edges could represent transactions or money transfers between these accounts.

Graph Neural Networks are designed to learn from data in this kind of graph structure by capturing both the features of the nodes and the patterns of their connections. They work by iteratively updating the representation of each node based on the features of its neighboring nodes and the structure of the graph itself. This process allows GNNs to capture complex dependencies and interactions that are difficult to model with traditional methods. The end result is a model that not only understands the individual characteristics of each entity but also the broader context in which these entities exist.

One interesting application of GNNs in finance that should help visualize the importance of not just tracking entities (nodes), but also the relationships between them is in their application for fraud detection. This is because the existence of an account is not in itself an indication of anything fraudulent, but the transactions that go into and out of the account and the other accounts that transact with this particular account could provide more detail that could link a particular account to fraudulent activity. Picture a network of financial transactions where each node represents a bank account and each edge represents a transaction between accounts. A straightforward analysis might look for individual accounts with unusual activity, but this could miss coordinated fraud schemes involving multiple accounts. GNNs, however, can analyze the entire transaction network, identifying suspicious subgraphs — clusters of nodes and edges that may represent fraudulent activity.

If a bad actor is using a network of seemingly unrelated accounts to move money in a way that evades detection by traditional methods, a GNN could identify subtle patterns in the way these accounts interact, such as unusual transaction chains, circular flows of money, or accounts that share similar transaction behaviors. By focusing on the structure of the network and the connections between entities, GNNs can spot these complex patterns and flag them for further investigation.

GNNs are highly adaptable and can be tailored to different types of graph data and fraud scenarios. For example, in e-commerce platforms, a graph might represent users and their purchasing behaviors, with edges representing shared devices, payment methods, or shipping addresses. A GNN could learn to identify clusters of users that, while appearing distinct, are actually part of a coordinated fraud ring.

Similarly, in telecommunications, GNNs could be used to detect fraud in networks of phone calls or messages, identifying suspicious patterns that suggest scam operations.

Let's dive in a little deeper into how a GNN could be used for fraud detection:

Graph Construction

The first step in setting up a GNN for fraud detection is to construct a graph representation of the financial data. In this graph, each node represents an account, and each edge represents a transaction between accounts. This structure allows the model to capture the relationships and interactions between accounts. Additional features, such as transaction amounts, timestamps, account types, and even geolocation data, can be incorporated as attributes of the nodes and edges. This enriched graph provides a detailed and dynamic view of the financial ecosystem, enabling the GNN to analyze complex transaction networks.

GNN Training

Once the graph is constructed, the GNN is trained on a large dataset of historical transaction graphs. During the training phase, the GNN learns to embed each node (account) into a low-dimensional vector space. The goal is to position nodes with similar neighborhood structures (those that engage in similar patterns of transactions) closer together in this space. Through this process, the GNN learns to recognize typical transaction behaviors, forming a baseline against which anomalies can be detected. If labeled fraud cases are available, supervised learning could be used to train the model. If labels are scarce, unsupervised learning techniques could be applied.

Anomaly Detection

GNNs can be used to detect potential fraud by embedding new, unseen transaction graphs into the same vector space. Nodes (accounts) that are embedded far from the majority of other nodes are flagged as potential anomalies. These accounts exhibit transaction patterns that deviate from the norm, suggesting possible fraudulent activity. This method allows for the identification of unusual behaviors even in the absence of explicit fraud labels, making it a powerful tool for proactive fraud detection.

Subgraph Analysis

Beyond identifying individual anomalous nodes, GNN embeddings can also be applied to analyze subgraphs within the transaction network. A subgraph consists of a group of nodes that are interconnected in some way. By examining these subgraphs, the GNN can identify clusters of nodes that, while not individually suspicious, together exhibit unusual connectivity patterns. These patterns may indicate coordinated fraudulent activity, such as a group of accounts engaging in a "money mule" scheme or a network of accounts involved in layering transactions to launder money. This subgraph analysis provides a deeper layer of fraud detection, capturing more sophisticated and coordinated schemes that might otherwise go unnoticed.

In financial networks, fraud is rarely isolated to a single transaction or account; instead, it often involves a web of interconnected activities spanning multiple entities. Traditional fraud detection methods, which might focus on individual accounts or straightforward transactional patterns, can miss these sophisticated schemes, especially when they involve intricate or indirect connections between accounts. But GNNs are able to capture and analyze complex, "multi-hop" relationships within transaction data.

GNNs are able to identify these multiple hops because the node representations are iteratively updated based on the features of their neighbors and the structure of the network as a whole. This process enables GNNs to capture relationships that span multiple "hops" across the network. For example, if a fraud scheme involves a series of transactions that move funds through a chain of accounts, a GNN can recognize this pattern by analyzing the connections across several layers of the graph. This ability to consider not just direct transactions but also the indirect relationships between accounts is crucial for identifying fraud that is deliberately spread across multiple entities to avoid detection.

GNNs also excel in identifying coordinated activities within a network, such as a group of accounts involved in circular transactions or accounts that share similar transaction patterns with a common central node. These complex patterns, which might be indicative of money laundering, Ponzi schemes, or other forms of organized fraud, can be difficult to detect with linear models that don't account for the network structure. GNNs, however, can model these patterns effectively, flagging suspicious subgraphs or clusters within the network that warrant further investigation.

GNNs are much better at detecting fraud than rule-based systems because as financial transactions are continuously generated, fraud tactics evolve, becoming more sophisticated and harder to detect. GNN models can be continuously updated with this new transaction data, allowing them to learn and adapt to these changing tactics in real-time. This continuous learning process ensures that the GNN remains effective at detecting fraud, even as fraudsters develop new strategies to exploit weaknesses in the financial system. By updating the model with the latest data, financial institutions can maintain a dynamic defense against fraud, staying ahead of the curve and reducing the window of opportunity for fraudulent activities to go undetected.

Customer Analytics

Data analytics unlocks insights from big data that would be impossible to discern through traditional human analysis. By leveraging advanced techniques such as machine learning and predictive modeling, financial institutions can uncover hidden patterns, correlations, and trends within their customer data. These insights reveal the underlying behaviors and preferences of customers, enabling institutions to anticipate needs, personalize offerings, and proactively address issues before they escalate. In this way, data analytics transforms overwhelming volumes of information into meaningful, actionable strategies that drive business success.

"Data is not information.
Information is not knowledge.
Knowledge is not understanding.
Understanding is not wisdom."

~ Clifford Stoll

While data forms the foundation, it is only through advanced analytics and interpretation that it evolves into wisdom that can drive informed and strategic business decisions.

As previously discussed, one of the key techniques in customer analytics is customer segmentation. By dividing customers into distinct groups based on shared characteristics, financial institutions can tailor their products, services, and marketing efforts to better meet the needs of each segment. This can lead to increased customer satisfaction, higher retention rates, and greater customer lifetime value.

Predictive modeling is also used extensively in customer analytics. By analyzing past customer behavior, predictive models can forecast likely future actions, such as the likelihood of a customer defaulting on a loan, closing an account, or responding to a marketing offer. This allows financial institutions to proactively address potential issues, target marketing efforts more effectively, and optimize resource allocation.

Techniques like sentiment analysis and text mining enable financial institutions to gain insights from unstructured digital data, including call center transcripts. By analyzing the language and emotions expressed in this text data, companies can gauge customer opinions, identify emerging trends and pain points, and adapt their strategies accordingly.

Deep-learning-powered recommender systems are highly effective in customer analytics. By analyzing patterns in customer behavior and preferences, recommender systems can suggest personalized product offerings, financial advice, or next best actions. This not only enhances the customer experience but also drives cross-selling and up-selling opportunities.

To leverage these techniques effectively, financial institutions need to integrate data from a wide range of sources. This would obviously include internal data from core banking systems, credit card transactions, and customer interaction logs, but also external data from credit bureaus, demographics providers, and social media platforms. Integrating and harmonizing this data is a major challenge that demands strong data governance, effective data quality management, and well-defined data integration strategies.

Once the data is integrated, companies can apply advanced analytics techniques to derive meaningful insights. This might involve segmenting customers based on their transaction patterns and engagement behaviors, predicting the likelihood of a customer churning, analyzing sentiment trends in customer feedback, or recommending personalized investment portfolios based on a customer's risk profile and goals.

The insights derived from customer analytics can inform a wide range of business decisions and strategies:

- **Product development**: By understanding the needs and preferences of different customer segments, financial institutions can develop targeted products and features that better meet those needs.
- **Marketing and sales:** Customer analytics can help identify the most effective marketing channels and messages for each customer segment, as well as the optimal times and frequencies for outreach. It can also help prioritize sales efforts based on a customer's likelihood to convert.
- **Customer service:** By predicting potential issues and understanding customer sentiment, financial institutions can proactively address concerns, personalize service interactions, and improve overall customer satisfaction.
- **Risk management:** Predictive analytics can help identify customers at high risk of default, fraud, or churning, enabling financial institutions to take preventative measures and mitigate potential losses.
- **Operational efficiency:** Customer analytics can help optimize resource allocation by predicting demand, identifying process inefficiencies, and automating routine tasks.

By better understanding and serving customers, financial institutions can increase customer acquisition, improve retention, drive revenue growth, and reduce costs. In an industry where customer relationships are key, this can provide a significant competitive advantage. But realizing this value requires more than just investing in advanced analytics technologies. This requires a cultural shift towards data-driven decision making, a commitment to data quality and governance, and a willingness to act on the insights derived from the data. It also requires a deep respect for customer privacy and data security, as well as compliance with increasingly stringent regulations around data use and protection.

Financial institutions that can successfully leverage their customer data to generate actionable, customer-focused insights will be well-equipped to thrive in this new era of data-driven finance. The future of finance will favor those who not only understand their customers but also can adapt and respond to their needs in real time. Deep learning and advanced analytics will be essential in achieving this, unlocking a level of customer understanding and engagement that was once out of reach.

Let's dive a little deeper ...

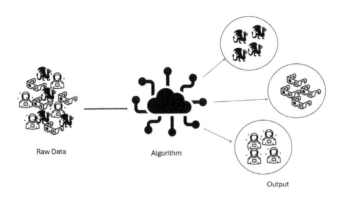

Raw Data — Algorithm — Output

Customer Segmentation with Clustering

Customer segmentation is dividing a company's customer base into distinct groups based on shared characteristics. The goal is to identify subsets of customers who have similar needs, behaviors, and preferences, enabling companies to tailor their products, services, and marketing strategies to better serve each segment. In the financial sector, effective customer segmentation can lead to improved customer satisfaction, higher retention rates, and increased lifetime value.

Traditional approaches to customer segmentation often rely on simple, manual rule-based systems or basic clustering algorithms like K-means. These methods typically use a limited set of predefined features, such as demographic data (age, gender, income) or basic transactional data (average balance, transaction frequency). While these approaches can provide some insights, they often fail to capture the full complexity of customer behavior and preferences. Deep learning algorithms, particularly deep clustering methods, can automatically learn rich, abstract representations of customers from raw data. This allows them to uncover complex, non-linear patterns and similarities that traditional methods might miss.

One of the key advantages of deep learning for customer segmentation is its ability to handle high-dimensional, heterogeneous data.

In the financial sector, customer data can come from a wide variety of sources:

- **Transactional data:** This includes data on purchases, payments, transfers, and other financial transactions. Deep learning can uncover patterns in transaction amounts, frequencies, and categories that can indicate distinct customer behaviors and needs.
- **Interaction data:** This encompasses data from customer interactions with the company, such as website visits, mobile app usage, customer service calls, and email communications. Deep learning can analyze patterns in the timing,

frequency, and nature of these interactions to identify distinct customer engagement styles.

- **Text data:** This includes data from customer reviews, social media posts, and other text-based communications. Deep learning techniques like natural language processing (NLP) can extract insights from this unstructured data, revealing customer sentiments, preferences, and concerns.
- **Demographic data:** While traditional segmentation often relies heavily on basic demographic data, deep learning can incorporate this data alongside other data types to paint a more comprehensive picture of each customer.

By integrating and analyzing these diverse data types, deep learning can uncover subtle, complex patterns that define distinct customer segments. For example, a deep clustering algorithm might identify a segment of "tech-savvy, mobile-first millennials" who frequently engage with the company's mobile app for day-to-day transactions and are responsive to mobile-based promotions. Another segment might consist of older, high-net-worth individuals who prefer in-person interactions and are interested in wealth management services.

The process of applying deep learning to customer segmentation typically involves several steps:

1. **Data Preparation:** The first step is to collect, clean, and preprocess the customer data. This can involve integrating data from multiple sources, handling missing values, normalizing data, and converting data into a format suitable for input into a deep learning model.
2. **Feature Learning:** Next, a deep neural network is used to learn a compact, informative representation of each customer. This is typically done in an unsupervised manner, using techniques like autoencoders or convolutional neural networks. The network learns to compress the high-dimensional customer data into a lower-dimensional space, capturing the most salient features and patterns in the process.
3. **Clustering:** The learned customer representations are then fed into a clustering algorithm, such as K-means or hierarchical clustering. The algorithm groups similar customers together based on their learned features, creating distinct customer segments.
4. **Interpretation and Profiling:** Once the customer segments have been identified, they are analyzed and interpreted by business users. Each segment is profiled based on its distinguishing characteristics, such as common demographics, behaviors, and preferences. These profiles provide a rich, data-driven understanding of each customer group.
5. **Strategy Development:** Based on the segment profiles, companies can develop targeted strategies for each group. This could involve tailoring product offerings, designing personalized marketing campaigns, or adapting customer service approaches to better meet the needs of each segment.

6. **Deployment and Monitoring:** Finally, the segmentation model is deployed into production, where it can be used to segment new customers in real-time. The performance of the model is continuously monitored and the model is periodically retrained on new data to ensure it remains accurate and relevant over time.

One of the challenges in applying deep learning to customer segmentation is the interpretability of the results. Deep neural networks are often seen as "black boxes," where it can be difficult to understand exactly how the network arrived at its outputs. This can be a concern in highly regulated industries like finance, where decisions need to be explainable. However, techniques for interpreting deep learning models are an active area of research, and methods like layer-wise relevance propagation and attention mechanisms are helping to improve the transparency of these models.

Another challenge is the need for large amounts of high-quality data. Deep learning models typically require significant amounts of data to learn effective representations. In the financial sector, data can be fragmented across different systems and silos, and data quality issues are common. Effective data governance and data integration strategies are crucial for successful deep learning applications.

Despite these challenges, the potential benefits of deep learning for customer segmentation are significant. By enabling more granular, dynamic, and actionable segmentation, deep learning can help financial institutions to better understand and serve their customers. This can lead to improved customer experiences, higher customer lifetime values, and ultimately, a competitive edge in an increasingly data-driven industry.

Here's a general approach to using deep clustering for customer segmentation:

1. **Data Preparation:** We start by collecting and preprocessing customer data. This could include demographic information, transaction histories, website interactions, and any other relevant data points. The data is typically normalized and transformed into a format suitable for input into a deep learning model.

2. **Feature Learning:** Next, we use a deep neural network (often an autoencoder or a convolutional neural network) to learn a low-dimensional representation of the customer data. This step is unsupervised - the network is trained to reconstruct the input data, learning to capture the most salient features in the process.

3. **Clustering:** The learned feature representations of the customers are then passed into a clustering algorithm, such as K-means. The algorithm groups similar customers together based on their learned features.

4. **Interpretation and Application:** Finally, the resulting customer segments are analyzed and interpreted by marketing and product teams. Each segment can be profiled based on its distinguishing characteristics, and these profiles can be used to guide targeted marketing campaigns, product recommendations, and customer service strategies.

Deep Learning for Churn Prediction

Customer churn, also known as customer attrition, refers to the phenomenon of customers stopping their use of a company's products or services. In the financial sector, this could mean closing an account, stopping the use of a credit card, or switching to a competitor's services.

Predicting and preventing churn is a major priority for companies across all industries. It is typically far more cost-effective to retain an existing customer than to acquire a new one. Fortunately, thanks to the ability of deep learning to learn complex patterns from large, diverse datasets, it can be deployed as a powerful tool for churn prediction.

A typical deep learning approach to churn prediction might look like this:

1. **Data Preparation:** The first step is to collect and preprocess historical customer data. This would include data points for customers who have churned in the past, as well as for those who have remained active. Relevant features might include demographic information, transaction patterns, customer service interactions, and product usage data.

2. **Model Training:** Next, a deep neural network is trained on this historical data to predict churn. The network takes in the various customer features as inputs and outputs a churn probability. The model is typically trained using a supervised learning approach, with the historical churn data serving as the labels.

3. **Model Evaluation:** The trained model is then evaluated on a held-out test set to assess its predictive accuracy. Key metrics include precision (what proportion of predicted churns are actual churns), recall (what proportion of actual churns are correctly predicted), and the AUC-ROC score (a measure of the model's ability to discriminate between churning and non-churning customers).

4. **Deployment and Action:** Once the model performance is satisfactory, it can be deployed to make churn predictions on the current customer base. Customers identified as high churn risks can then be targeted with retention strategies, such as special offers, personalized communications, or improved customer service.

Recommender Systems with Deep Learning

A recommender system is a type of software or algorithm that analyzes data to suggest products, services, or content to users based on their preferences, behavior, and past interactions. These systems are widely used in platforms like e-commerce websites, streaming services, and social media to personalize the user experience, helping users discover items they might be interested in (e.g. movies, books, or products). By leveraging data from user behavior and other sources, recommender systems aim to increase engagement, satisfaction, and sales by delivering more relevant and appealing suggestions.

In finance, recommender systems can be used to suggest products (credit cards, investment options), services (financial planning, wealth management), or actions (budget adjustments, balance transfers) to customers based on their individual needs and preferences.

Deep learning-based recommender systems, particularly those based on neural collaborative filtering, have shown state-of-the-art performance on many benchmarks.

Here's a high-level overview of how a deep learning recommender system might work:

1. **Data Preparation:** The input data for a recommender system typically consists of a matrix of user-item interactions. In a financial context, the users might be customers, and the items might be financial products. The interactions could be purchases, clicks, or any other relevant metrics. Additional side information, such as user demographics or product attributes, can also be included.

2. **Embedding Learning:** The key idea behind neural collaborative filtering is to learn low-dimensional vector representations (embeddings) for each user and item. These embeddings are learned such that they capture the latent preferences of users and the latent attributes of items. This is typically done using a deep neural network, often with separate subnetworks for users and items, which are then combined to predict interaction likelihoods.

3. **Model Training:** The model is trained on the historical user-item interaction data. It learns to predict the likelihood of a user interacting with an item, given their respective embeddings. The model is typically trained using a loss function that compares the predicted likelihoods to the actual interactions.

4. **Recommendation Generation:** Once trained, the model can be used to generate recommendations for each user. This is done by computing the predicted interaction likelihood for a user with each item they haven't interacted with yet, and recommending the items with the highest predicted likelihoods.

5. **Online Updates:** As new user-item interactions occur, the model can be updated in real-time. This allows the recommendations to stay up-to-date with changing user preferences and new product additions.

Deep learning recommender systems can learn complex, non-linear user-item interaction patterns, incorporate side information seamlessly, and scale to massive datasets. This can lead to more personalized, relevant recommendations, which can drive customer engagement and satisfaction.

Deep learning is already making a strong impact in customer analytics, revolutionizing areas like segmentation, churn prediction, and recommendations. Financial institutions are now equipped with powerful tools to better understand and serve their customers.

Chapter Six

CHALLENGES AND FUTURE DIRECTIONS

As deep learning models become more prevalent in financial applications, the black box problem becomes an increasingly significant issue. Deep learning models, particularly complex neural networks, can be highly accurate predictors, but their inner workings are often opaque. This lack of transparency can be problematic in the heavily regulated financial industry, where understanding and explaining model decisions is crucial for compliance, risk management, and customer trust.

In this section, we'll dive into the challenges of interpretability and explainability in deep learning models, explore techniques for interpreting these models, and discuss the regulatory environment surrounding explainable AI in finance.

The Black Box Problem

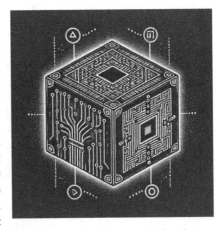

Deep learning models have achieved remarkable performance in tasks like image recognition, natural language processing, and time series forecasting, but the complexity that enables this performance also makes these models difficult to interpret.

Consider a deep neural network used to assess loan default risk. The model might ingest hundreds of features about the applicant and their financial history, pass these through dozens of hidden layers with millions of parameters, and output a default probability. While the model's prediction may be highly accurate, understanding how it arrived at this prediction can be challenging.

- Which features were most important?
- How did different features interact?

- What would need to change about the applicant's profile to get a different prediction?

This opacity is the core of the "black box" problem. In many financial applications, simply having an accurate model isn't enough. Stakeholders, from regulators to customers to internal risk managers, often demand an understanding of why the model made a particular decision.

The black box problem is particularly acute in finance for several reasons:

- **Regulatory requirements:** Financial institutions operate in a heavily regulated environment. Many regulations, such as the Equal Credit Opportunity Act (ECOA) in the US or the General Data Protection Regulation (GDPR) in the EU, have provisions related to explainability in automated decision-making.
- **Risk management:** Understanding how a model arrives at its predictions is crucial for assessing and managing the risks associated with using that model. If a model is making decisions based on spurious correlations or is overly sensitive to certain features, that needs to be known and addressed.
- **Customer trust:** Financial decisions, such as loan approvals or insurance underwriting, can have a significant impact on customers' lives. Customers may demand explanations for decisions that affect them, and being able to provide these explanations can be key to maintaining trust.
- **Debugging and improvement:** When a model makes an error, understanding why it made that error is the first step to improving the model. Without interpretability, debugging and refining models can be a significant challenge.

The black box problem isn't unique to finance, but the high stakes and heavy regulation of the financial industry make it particularly pressing. As deep learning models become more widely adopted in finance, developing techniques to interpret and explain these models is becoming a critical area of research and development.

"As we know, there are known knowns;
there are things we know we know.
We also know there are known unknowns;
that is to say we know there are some things we don't know.
But there are also unknown unknowns —
the ones we don't know we don't know."

~Donald Rumsfeld

Techniques for Interpreting Deep Learning Models

While deep learning models can be opaque, there are a variety of techniques to help interpret and explain them. These techniques can be broadly categorized into two groups: intrinsic interpretability methods, which attempt to build models that are inherently interpretable, and post-hoc interpretability methods, which attempt to explain a model's predictions after it has been trained.

Intrinsic Interpretability Methods

Intrinsic interpretability methods aim to create models that are inherently interpretable, meaning that their decision-making process can be easily understood by humans.

Some key intrinsic interpretability methods include:

Linear Models

Linear models are a straightforward approach where the relationship between input features and the output is represented as a straight line, making them easy to interpret. For example, in logistic regression, each feature in the dataset is assigned a coefficient that directly reflects its influence on the output. The simplicity of this approach is its greatest strength — any stakeholder can easily understand how different features affect predictions. Although linear models may not capture complex patterns as effectively as deep learning models, their transparency makes them invaluable in applications where interpretability is crucial, such as in regulatory environments or high-stakes decision-making scenarios.

Decision Trees

Decision Trees also work well for intrinsic interpretability. In decision trees, decisions are made by following a tree-like structure of if/then rules. Each node in the tree represents a decision based on a particular feature, and branches lead to outcomes or further decisions. This structure is highly interpretable, as the entire decision process can be visualized, showing exactly how each input leads to the final prediction. While single decision trees are easy to understand, ensemble methods like random forests or gradient boosted trees, which combine multiple decision trees, can be more powerful but less transparent. But even these ensembles can sometimes be interpreted through methods that summarize their decision processes.

Rule-Based Models

Rule-Based Models operate on a set of predefined or learned rules that explicitly dictate how decisions are made. These rules can be manually crafted by experts or derived from data using algorithms. The key advantage of rule-based models is their transparency — each decision is traceable back to a clear and understandable rule. This transparency makes rule-based models particularly useful in fields where decision-making needs to be explainable, such as in legal or medical domains. However, the complexity of these models can grow with the number of rules, potentially making them harder to manage.

Attention Mechanisms

Attention Mechanisms are used in sequence models such as Recurrent Neural Networks (RNNs) to highlight which parts of the input data are most important for each output. In models where input data consists of sequences (such as text or time series) attention mechanisms allow the model to focus on specific parts of the sequence when making predictions. This provides insight into the model's decision-making process by showing what it "pays attention to" during prediction, enhancing interpretability. Attention mechanisms are particularly useful in complex models like those used for natural language processing, where understanding the basis for the model's predictions is essential.

Intrinsic interpretability methods offer the advantage of models that are inherently understandable. However, these methods often involve a trade-off between interpretability and predictive power. The most interpretable models, like linear models and decision trees, may not be able to capture the complex, non-linear relationships that deep learning excels at.

Post-hoc Interpretability Methods

Post-hoc interpretability methods seek to explain a model's predictions after it has been trained. Rather than modifying the model itself, these methods treat the model as a "black box" and attempt to infer its decision-making process. Some key post-hoc interpretability methods include:

Feature Importance

Feature Importance is a post-hoc method that assesses which features most significantly influence a model's predictions. It does this by measuring how the model's performance changes when a particular feature is altered or removed. One common approach is permutation importance, where the values of a feature are randomly shuffled and the resulting impact on the model's performance is observed. A drop in performance indicates that the feature was important to the model's decisions. Another advanced technique is SHAP (Shapley Additive Explanations), which assigns each feature an importance value for each prediction, offering a more detailed insight into how features contribute to the model's decisions across different instances.

Partial Dependence Plots

Partial Dependence Plots (PDPs) are visual tools that help to understand the relationship between specific features and the model's predictions. By plotting the average predicted outcome as a function of one or two features while holding others constant, PDPs reveal the nature of the relationship — whether it is linear, monotonic, or more complex. These plots are particularly useful for identifying the general trend of a model's predictions as a particular feature changes, giving a clearer understanding of the model's behavior in response to individual features.

Individual Conditional Expectation (ICE) Plots

Individual Conditional Expectation (ICE) Plots extend the concept of Partial Dependence Plots by showing how a model's predictions vary across different instances in the dataset. Unlike PDPs, which average over all data points, ICE plots display a line for each instance, highlighting heterogeneous effects that may be obscured in aggregate plots. This can be especially valuable for detecting interactions between features or identifying cases where a model's prediction mechanism is not consistent across different data points.

Surrogate Models

Surrogate Models are simplified, interpretable models that are trained to mimic the predictions of a more complex black box model. By interpreting the surrogate model, analysts can gain insights into how the black box model makes its decisions. The surrogate model acts as a stand-in that approximates the original model's predictions while being more transparent, making it easier to understand and explain the underlying patterns and rules that the black box model uses.

Local Interpretable Model-Agnostic Explanations (LIME)

Local Interpretable Model-Agnostic Explanations (LIME) is a technique designed to explain individual predictions of a black box model. LIME works by approximating the black box model with a simple, interpretable model — like linear regression — specifically in the vicinity of the instance being analyzed. By understanding this local model, one can discern why the black box model made a particular decision for that instance. This method is particularly effective in scenarios where understanding the rationale behind a single prediction is crucial, such as in credit scoring or medical diagnostics.

Post-hoc interpretability methods offer the advantage of being applicable to any machine learning model, including complex deep learning models. They allow us to benefit from the predictive power of these models while still being able to interpret and explain their predictions. However, post-hoc methods can be computationally intensive, and there's always a risk that the explanations they provide are not a faithful representation of the model's true decision-making process.

Regulatory Requirements for Explainability

Several existing and proposed regulations have provisions related to the explainability of deep learning models.

In the United States, the Equal Credit Opportunity Act (ECOA) requires that applicants who are denied credit must be given specific reasons for the denial. If a machine learning model was used in the decision, this implies that the model's decision-making process must be interpretable enough to provide these reasons.

Similarly, the Fair Credit Reporting Act (FCRA) requires that consumers be able to access and correct the information used to make credit decisions about them. If this information includes the outputs of a machine learning model, the model must be explainable enough for consumers to understand and potentially challenge its decisions.

In the European Union, the General Data Protection Regulation (GDPR) includes provisions on "automated individual decision-making," including profiling. Under these provisions, individuals have the right to receive "meaningful information about the logic involved" in fully automated decisions that significantly affect them. This implies a requirement for explainability in machine learning models used for these types of decisions.

The EU Artificial Intelligence Act classifies AI systems used in financial services as "high-risk." These systems are subject to stringent requirements, including the obligation to provide clear and sufficient information about their capabilities and limitations, and to ensure that the system's decisions are traceable. Full enforcement of the Act is expected by 2026, impacting companies within and outside the EU that offer AI services to the European market.

At the time of this writing, other jurisdictions, including Singapore, Hong Kong, and Brazil, are also developing AI governance frameworks that include principles of transparency and explainability.

Complying with these regulatory requirements is a significant challenge for financial institutions looking to deploy deep learning models. It requires not only technical solutions for interpreting these models, but also clear communication and collaboration with regulators to ensure that the provided explanations are sufficient.

Some key considerations for financial institutions include:

Choosing the Right Interpretability Methods

Selecting the appropriate interpretability methods is crucial for financial institutions to ensure that their AI models provide clear and compliant explanations. Different models and use cases may require different approaches to interpretability. For instance, while linear models are naturally interpretable, more complex models like deep learning networks may require specific techniques such as SHAP (Shapley Additive Explanations) or LIME to elucidate their decision-making processes. Financial institutions must carefully evaluate these methods to determine which will offer the most meaningful insights for the particular model in question, while also satisfying regulatory expectations for transparency and explainability.

Documenting and Auditing Models

Clear and comprehensive documentation is vital for ensuring transparency and regulatory compliance in the AI models deployed by financial institutions. This process involves meticulously recording every aspect of the model's development, including the data used for training, the architecture of the model, and the interpretability methods employed. Beyond initial documentation, regular audits are necessary to ensure that models continue to meet interpretability standards over time. These audits should check for alignment with regulatory requirements and assess whether the models remain interpretable as they evolve with new data inputs or algorithmic adjustments.

Engaging with Regulators

To ensure their AI models meet all necessary explainability standards, financial institutions should proactively engage with regulators. By working with regulatory bodies, companies will better understand the specific expectations for model transparency and explainability. Collaborative initiatives, such as Singapore's Veritas initiative, exemplify how financial institutions can work alongside regulators to establish industry-wide practices that align with regulatory standards. This engagement not only helps in meeting current regulatory demands but also positions institutions as active participants in shaping the future landscape of AI governance in finance.

Balancing Interpretability and Performance

One of the major challenges in deploying AI in finance is striking the right balance between model interpretability and performance. Highly interpretable models, such as decision trees or linear regression, may offer clear insights ... but might not always deliver the highest predictive accuracy. On the other hand, complex models like neural networks may excel in predictive power but can be opaque in their decision-making processes. Financial institutions must navigate this trade-off carefully, ensuring that their chosen models provide sufficient interpretability to satisfy regulatory scrutiny, while also delivering robust performance that meets business needs. Institutions should be prepared to justify their decisions to regulators, explaining how they have balanced these sometimes conflicting demands.

The black box problem is a significant hurdle in adopting deep learning for finance, as the lack of transparency in these models conflicts with the industry's need for clarity, accountability, and compliance. However, emerging interpretability techniques, both built into the models and applied after training, are helping to shed light on how these models make decisions, making them more suitable for financial applications.

As regulations around AI transparency and explainability continue to evolve, it will be crucial for financial institutions to stay abreast of these developments and proactively incorporate interpretability into their model development and deployment workflows. By doing so, they can harness the predictive power of deep learning while still meeting the high standards of explainability and accountability required in the financial domain.

Dealing with Limited and Noisy Financial Data

Deep learning models in finance face challenges due to the nature of financial data. These models require large amounts of high-quality, labeled data to perform well, but financial data is often limited, noisy, and expensive to obtain. Historical records may only cover a few decades, events like financial crises are rare, and labeling requires significant human expertise, making it difficult to achieve the desired results in financial applications. Financial data often has characteristics that can be challenging for deep learning models. It can be highly non-stationary (the statistical properties of the data change over time), it can contain complex, non-linear relationships, and it can be sensitive to external events and noise.

In this section, we'll explore techniques for dealing with these data challenges, including data augmentation, transfer learning, and unsupervised pre-training.

"Distinguishing the signal from the noise requires both scientific knowledge and self-knowledge."

~Nate Silver

Data Augmentation Techniques

Data augmentation increases the size and diversity of a training dataset by creating new examples from the existing data. By applying transformations to existing data points, we can create new, synthetic data points that retain the essential characteristics of the original data. This approach is commonly used in fields like computer vision and natural language processing, where techniques like image rotation, cropping, and synonym replacement can significantly increase the size of a dataset.

In finance, data augmentation techniques need to be carefully designed to ensure they create realistic and meaningful synthetic data.

Some potential data augmentation techniques for financial data include:

Time-Series Augmentation

Time-series data, such as stock prices or economic indicators, can be enriched through various augmentation techniques. Data augmentation expands and diversifies a training dataset by generating new examples from the existing data. This can help simulate different market conditions or account for temporal anomalies. Another approach is magnitude scaling, where the entire series is multiplied by a constant factor, creating variations in the scale of data, which can be useful for stress-testing models. Additionally, time warping, which stretches or compresses parts of the series, can introduce variability in time, helping the model to generalize better across different timeframes.

Noise Injection

Introducing noise into financial data strengthens a model's robustness by helping it learn to handle variations and uncertainties more effectively. By adding random noise to numerical features, a model can learn to handle the inherent variability and imperfections present in real-world data. Other noise injection methods include randomly dropping out certain features, which forces the model to focus on the most relevant data, and randomly shuffling a small proportion of the data, which helps prevent overfitting by making the model less reliant on specific data sequences.

Synthetic Minority Over-Sampling Technique (SMOTE)

In many financial datasets, there is an imbalance where certain classes, like fraudulent transactions or defaulted loans, are underrepresented. SMOTE addresses this issue by generating synthetic examples of the minority class. It does this by interpolating between existing examples, effectively creating new data points that help balance the class distribution. This technique improves the model's ability to recognize and learn from rare events, leading to better overall performance in tasks like fraud detection or credit risk assessment.

Adversarial Data Generation

Generative Adversarial Networks provide an advanced approach for generating synthetic financial data, enabling the creation of realistic data samples for training and testing financial models. Thy are particularly useful in scenarios where obtaining large amounts of high-quality financial data is challenging, as GANs can generate synthetic datasets that closely mimic real-world financial data, enhancing model training and performance.

When applying data augmentation, it's important to ensure that the synthetic data is truly representative of the real data. Augmentation techniques should be designed based on a deep understanding of the domain and the specific characteristics of the data. It's also important to thoroughly validate models trained on augmented data to ensure they generalize well to real data.

Transfer Learning from Other Domains

Transfer learning is the technique of taking a model trained on one task or domain and applying it to a different but related task or domain. The idea is that the knowledge a model has learned in one context can be useful in another – even if the specific tasks or data are different.

In deep learning, transfer learning often involves using a pre-trained neural network as a starting point, rather than training a new network from scratch. The pre-trained network may have been trained on a large, general dataset (like ImageNet for image classification), and its learned features can be useful for many related tasks.

In finance, transfer learning can be particularly valuable given the often limited availability of labeled data.

Some potential applications of transfer learning in finance include:

Cross-Asset Prediction

In financial modeling, a model trained to predict returns for one asset class, such as stocks, can often be repurposed to predict returns for another asset class, like bonds. This is because the model may have learned generalizable features and patterns about financial time series, such as trends, volatility, and mean reversion, that are applicable across different types of assets. By leveraging these learned characteristics, the model can provide insights into how various asset classes might behave under similar market conditions, enhancing its utility in multi-asset portfolio management.

Cross-Market Prediction

Similarly, a model initially trained on data from one market, such as the US stock market, may be transferable to another market, like the European stock market. Despite differences in specific companies and economic conditions between these markets, the model may have captured broader patterns of market behavior, such as responses to macroeconomic indicators or shifts in investor sentiment. This cross-market transferability can be particularly valuable for global investors looking to apply a consistent strategy across diverse geographical regions.

Sentiment Analysis

In sentiment analysis, neural networks pre-trained on general text data, like Wikipedia articles or news stories, can be fine-tuned for financial applications. This process allows these models to adapt and predict stock movements based on financial news or other online content, making them highly effective in understanding the specific language and context of finance. The pre-trained network already understands language and semantics, which provides a strong foundation for interpreting the nuances of financial sentiment. By fine-tuning this network on domain-specific data, such as financial news articles, the model becomes adept at recognizing the sentiments and opinions that are likely to influence market movements.

Anomaly Detection

For anomaly detection in financial data, unsupervised learning models like autoencoders are highly effective. These models are trained on a wide range of financial data to recognize "normal" patterns, including typical transaction behaviors, market trends, and pricing variations. When new data deviates from these learned norms, the model can flag potential anomalies, helping to identify unusual or suspicious activity. Once trained, the model can then identify deviations from this norm, flagging potential anomalies such as fraudulent transactions or unusual market activities. The autoencoder's ability to reconstruct typical data patterns makes it particularly suited for detecting subtle irregularities that might escape traditional rule-based systems.

When applying transfer learning, it's important to consider how similar the source and target domains are. The more similar the domains, the more likely it is that the learned features will be useful. It's also important to fine-tune the model on the target domain, rather than just using the pre-trained model directly. This allows the model to adapt its learned features to the specifics of the new domain.

Unsupervised Pre-Training

Unsupervised learning is a type of machine learning where the model identifies patterns in unlabeled data without specific guidance on what to look for. Models like autoencoders, which compress and reconstruct data, and generative adversarial networks (GANs), which generate data similar to the training set, are examples of this approach. In deep learning, unsupervised pre-training is used to initialize neural network weights by learning general features from data, which can then be fine-tuned for specific tasks in a supervised learning phase, improving performance.

Unsupervised pre-training can be particularly useful in finance, where labeled data can be scarce but unlabeled data is often abundant.

Some potential applications of unsupervised pre-training in finance include:

Representation Learning for Time Series

In financial modeling, autoencoders can be effectively utilized for representation learning of time series data. An autoencoder is trained to compress and then reconstruct financial time series, such as stock prices or trading volumes. The learned compressed representation — often capturing essential patterns and underlying structures within the data — can then serve as input features for supervised learning tasks like stock price prediction. This approach allows the model to leverage complex temporal patterns that might not be immediately apparent from raw data, thereby improving predictive accuracy.

Anomaly Detection Pre-Training

Autoencoders or GANs can be pre-trained on large datasets containing normal financial transactions. During this pre-training phase, the model learns to recognize typical patterns and behaviors within the data. This pre-trained model can then be used to initialize an anomaly detection system, which is subsequently fine-tuned on a smaller, labeled dataset of both anomalous and non-anomalous transactions. The advantage of this approach is that the model starts with a solid understanding of what constitutes "normal" transactions, making it more adept at identifying deviations that signify potential anomalies or fraud.

Domain Adaptation Pre-Training

Domain adaptation is particularly valuable in financial modeling when there is ample data available in one domain, such as stock market data, but limited data in a related domain, like bond market data. This technique allows models to leverage the abundant data from the well-established domain to improve performance in the less populated domain, effectively transferring learned patterns and features, which can lead to more accurate predictions and insights in the target domain.

A model can first be pre-trained on the data-rich domain to learn general features and patterns about financial markets. After this pre-training, the model is fine-tuned on the data-poor domain, allowing it to apply the learned general features to more specific tasks, such as predicting bond prices or yields. This approach enhances the model's ability to perform well even when the available data in the target domain is scarce, making it a powerful technique for financial forecasting and analysis across different markets.

When applying unsupervised pre-training, the choice of unsupervised learning task should be guided by the nature of the data and the ultimate supervised learning goal. The unsupervised task should encourage the model to learn features and representations that are likely to be useful for the supervised task. It's also important to validate that the unsupervised pre-training actually improves performance on the supervised task, as not all unsupervised tasks will be equally useful for all supervised tasks.

Emerging Trends in AI for Finance

Applications of AI in finance are becoming increasingly common, with new techniques and technologies continually emerging.

While many of the innovations discussed in the next section are still in early stages, they have the potential to transform financial AI. Staying informed about these emerging trends will help us stay ahead of the curve and capitalize on new opportunities as they arise.

Federated Learning for Data Privacy

Balancing AI's potential with data privacy concerns requires careful management, especially given the strict regulations and competitive nature of financial data. The emerging federated learning approach could offer a promising solution to this problem. Federated learning allows multiple parties to collaboratively train machine learning models without sharing their raw data, addressing privacy concerns while still leveraging the power of AI. The key advantage of federated learning is that it allows institutions to benefit from each other's data without actually sharing that data, which can help overcome data silos and enable more powerful models while still preserving data privacy and confidentiality.

Some potential applications of federated learning in finance include:

- **Credit risk modeling:** Banks could collaboratively train credit risk models without sharing sensitive customer data. Each bank would train the model on their own customer data, and the resulting global model would benefit from the diverse data of all participating banks.
- **Fraud detection:** Financial institutions could share fraud patterns and techniques without revealing sensitive transaction data. A federated fraud detection model could learn from the collective experience of all participants, making it more robust and adaptive.
- **Market forecasting:** Investment firms could share their market insights and predictions without revealing their proprietary trading strategies. A federated market forecasting model could aggregate the knowledge of multiple firms to make more accurate predictions.

Implementing federated learning comes with its own set of challenges. Participants need to agree on the model architecture and training protocol, and there needs to be a trusted central authority to coordinate the learning process. There are also potential security risks, as the shared model updates could potentially leak information about the underlying data. Despite these challenges, federated learning is a promising technique for enabling collaborative AI in finance while preserving data privacy. As the technique matures and more robust frameworks and protocols are developed, we can expect to see more widespread adoption in the financial industry.

Quantum Machine Learning

Quantum computing is an emerging field that builds on quantum mechanics to enhance computational power, targeting problems that challenge classical computers. Though still in its early stages and not widely used, it shows promise in advancing areas like AI and finance. Quantum machine learning, a key focus of quantum computing research, leverages quantum computing to improve machine learning algorithms, particularly in optimization and linear algebra, potentially leading to faster, more efficient solutions for complex problems and opening new avenues in computational research.

Some potential applications include:

Portfolio Optimization

Quantum algorithms like the Quantum Approximate Optimization Algorithm (QAOA) can significantly accelerate portfolio optimization by solving complex problems faster than classical algorithms. Traditional portfolio optimization often involves balancing risk and return across a variety of assets, a task that grows exponentially more difficult as the number of assets increases. QAOA and similar quantum algorithms could process this information more efficiently, allowing for more dynamic and responsive portfolio management. This capability could be particularly advantageous in volatile markets where timely adjustments to asset allocations are critical for maintaining optimal portfolio performance.

Risk Simulation

Quantum computing also holds potential for transforming risk simulation, particularly in generating random numbers and simulating complex financial systems. Quantum computers can produce truly random numbers, a key requirement for accurate Monte Carlo simulations, which are commonly used for pricing complex derivatives and assessing risk. Additionally, quantum computers could simulate complex financial systems at speeds unattainable by classical computers, leading to more accurate risk assessments. These improvements in risk simulation could provide financial institutions with a more detailed understanding of potential market scenarios and enhance their ability to manage financial risk.

Fraud Detection

In fraud detection, quantum algorithms could greatly improve the speed and accuracy of anomaly detection and pattern recognition. Quantum computing's ability to process and analyze large datasets more efficiently than classical computing could enable financial institutions to identify fraudulent activities more quickly. This capability is crucial in detecting subtle and complex patterns of fraud that might go unnoticed by classical algorithms. By improving the timeliness and precision of fraud detection, quantum computing could help reduce financial losses and strengthen the security of financial systems.

However, realizing the potential of quantum machine learning in finance faces significant challenges. Quantum computers are still in their infancy, and most current devices are noisy and error-prone. Quantum algorithms often require specific problem formulations and can be difficult to adapt to real-world financial data. Further, there is a pretty wide skills gap from quantum computing and quantum machine learning to finance. It is unlikely that many financial professionals have the necessary quantum computing expertise to apply this technology, and few quantum computing experts have deep financial domain knowledge.

But the development of quantum computing lies out there – somewhere – on the horizon, and as quantum computers continue to improve and become more widely available, and as more research is done on applying quantum algorithms to financial problems, we can expect to see more practical applications emerge. If you're looking for some advice for your yet unborn granddaughter, you might recommend she pursue this dual path. It would probably be a pretty nice job to have in the future.

Integration of Deep Learning with Other Technologies

Deep learning doesn't exist in a vacuum - it is part of a wider ecosystem of technologies that are transforming the financial industry. Two particularly exciting areas of integration are blockchain and the Internet of Things (IoT).

Blockchain and Deep Learning

Blockchain technology has often been vilified or at least misunderstood by many due to its close association with volatile cryptocurrencies. However, beyond its use in digital currencies, blockchain offers several potential benefits, including enhanced security, transparency, and efficiency in various industries.

Blockchain is a distributed ledger technology that allows multiple parties to securely and transparently record transactions without the need for a central authority. While it is most commonly associated with cryptocurrencies, blockchain has many potential applications in finance, ranging from trade settlement to identity verification. By providing a tamper-resistant and decentralized record-keeping system, blockchain could revolutionize the way transactions are conducted and verified across various sectors.

The integration of deep learning with blockchain holds promise for creating more intelligent, automated, and secure financial systems. Some potential applications include:

Smart Contract Optimization

Deep learning could greatly improve the efficiency of executing smart contracts on blockchain platforms. By training models to predict the optimal gas price for swift transaction processing on networks like Ethereum, deep learning can minimize costs while ensuring timely execution. Additionally, it can optimize the sequence of transactions, reducing overall gas fees, which is particularly valuable in volatile environments where transaction costs can heavily impact the efficiency and profitability of decentralized applications.

Fraud Detection in Blockchain Networks

Blockchain networks, while secure by design, are not immune to fraudulent activities such as double-spending attacks or exploitation of vulnerabilities in smart contracts. Deep learning models can be trained to detect these types of malicious behaviors by analyzing patterns within the blockchain data. For example, a deep learning model could detect unusual transaction patterns that suggest a double-spending attempt or identify anomalies in smart contract execution that indicate an exploit. By deploying deep learning-based fraud detection systems, blockchain networks can bolster their security, safeguarding users and assets against increasingly sophisticated attacks.

Decentralized AI Marketplaces

Blockchain technology can also facilitate the creation of decentralized marketplaces for AI models and services, enabling the secure and transparent exchange of AI capabilities. In such a marketplace, deep learning models could be trained, validated, and sold directly on the blockchain platform. Smart contracts would automate the transactions, ensuring that payments are made only when predefined conditions—such as model performance metrics—are met. This decentralized approach allows for greater trust and reduces the need for intermediaries, fostering a more open and accessible market for AI innovations.

Additionally, the use of blockchain ensures that all transactions and ownership transfers are immutably recorded, providing transparency and reducing the risk of disputes.

Integrating deep learning with blockchain also presents challenges. Blockchain platforms often have limited computational resources, which can make it difficult to train and deploy large deep learning models. There are also questions around data privacy and ownership when training models on decentralized data.

IoT and Deep Learning

The Internet of Things refers to the growing network of connected devices and sensors that are collecting and exchanging data. In finance, IoT data can provide valuable insights into consumer behavior, economic activity, and risk factors.

Deep learning is well-suited to analyzing the immense, complex, and often unstructured data generated by IoT devices.

Some potential applications of deep learning and IoT in finance include:

- **Insurance risk assessment:** IoT sensors in homes, vehicles, and wearable devices can provide detailed data about individual risk factors. Deep learning models can analyze this data to provide more personalized and dynamic insurance pricing.
- **Real-time fraud detection:** IoT devices can capture real-time data about financial transactions, such as the location of a point-of-sale terminal. Deep learning models can analyze this data in real-time to detect and prevent fraudulent transactions.
- **Economic forecasting:** IoT data can provide real-time indicators of economic activity, such as energy consumption, traffic patterns, or shipping volumes. Deep learning models can incorporate this data to make more accurate and timely economic forecasts.

Integrating deep learning with IoT also comes with challenges, particularly around data quality, privacy, and security. IoT data can be noisy and unreliable, and the sheer volume of data can make it difficult to process and analyze in real-time. There are also significant privacy concerns around the collection and use of personal data from IoT devices.

Chapter Seven

COMPUTER VISION IN FINANCE

While its relevance to finance may not be immediately obvious, computer vision is already being applied in practical ways by innovative companies, particularly in areas like asset monitoring, portfolio management, and risk assessment.

For example, in asset monitoring and risk assessment, computer vision techniques are being used to analyze satellite imagery, monitor agricultural production, track urban economic activity, and assess the impacts of natural disasters. These applications can offer early indicators of market trends, giving investors and analysts an edge.

Companies like SpaceKnow (www.spaceknow.com) analyze satellite images of ports to predict industrial activity, which has shown efficacy in forecasting stock index returns. Similarly, Apollo Agriculture (www.apolloagriculture.com) uses satellite data to monitor crop health, which supports the assessment of creditworthiness and risk management in the agricultural sector.

In China, startups like TerraQuanta (www.terraqt.ai) are pushing the envelope further, providing private equity firms and traders with advanced insights into agricultural yields through cutting-edge satellite imaging. This blend of computer vision and AI is allowing investors to track economic activities and monitor agricultural outputs almost in real-time, giving them a significant edge in financial decision making.

In business, where companies are always looking for a competitive edge, it is important to note the creative applications of technology to solve problems or gain greater business insights.

Let's dive into the technology to gain an understanding of how it works and areas where it is already being applied today – with the idea that by understanding how computer vision works, we might be able to find new and innovative applications for our own companies and industries.

Computer vision is also transforming how financial documents are processed.

Optical Character Recognition (OCR) has been around for decades, but didn't truly become practical until the 1990s – coinciding with the increased computing power and algorithms that became available in that era. Now, with the integration of computer vision, OCR has significantly improved how financial documents are processed. Tasks like reading invoices and regulatory filings that once took significant time and effort and were prone to human error are now automated with high accuracy.

Economic Forecasting through Satellite Imagery

By applying computer vision techniques to satellite imagery, analysts can now extract detailed information on a wide range of economic indicators, including agricultural productivity, urban development, and industrial activity. Satellite imagery is widely used today in agricultural forecasting, with its application becoming more accessible due to advancements in technology and the commercial availability of high-resolution images from various providers. This abundance of data, combined with advanced computer vision algorithms, offers unprecedented capabilities in assessing vegetation health, analyzing weather patterns, and incorporating historical yield data to predict crop production with a speed and precision that surpasses human capabilities. These insights are invaluable for making informed decisions across multiple sectors, from agriculture to urban planning and industrial analysis.

These insights are particularly valuable for commodity traders, agribusinesses, and investors, who rely on accurate data to inform their decisions and strategies. The ability to process and analyze satellite imagery at scale allows stakeholders in the agricultural sector to gain a competitive edge by making more informed predictions and mitigating risks associated with crop yields.

Consider a hedge fund evaluating a position in wheat futures. By analyzing satellite imagery of global wheat crops, the fund can gain early insights into potential yield levels. If the imagery analysis indicates that yields may be lower than market expectations, the fund might short wheat futures, anticipating price increases due to a constrained supply, and potentially profiting from the market shift.

Satellite imagery obviously extends beyond agricultural forecasts. It can be used, for example, to gauge economic activity. By tracking indicators such as construction activity, traffic volumes, and energy usage, investors can uncover promising opportunities and evaluate the economic health of specific regions. For example, a real estate investment trust (REIT) with properties in a particular city could use satellite data to monitor development in the surrounding area. If the analysis reveals increased construction and traffic near the REIT's holdings, it could indicate rising demand for real estate, signaling a potential for further investment in that locality.

Satellite imagery has also been applied by insurance companies that use it to assess the economic impact of natural disasters. By comparing images from before and after an event, insurers can quickly determine the extent of damage to policyholders' properties, which allows for rapid, accurate estimates of potential claims, and helps insurers plan for adequate reserves to cover payouts. Real-time satellite imagery could enable insurers to assess damage across a wide area in a matter of hours, streamlining the claims process and improving response times. This not only enhances operational efficiency but also strengthens the insurer's ability to support policyholders during critical times.

"The world itself looks cleaner and so much more beautiful.
Maybe we can make it that way ...
by giving everyone, eventually, that new perspective from out in space."
~ Roger B. Chaffee, Apollo astronaut

To effectively leverage satellite imagery analysis, financial institutions need to focus on building the right expertise and forming strategic partnerships. Access to high-quality satellite imagery often comes through collaborations with specialized providers who offer the necessary data. The real value, however, lies in assembling multidisciplinary teams that combine skills in computer vision, data science, and financial analysis. These teams must be adept at interpreting the outputs from advanced computer vision algorithms and turning them into actionable insights that can guide investment decisions.

Document Analysis and Automated Reading

Financial institutions still process a significant number of physical documents daily, from invoices and contracts to financial statements and regulatory filings. Manually reading and extracting data from these documents is a time-consuming and error-prone process. However, advances in computer vision are enabling the automation of this task, promising significant improvements in efficiency and accuracy.

Combining OCR with advanced computer vision techniques transforms the way financial documents are processed, far surpassing the capabilities of analog methods with human analysts. While traditional OCR can convert text into machine-readable data, it often falls short when dealing with complex documents that include tables, varied layouts, or multiple columns. This is where computer vision steps in, enabling the automated analysis of document structures, such as identifying headers, paragraphs, and tables, and accurately extracting relevant information.

Banks and financial institutions are increasingly turning to SaaS accounts payable (AP) solutions like Tipalti and Bill to automate invoice processing. Traditionally, this would involve manual data entry, with employees reading each invoice and keying in relevant information. Now, these platforms leverage OCR and computer vision to streamline the process.

Invoices can be scanned or digitally received, and OCR technology converts the printed or handwritten text into machine-readable data. Meanwhile, computer vision algorithms analyze the layout of the document, identifying structures like supplier names, invoice numbers, amounts due, and payment terms. This extracted data is then seamlessly integrated into the bank's AP system, where it triggers automated workflows—such as routing invoices for approval, scheduling payments, and updating financial records.

By using these technologies, banks can significantly reduce the time and effort required for invoice processing, minimize errors, and ensure timely payments. This automation enhances operational efficiency and allows financial institutions to manage large volumes of transactions with greater accuracy and speed.

Haven't we seen this before?

Robotic Process Automation (RPA) has been a valuable and widely used tool in automating routine, rule-based tasks within the financial sector, but it has limitations when it comes to handling unstructured or complex documents. RPA relies on structured data and predefined workflows, making it less effective for tasks that require understanding and interpreting more intricate document layouts.

The integration of computer vision techniques, such as OCR and layout analysis, offers a more advanced alternative to traditional RPA. Unlike RPA, which is primarily designed for repetitive tasks based on structured inputs, computer vision can process and extract meaningful data from unstructured documents with greater precision and flexibility. This next level of automation allows financial institutions to move beyond the constraints of RPA, enabling them to handle a wider variety of document types and more complex data extraction tasks with improved accuracy.

AI-driven document analysis is increasingly being used to process financial statements released regularly by public companies. These detailed documents are essential for investors, analysts, and financial institutions, but their sheer volume and complexity make them challenging and time-consuming to analyze. By leveraging AI, this process can be streamlined, making it more efficient to extract and interpret the critical data within these statements.

AI algorithms can be trained to recognize and extract key financial metrics, such as revenue, profits, assets, and liabilities. Additionally, these algorithms can identify and highlight important qualitative information, such as risk factors and management commentary. This automated extraction process enables faster and more comprehensive analysis of financial statements, allowing an investment firm, for instance, to quickly process the financial statements of hundreds of companies and identify potential investment opportunities or red flags based on predefined criteria.

Generative AI is already doing this today with even greater efficacy by not only extracting information but also synthesizing and generating insights from financial documents. Today, generative AI models can be trained to read and understand financial statements in the same way a human analyst would. These models can generate summaries, create detailed reports, and even draft commentary that highlights key trends and anomalies within the data. This capability allows for the automation of more complex and nuanced tasks, such as forecasting future performance based on historical data, identifying discrepancies, or generating insights that might otherwise require a deep understanding of the financial context.

By automating these lower-level tasks, generative AI is changing the way financial institutions and analysts approach document processing. They can handle ever-larger datasets with greater accuracy and efficiency, providing more timely and actionable insights. This advancement is particularly valuable in an environment where speed and accuracy are critical for decision-making, further enhancing the competitive edge for those who leverage these technologies in their financial operations.

As with any process that involves a company's financial information, data security and privacy must be taken into account. Financial documents often contain sensitive information that must be protected. As financial institutions automate document processing, they must ensure that strong data security measures are in place and that all activities comply with relevant privacy regulations. Despite these challenges, the benefits of automating document analysis in finance are substantial. Automation can significantly reduce manual processing time and improve data extraction accuracy, leading to efficiency gains, cost savings, and more timely, data-driven decision-making.

Customer Identification and Verification

Verifying customer identities is the backbone of anti-money laundering (AML) and know-your-customer (KYC) regulations. Traditionally, this process involved manual checks of government-issued IDs—a method that is both time-consuming and prone to error. However, computer vision has introduced more efficient and secure methods for customer identification, with facial recognition emerging as a key application. By analyzing an image or video of a person's face and comparing it to a database of known faces, facial recognition algorithms can quickly and accurately verify identities. In practice, this could mean a customer submitting a selfie or video, which is then matched to the photo on their government-issued ID, streamlining the verification process.

When a new customer wants to open an account with an online bank, they could be asked to provide a photo of their government ID and a live selfie. The bank's computer vision system would then compare the face in the selfie to the photo on the ID to verify that they match. This process can be completed in real-time, providing a seamless and secure onboarding experience for the customer.

Facial recognition can also be used for ongoing authentication in certain high-risk transactions. For instance, when a customer wants to make a large funds transfer, they could be prompted to provide a live facial scan, which would be compared to the bank's records to confirm their identity before processing the transaction.

Another area where computer vision is being applied is in the verification of document authenticity. When a customer provides a scan or photo of their ID, computer vision algorithms can analyze the document for signs of tampering or forgery. This may involve checking for the presence of security features like holograms or microprinting, analyzing the document's layout and fonts, or comparing the document to a database of known genuine and fake IDs.

By automating the process of document verification, financial institutions can reduce the risk of accepting fraudulent IDs and improve the efficiency of their KYC processes. An insurance company, for example, could use computer vision to automatically verify the authenticity of driver's licenses submitted with policy applications, flagging any suspicious documents for further manual review.

The use of computer vision in customer identification and verification offers several key benefits. It significantly speeds up the process, enabling real-time onboarding and authentication without the need for physical branch visits or manual checks, thus enhancing the customer experience. Additionally, computer vision improves the accuracy of identity verification by reducing human error, leading to more consistent and reliable outcomes. Finally, by minimizing manual intervention, it helps lower costs, particularly for financial institutions with large customer bases or high transaction volumes.

On the flip side, there are potential risks of bias and discrimination in facial recognition systems. Research has shown that some facial recognition algorithms can have higher error rates for certain demographics – particularly people of color. Financial institutions need to be vigilant in testing their systems for such biases and taking steps to mitigate them.

Another challenge is the need to continuously update and improve the algorithms as criminals develop new techniques for creating fake IDs or spoofing facial recognition systems. This requires ongoing investment in research and development, as well as regular testing and updating of the systems in place.

Despite these challenges, the use of computer vision in customer identification and verification is likely to grow in the coming years. The efficiency and security benefits are compelling, and as the technology continues to improve, it will likely become an increasingly standard part of the KYC process.

In the future, we may see the integration of computer vision with other biometric technologies, such as voice recognition or fingerprint scanning, to create even more robust multi-factor authentication systems. We may also see the development of industry-wide databases of verified customer identities, allowing for more seamless and secure identification across different financial institutions.

In each of these applications, computer vision is providing powerful new tools for gathering and interpreting data, enabling financial institutions to make more informed decisions, improve efficiency, and enhance security.

Chapter Eight

NATURAL LANGUAGE PROCESSING IN FINANCE

NLP allows financial institutions to extract valuable insights from the continuous firehose of unstructured text data generated daily. From real-time market sentiment analysis to automating customer interactions through chatbots, NLP enhances decision-making and operational efficiency while fostering more natural communication with customers and stakeholders.

Sentiment Analysis and Market Prediction

In finance, quickly gauging market sentiment and predicting trends directly impacts forecasting accuracy. Historically, analysts would manually sift through financial news, company reports, and economic data to form market opinions. But now, with the overwhelming surge of digital data, especially from social media and news outlets, sentiment analysis can actively manage and interpret troves of data, allowing for real-time insights that were previously unattainable with manual methods.

Sentiment analysis is an NLP technique used to determine the emotional tone or attitude expressed in a piece of text. It involves analyzing and categorizing opinions, emotions, or sentiments in written content into positive, negative, or neutral categories. In finance, sentiment analysis is particularly useful in assessing market sentiment by processing large volumes of unstructured data to gauge public opinion about stocks, companies, or economic conditions, which can then inform trading strategies, investment decisions, and risk management.

One of the primary uses of sentiment analysis in finance is to predict stock market movements. By analyzing the sentiment of text data mentioning a particular company or sector, investors and traders can gain insights into how the market is likely to react. For example, if there is a sudden surge of negative sentiment around a company, it may indicate that the company's stock price is likely to decline in the near future.

Several studies have demonstrated the predictive power of sentiment analysis in the stock market, highlighting how public sentiment, particularly from highly active platforms like Reddit or X (formerly Twitter), can influence market movements.

Bollen, Mao, and Zeng (2011) Study

An academic paper by Bollen, Mao, and Zeng (2011) explored the relationship between public mood and stock market performance, specifically focusing on the Dow Jones Industrial Average (DJIA). The researchers analyzed millions of tweets, categorizing the overall sentiment into various mood states such as calm, happy, and anxious using a mood-tracking tool called the Google-Profile of Mood States (GPOMS). They discovered a strong correlation between certain mood states and market performance. Remarkably, they found that shifts in public mood could predict the direction of the DJIA with an accuracy of 87.6%. Their findings suggested that collective sentiment on social media could be a leading indicator of stock market trends, potentially offering a new dimension to market forecasting.

Pagolu et al. (2016) Study

Another influential study by Pagolu et al. (2016) further validated the predictive potential of sentiment analysis for stock market indices. The researchers focused on sentiment analysis of Twitter data, examining the sentiment expressed in tweets about specific companies and their stocks. By applying machine learning techniques to categorize these sentiments as positive, negative, or neutral, they correlated the overall sentiment with movements in stock market indices. Their model achieved an accuracy of around 70% in predicting stock market trends, demonstrating that sentiment analysis could provide valuable insights for investors and traders.

The implications of these findings are significant for both individual investors and large financial institutions. By integrating sentiment analysis into their trading strategies, investors can potentially enhance their decision-making processes, identify emerging trends earlier, and better manage risks associated with market volatility. Moreover, as sentiment analysis tools continue to evolve with advancements in natural language processing and machine learning, their predictive accuracy is likely to improve, making them an increasingly vital component of modern financial analysis.

Financial institutions are increasingly incorporating sentiment analysis into their trading strategies. Hedge funds, for instance, may use sentiment analysis to inform their long or short positions in particular stocks or sectors. If the sentiment around a company is consistently positive, a fund may take a long position, betting that the stock price will rise. Conversely, if the sentiment is negative, the fund may short the stock, expecting the price to fall.

Sentiment analysis can also be used for risk management. By monitoring the sentiment around the companies or industries they are invested in, financial institutions can identify potential risks early and take steps to mitigate them. For example, if a bank detects a sudden increase in negative sentiment around a company it has lent money to, it may increase its provisions for loan losses or take other steps to reduce its exposure.

Implementing sentiment analysis in finance does present challenges. One issue is dealing with the noisy and unstructured nature of text data, particularly from social media. Tweets and other social media posts often contain slang, sarcasm, and other language that can be difficult for algorithms to interpret correctly. There's also the issue of distinguishing between relevant and irrelevant information. Not every mention of a company on social media will be relevant to its financial performance.

To address these challenges, financial institutions need to invest in robust NLP pipelines that can effectively preprocess and filter text data. This may involve techniques like text cleaning (removing HTML tags, special characters, etc.), tokenization (breaking text into individual words or phrases), and stop word removal (filtering out common words like "the" or "and"). Institutions may also need to develop domain-specific sentiment lexicons that capture the unique language and jargon of the financial world.

Another key consideration is the real-time nature of financial markets. For sentiment analysis to be useful for trading or risk management, it needs to be able to process and analyze data in near real-time. This requires significant computational resources and optimized algorithms that can handle the volume and velocity of financial text data.

Despite these challenges, there are significant potential benefits from sentiment analysis. By harnessing the power of NLP to gauge market sentiment in real-time, financial institutions can make more informed trading decisions, better manage risk, and ultimately, generate higher returns. As the volume of digital text data continues to grow, the ability to effectively analyze and interpret this data will likely become an increasingly important competitive advantage in the finance industry.

Looking forward, we can expect to see continued innovation in the application of sentiment analysis to finance. One promising area is the integration of sentiment analysis with other forms of alternative data, such as satellite imagery or geospatial data. By combining insights from multiple non-traditional data sources, investors may be able to gain an even more comprehensive and nuanced view of market sentiment and risk.

We may also see the development of more sophisticated sentiment analysis techniques that go beyond simple polarity classification (positive/negative/neutral) to capture more complex emotional states or even predict the intensity of market reactions. Advancements in deep learning, particularly in the field of transfer learning, may enable the development of more powerful and generalizable sentiment analysis models.

News Analytics and Real-Time Data Processing

The financial markets are continuously generating textual data, from news articles and press releases to regulatory filings. This data often contains a treasure trove of valuable information that can influence the prices of financial assets, but its sheer volume makes it impossible to manually process and analyze it quickly enough for it to be at all useful.

As with other analytics pipelines, the process of news analytics starts with data collection and preprocessing. This involves gathering text data from various sources (financial news websites, company websites, and regulatory databases), cleaning and formatting it to remove any irrelevant or noisy information, and then applying various NLP techniques to analyze the content.

These techniques can include:

Named Entity Recognition (NER)

Named Entity Recognition (NER) involves identifying and extracting the names of specific entities mentioned in the text, such as companies, people, locations, or products. In finance, NER helps pinpoint key players like corporations, executives, and financial institutions. For example, if analyzing a news article about a merger, NER would identify the companies involved, key stakeholders, and relevant locations, and then cross-reference them with other data sources.

Event Detection

Event Detection identifies specific actions or occurrences, such as mergers and acquisitions, earnings announcements, changes in management, or other significant business events that are described within the data. This technique allows organizations to track and respond to important developments quickly – providing insights that can influence investment decisions, risk assessments, or strategic planning. This could be something like a CEO's resignation, which would likely prompt a reassessment of a company's stock value or risk profile.

Sentiment Analysis

Sentiment analysis identifies the overall tone or emotion expressed in a text regarding specific entities or events. It categorizes the sentiment as positive, negative, or neutral. This approach allows users to gauge public or market reaction to specific events. For example, if a press release about a company's earnings report is analyzed, sentiment analysis can reveal whether the market's response is generally optimistic, pessimistic, or indifferent, which can inform trading strategies or investor relations efforts.

"But reason always cuts a poor figure beside sentiment;
the one being essentially restricted,
like everything that is positive, while the other is infinite."
~ Honoré de Balzac

Relation Extraction

Relation Extraction identifies and maps the relationships between entities mentioned in a corpus of text. This technique helps to understand the context and connections among events (e.g. company acquisitions, partnership announcements, or leadership changes), and maps a network of interactions within the financial ecosystem. This provides a clearer picture of how different entities are connected and how these relationships might influence the market or industry trends.

Relation extraction turns unstructured text into structured, machine-readable data that can be further analyzed and incorporated into various financial models and trading algorithms.

Timing is critical in financial markets. The sooner an investor or trader can act on new information, the greater the potential for profit or risk mitigation. NLP-powered news analytics systems can process data as soon as it becomes available, allowing financial institutions to quickly identify and react to potential market-moving events.

This real-time capability is particularly valuable in algorithmic trading. By incorporating news analytics into these algorithms, traders can automatically adjust their positions based on the sentiment and events extracted from news, which gives them the opportunity to capitalize on market inefficiencies before other participants.

Algorithmic Trading and Arbitrage

Arbitrage traditionally involves taking advantage of price differences for the same asset across different markets. Traders buy an asset where it's undervalued and sell it where it's overvalued, profiting from the discrepancy. This classic form of arbitrage relies on speed, as market forces quickly close these gaps.

But algorithmic trading takes arbitrage a step further by targeting temporary mispricings within a single market before they are widely recognized. Unlike traditional arbitrage, which focuses on cross-market comparisons, algorithmic trading uses sophisticated algorithms to scan vast amounts of data in real time, identifying subtle patterns and anomalies that suggest an asset is momentarily mispriced.

These algorithms can execute trades with remarkable speed and precision, often capitalizing on these brief windows of opportunity before the market corrects itself. This approach is not just about comparing prices across different markets; it's about understanding and predicting when an asset's price will adjust based on emerging information or market inefficiencies.

In essence, while traditional arbitrage exploits price differences between markets, algorithmic trading leverages advanced technology to identify and act on momentary mispricings within a market, providing traders with a powerful tool to maximize profits in a rapidly changing environment.

News analytics can also be used in risk management. By continuously monitoring news sources for potential risks related to invested assets, risk managers can quickly identify emerging threats and take proactive measures to mitigate potential losses.

A news analytics system could detect a significant increase in negative sentiment towards a particular sector or geography, for example, which would give risk managers access to advanced information, enabling them to reduce exposure to those areas or hedge their positions.

There are challenges, however, to implementing a news analytics system. The noise and overwhelming irrelevance in the broad sea of textual data is hard to sift through. Things like customer reviews, random mentions, and vague mentions can clog the data pipeline, but don't move markets. News analytics systems need to be designed to filter out the noise and focus on the most pertinent and impactful information.

This requires the development of powerful data preprocessing pipelines and the application of domain-specific knowledge to train the NLP models. The models need to understand the nuances and context of financial language, distinguishing between relevant and irrelevant information. Building comprehensive knowledge bases and ontologies that capture the relationships between financial concepts, companies, and events can help improve the accuracy and relevance of the extracted insights.

Another challenge is ensuring the reliability and correctness of the generated insights. NLP models, while powerful, are not perfect and can sometimes misinterpret or miss important information. In finance, where decisions can have significant monetary consequences, the accuracy of the insights is paramount. Rigorous testing, validation, and continuous monitoring of the news analytics system are essential to ensure its reliability and effectiveness.

Chatbots and Document Automation

Financial institutions are increasingly turning to NLP to handle the heavy lifting in customer interaction and document processing. Traditionally, these tasks involved manual work, which was slower, costlier, and more prone to human error. But as NLP technology advances, chatbots and document automation are stepping in to streamline these processes.

NLP-powered chatbots are increasingly used for handling routine customer service tasks like answering common questions and processing simple requests. Meanwhile, NLP-driven document automation systems are transforming how financial institutions extract and process data from complex documents, significantly reducing errors and improving efficiency. This shift is part of a broader move towards more intelligent, automated systems that enhance the speed, accuracy, and responsiveness of financial services.

Chatbots

Chatbots never sleep. Unlike human customer service representatives, chatbots can operate around the clock, providing instant assistance to customers at any time. This is particularly beneficial for financial institutions with a global customer base spanning different time zones.

NLP plays a crucial role in enabling chatbots to understand and respond to customer queries in a natural, human-like manner. Through techniques such as text classification, named entity recognition, and sentiment analysis, chatbots can interpret the intent behind a customer's message, extract relevant information, and provide appropriate responses.

For example, if a customer asks a chatbot about their account balance, the NLP algorithms can identify the intent (request for account information), recognize the relevant entity (the customer's account), and formulate a response that provides the requested information. If the chatbot detects a negative sentiment in the customer's message, it can adjust its response to be more empathetic or escalate the conversation to a human agent if necessary.

In addition to handling routine queries, NLP-powered chatbots can also assist customers with more complex tasks, such as filling out application forms or navigating through a financial institution's products and services. By asking relevant questions and providing guidance, chatbots can help customers complete these tasks more efficiently, reducing the need for human intervention.

Implementing effective NLP-based chatbots requires careful design and training. The chatbot's language model needs to be trained on a large corpus of financial domain-specific data to understand the terminology, concepts, and common customer queries. The model also needs to be continuously updated and refined based on real-world interactions to improve its accuracy and effectiveness over time.

Document Automation

Financial institutions handle an inordinate amount of textual data, including contracts, reports, and regulatory filings. Processing and analyzing these documents manually is not only time-consuming, but also prone to errors. By automating these tasks, NLP allows for faster, more accurate analysis, reducing the manual burden and improving overall operational efficiency.

By automatically scanning documents for required clauses or disclosures, NLP algorithms can quickly identify missing or inconsistent information, reducing the risk of compliance issues; and when combined with machine learning, it can automate many aspects of document processing. In contract review, NLP algorithms extract key information such as the parties involved, terms and conditions, and expiration dates. This data is then structured and stored in a database, making it easily accessible for retrieval and analysis.

Implementing this technology requires a blend of technical expertise and industry knowledge: NLP models must be trained on extensive datasets of financial documents to understand the specific language patterns, terminologies, and structures unique to the industry. Additionally, these models need to be fine-tuned for tasks like information extraction or report generation to ensure high accuracy and relevance.

One of the biggest challenges in deploying NLP for document analysis is dealing with the diversity and complexity of financial documents. Contracts like purchase agreements, employment contracts, and partnership agreements can vary widely in structure, language, and formatting across different jurisdictions and counterparties.

Developing NLP models capable of handling this variability requires training data and continuous refinement.

It can also be difficult to integrate NLP-based document automation into existing workflows and systems. Financial institutions need to ensure that the automated processes integrate seamlessly with their current IT infrastructure and that there are proper validation and oversight mechanisms in place to review the outputs of the NLP models.

Despite these challenges, the potential benefits of both chatbots and document automation in finance are significant. By automating routine customer interactions and document processing tasks, financial institutions can reduce operational costs, improve efficiency, and provide faster, more consistent service to their customers. By leveraging the insights generated from automated document analysis, financial institutions can make more informed business decisions, identify potential risks and opportunities, and respond more quickly to changing market conditions.

The integration of NLP with other AI technologies, such as computer vision for processing scanned documents or blockchain for secure document storage and verification, could open up new possibilities for end-to-end automation of financial processes.

Chapter Nine

REINFORCEMENT LEARNING IN FINANCE

Reinforcement learning (RL) differs from other machine learning methods in the way it learns by interacting with its environment. This means the algorithm makes decisions, observes the outcomes, and adjusts its strategy based on the feedback it receives, continuously refining its approach over time, which is particularly suited for the dynamic, unpredictable nature of financial markets.

In this chapter, we will examine the application of reinforcement learning in algorithmic trading, where it empowers the creation of trading strategies that progressively improve through ongoing feedback from the market. Additionally, we will investigate how reinforcement learning is enhancing portfolio management by dynamically adjusting asset allocations to maximize returns while carefully managing risk.

Algorithmic Trading

Reinforcement learning is a machine learning method that enables algorithms to learn and improve their decision-making processes through repeated interactions with the environment. In algorithmic trading, the environment is the financial market, and the decisions relate to trading actions such as buying, selling, or holding assets.

The fundamental concept behind reinforcement learning is the notion of an agent learning to make optimal decisions by maximizing a cumulative reward signal. The agent (trading algorithm in this case), receives feedback in the form of rewards or penalties based on the outcomes of its trading actions. This feedback loop is what allows the agent to learn from its experiences and adapt its strategies.

While traditional rule-based or even supervised learning approaches can struggle to deal with the dynamic nature of market conditions, RL models are able to navigate the inherent uncertainty and non-stationarity of financial markets by continuously updating their knowledge and adapting their strategies based on the changing market dynamics.

The components of RL for algorithmic trading are:

1. **State Representation:** The current state of the market, including price data, technical indicators, and other relevant features, is encoded into a suitable representation for the reinforcement learning algorithm.
2. **Action Space:** The algorithm considers a set of possible trading actions, such as buying, selling, or holding a specific quantity of an asset.
3. **Reward Function:** A reward function is defined to evaluate the performance of the trading actions. This can be based on metrics such as profit, risk-adjusted returns, or other domain-specific objectives.
4. **Learning Algorithm:** The reinforcement learning algorithm, such as Q-learning, SARSA, or policy gradients, is employed to learn the optimal trading policy based on the state, action, and reward interactions.
5. **Training and Evaluation:** The trading algorithm is trained on historical market data and evaluated on out-of-sample data to assess its performance and robustness.

RL is being applied today in models used to predict everything from equities and foreign exchange to derivatives; but its effectiveness is bound by the choice of hyperparameters, reward functions, and risk constraints used in the models. That said, as research advances and more sophisticated algorithms are developed, reinforcement learning is likely to continue to play an increasingly significant role in shaping the future of trading.

Portfolio Optimization

Portfolio managers face the ongoing challenge of navigating the intricate and ever-shifting financial markets. The task of maximizing returns while effectively managing risk requires constant adaptation and informed decision-making. Reinforcement learning offers a powerful solution, equipping managers with advanced tools for dynamic portfolio optimization.

In portfolio management, the algorithm learns to make optimal asset allocation decisions based on the rewards it receives, such as maximizing returns or minimizing risk.

One of the key advantages of applying reinforcement learning to portfolio optimization is its ability to adapt to changing market conditions. Traditional optimization methods, such as mean-variance optimization, rely on historical data and assume that the future will resemble the past. However, financial markets are notoriously unpredictable, and what worked yesterday may not work today. Reinforcement learning algorithms, on the other hand, can continuously learn and adjust their strategies based on real-time market feedback, allowing them to adapt to new patterns and trends.

Here's how reinforcement learning works in portfolio optimization:

State Representation

The foundation of any reinforcement learning algorithm in financial markets begins with state representation. This involves defining the state of the environment, which encapsulates relevant market information. This information typically includes asset prices, economic indicators, risk factors, and other variables that influence market conditions. The state representation acts as the input to the algorithm, providing it with a snapshot of the market environment at any given time, allowing the algorithm to make informed decisions based on the current market state.

Action Space

Once the state is defined, the algorithm needs to know what actions it can take. The action space represents the set of all possible portfolio allocation decisions the algorithm can make. These actions can include buying, selling, or holding specific assets. The complexity of the action space can vary depending on the investment strategy — ranging from simple binary decisions (buy or sell) to more complex multi-asset allocations.

Reward Function

The reward function determines the feedback the algorithm receives based on its actions. This function is designed to guide the algorithm toward the desired outcomes by rewarding successful actions. In the context of portfolio management, the reward function can be based on various metrics such as portfolio returns, risk-adjusted performance (e.g., Sharpe ratio), or other custom objectives that align with the investor's goals.

Learning Algorithm

The learning algorithm lies at the heart of reinforcement learning. This algorithm is responsible for updating the investment strategy based on the rewards observed from previous actions. Popular learning algorithms in this context include Q-learning, SARSA (State-Action-Reward-State-Action), and policy gradient methods. Each of these algorithms has its strengths and weaknesses, and the choice of algorithm often depends on the specific requirements of the investment strategy and the complexity of the environment.

Training and Evaluation

Finally, the reinforcement learning algorithm undergoes a rigorous training and evaluation process. During training, the algorithm is exposed to historical market data, where it learns to optimize its actions to maximize the reward function. Once the algorithm is trained, it is then evaluated on out-of-sample data to assess its performance and robustness in real-world scenarios. This evaluation helps ensure that the algorithm generalizes well to unseen data and can perform effectively under different market conditions.

One popular approach to implementing reinforcement learning in portfolio optimization is using Q-learning, a model-free algorithm that learns to make optimal decisions based on the expected future rewards. Q-learning estimates the value of taking a specific action in a given state and updates these estimates based on the actual rewards received. By iteratively updating its Q-values, the algorithm learns to make better decisions over time.

Another approach is policy gradient methods, which directly optimize the policy (i.e., the strategy for making decisions) based on the expected rewards. Policy gradient methods aim to find the optimal policy that maximizes the expected cumulative reward over time. These methods are particularly well-suited for continuous action spaces, such as adjusting portfolio weights.

Reinforcement learning has shown promising results in various portfolio optimization studies. For example, a study by Jiang et al. (2017) applied deep reinforcement learning to portfolio management and demonstrated that the algorithm could outperform traditional optimization methods, particularly in volatile market conditions. Another study by Yu et al. (2019) used reinforcement learning to optimize a multi-asset portfolio, considering transaction costs and market impact, and showed improved risk-adjusted returns compared to benchmark strategies.

It is important to understand that financial markets are complex and noisy environments, and the algorithm's performance can be sensitive to the choice of reward function, state representation, and hyperparameters. Moreover, the interpretability of the learned strategies may be limited, which can be a concern for investors and regulators who prefer transparent and explainable models.

As research in this area continues to advance, we can expect to see more sophisticated reinforcement learning algorithms that can handle a wider range of market conditions, incorporate transaction costs and constraints, and adapt to changing investor preferences and risk tolerances. The integration of reinforcement learning with other techniques, such as deep learning and transfer learning, may further enhance its capabilities in portfolio optimization.

By enabling algorithms to learn and adapt based on real-time market feedback, reinforcement learning has the potential to revolutionize the way asset allocation and investment decisions are made. While challenges remain, the promise of reinforcement learning in portfolio management is clear, and it is poised to play an increasingly important role in the future of investment management.

Risk Management

Financial firms and companies across industries constantly navigate market uncertainties, credit risks, and operational challenges to safeguard investments and optimize returns. Traditionally, risk management has relied on historical data, statistical models, and human expertise, but these methods often fall short in capturing the intricate, ever-shifting dynamics of modern markets.

Reinforcement learning has its place here, too. In this section, we'll dig deeper into how RL works along with its benefits and challenges.

Understanding Reinforcement Learning

Think of reinforcement learning as training a model the same way you might train a dog to do new tricks. You can't just tell it what to do. You have to guide it through rewards and feedback. When the dog performs the desired action, you give it a treat. Over time, the dog learns to associate certain behaviors with positive outcomes. RL operates on a similar principle, but with algorithms instead of furry companions.

The goal of reinforcement learning is to learn a policy that maximizes its cumulative reward over time. Through repeated interactions and trial-and-error, the agent gradually refines its policy, learning to make optimal decisions in complex, dynamic situations.

Applying RL to Risk Management

So, how does this AI dog trainer help with financial risk management?
Let's break it down:

Environment Modeling

The first step in developing a financial RL system is building its environment. This involves creating a virtual simulation that closely mimics real-world financial markets. It incorporates all the critical variables that influence risk: market conditions, portfolio positions, and regulatory constraints. And by accurately modeling these factors, the environment works as a realistic playground where the RL agent — acting as a risk manager — can learn and experiment with different strategies in a controlled setting.

State Space

In a simulated RL environment, the system occupies a specific "state" at any given moment, representing a snapshot of the risk landscape at that point in time. This state encompasses all relevant risk factors, including variables like current asset prices, volatility levels, and portfolio allocations. By defining this state space, the RL agent gains the context needed to make informed decisions, enabling it to accurately assess risk and adapt to changing market conditions.

Action Space

While the state space defines all possible situations the RL agent can observe in the environment, the action space contains all potential decisions the agent can make in response. In financial risk management, these actions might include adjusting exposure limits, hedging positions, or implementing mitigation strategies. Each action influences the environment's state and impacts the rewards the agent receives. The design of the action space is critical, as it shapes the range of strategies the agent can explore and optimize.

Reward Function

The reward is the carrot for which RL aspires, driving it to become an effective risk manager. In RL, the reward function is a mathematical formula that assigns a score to each action based on its impact on key performance indicators. For a financial RL agent, this means being incentivized to maximize profits. By carefully designing the reward function, developers can steer the agent toward strategies that align with broader risk management goals.

Learning Algorithms

With the environment configured and reward function identified, the final step is to deploy reinforcement learning algorithms. These algorithms are the "thought process" by which the RL agent learns. Through repeated exposure to various simulated scenarios, the agent gradually improves its ability to navigate the simulated risk landscape, where it develops the risk management strategies that can be applied in real-world financial markets.

Benefits and Challenges

RL's greatest strength is its ability to address complex, multidimensional problems that often overwhelm traditional models by learning from interactive simulations. RL algorithms can uncover subtle patterns and relationships that might otherwise be invisible to human analysts or conventional statistical methods. These algorithms thrive in dynamic environments, continuously refining their strategies based on new data inputs, making them inherently adaptive to the ever-shifting conditions of financial markets and regulatory environment. But there are constraints: RL algorithms are data-intensive, requiring large volumes of high-quality data to function optimally. When the data is insufficient, incomplete, or noisy, the performance of these algorithms can be significantly compromised, leading to suboptimal or even erroneous outcomes.

Chapter Ten

GENERATIVE MODELS IN FINANCE

While data scientists and engineers have been using AI at scale for more than a decade, the broader world hasn't paid much attention until the last couple of years, as generative AI has emerged. The reason generative AI has caught the world's attention is because it has brought the power of artificial intelligence to the masses via its ability to interact with humans in natural human language. While access to AI was previously the domain of engineers and programmers who knew odd-sounding secret languages like Python, Java, and C++, generative AI has made the power of this technology accessible to the rest of the world.

Generative AI creates novel (new) unseen content based on the prompts it receives. AI-powered chatbots like ChatGPT, Claude, and Llama use this technology to interact with humans in language we understand, making powerful AI tools directly accessible to nonprogrammers.

Further, the technology's ability to create new data that resembles the patterns of the data it was trained on gives it a lot of potential applications in finance. These models' ability to create synthetic financial data that closely mirrors real-world market conditions make them ideal for tasks like stress testing, model training, and scenario analysis. By using synthetic data in these applications, finance professionals can avoid risking sensitive, proprietary information while simultaneously expanding the size of their training sets.

Generative AI could also be used to help develop new, innovative financial products by simulating various market behaviors and conditions.

Synthetic Data Generation with Generative Models

We talked previously about Generative Adversarial Networks (GANs), and how they generate realistic synthetic data, which has powerful applications in finance, where they can be applied to ML model development and testing without compromising privacy or relying on sensitive, proprietary information.

In financial applications, GANs can generate synthetic datasets that capture the statistical properties and patterns of real financial data, such as time series of stock prices, customer transaction records, or loan default histories.

Applications of this synthetic data include:

Synthetic data can be used throughout the process of model training and validation, particularly when real data is limited, incomplete, or unbalanced. By augmenting or replacing actual data with synthetic data, machine learning models can be trained to better recognize the hidden generalizable patterns and improve performance. GANs also make it easier to run scenario analysis and stress testing on forecasts by simulating extreme or hypothetical scenarios (black swan events) that are rarely observed in historical data.

Synthetic data also provides a solution to privacy and confidentiality concerns associated with sharing or accessing real financial data, which often contains sensitive, personal, or competitive information. By using synthetic data, institutions can collaborate and innovate without exposing proprietary datasets. Researchers can also use synthetic data to address fairness and bias issues in their models by generating data with specific statistical profiles or demographic distributions. This would allow thorough testing and mitigation of potential biases before deploying models in real-world applications.

As with any AI model, GAN implementation requires careful model design and validation. The choice of GAN architecture, loss functions, and training procedures can significantly impact the quality and diversity of the generated samples. Synthetic data is useless if it doesn't faithfully represent the relevant statistical properties and relationships of the real data – without introducing unintended artifacts or distortions. And for use in finance, its application should be accompanied by appropriate governance and risk management practices. While synthetic data mitigates some privacy and security risks, it may still be subject to regulatory scrutiny and ethical considerations – especially if used in decision-making processes that impact real individuals or markets.

As we're still in the early stages of this technology, we can expect the power of these models will only grow as they are further developed and refined, and that we will continue to see increasingly sophisticated and diverse applications in synthetic financial data generation in the coming years.

Financial Product Development with Generative Models

Generative AI has applications in finance beyond data creation. It could also be used to help create new financial products. By learning to simulate and manipulate complex financial structures and market dynamics, these models can assist in the development of novel financial instruments and investment strategies.

Consider the creation of new derivative products. Derivatives are complex financial instruments whose value is derived from an underlying asset or benchmark. Due to their complexity, designing effective derivatives requires a deep understanding of the underlying market dynamics and the ability to effectively model various risk factors and payoff structures. While difficult for human finance professionals, these requirements are perfectly suited for AI. Generative models can be trained on historical data of existing derivatives to learn the key features and relationships that drive their value. They can then be used to generate new derivative structures with desired characteristics, such as enhanced risk-return profiles, customized payoffs, or exposure to specific market factors.

By training a GAN on historical option prices and their underlying stock prices, the model could learn implied volatility surfaces and the relationships between option prices and market variables. The model could then generate new option contracts with custom strike prices, expiration dates, and payout structures. These synthetic options could be tailored to specific investor preferences or market conditions.

Generative AI could also be applied to creating structured products – pre-packages investment strategies that combine different financial instruments that balance risk-return objectives. These investment tools generally involve complex combinations of derivatives, fixed income securities, and equities, with payoffs tied to various market indices or triggers. Generative AI is well suited to simulate and optimize the performance of these multi-asset portfolios under different market scenarios. By using specific inputs, such as market conditions, investor needs, or risk limitations, generative models can create and evaluate a wide variety of financial products. This process helps identify the most promising options more quickly, leading to faster development of new financial products and allowing for better customization and management of risks to suit different investor profiles or market scenarios.

These models can also assist in the backtesting and stress testing, identifying potential weaknesses and allowing for iterative refinement and risk mitigation. By simulating realistic market scenarios and generating synthetic time series data, they can develop a more comprehensive assessment of a product's performance and risk profile before its actual launch.

While finance pros have traditionally relied on theoretical assumptions and historical precedents to develop these instruments, generative models offer a more data-driven and empirical approach. This can inspire new product ideas and challenge conventional wisdom about what is possible or desirable in the market.

But the complexity and opacity of these models can make it difficult to interpret and explain the rationale behind the generated products. There is a risk of creating products that are overly complex, misaligned with investor needs, or exposed to unexpected risks. Robust governance frameworks and interpretability techniques will be crucial to ensure the transparency, fairness, and stability of AI-driven product innovation.

Regulators and policymakers will also need to adapt to the new realities of AI-generated products. They will need to develop guidelines and oversight mechanisms to ensure these models are used responsibly and that the resulting products comply with consumer protection, market integrity, and financial stability objectives.

Risk Simulation and Scenario Analysis

By learning to simulate realistic market conditions and generate plausible future scenarios, generative models enable a more proactive and comprehensive assessment of potential risks and opportunities.

Statistical models have long been a mainstay of risk management, but even the most complex models pale in comparison to modern deep learning approaches. Standard statistical models aren't able to capture the complex, non-linear dynamics of financial markets, particularly in extreme or unprecedented events. Deep learning, on the other hand, excels in identifying intricate patterns and relationships within datasets, making it better suited for understanding and predicting market behavior under a wide range of conditions, including those that deviate significantly from historical norms.

> *"The biggest risk is not taking any risk ...*
> *In a world that is changing really quickly,*
> *the only strategy that is guaranteed to fail is not taking risks."*
>
> *~ Mark Zuckerberg*

Generative models can create synthetic time series that exhibit similar statistical properties and correlations to real market data, but with the flexibility to explore alternative paths and stress scenarios. For example, a GAN trained on historical stock prices, interest rates, and macroeconomic variables could generate a diverse set of future market scenarios, each representing a different combination of risk factors. These scenarios could include both typical market conditions and extreme events, such as market crashes, inflationary spikes, or geopolitical shocks. By simulating the performance of investment portfolios or risk models under these different scenarios, institutions can gain a more comprehensive understanding of their risk exposures and potential losses.

Generative models can also enhance the realism and granularity of scenario analysis by incorporating additional data sources and dimensions. For instance, by training on news articles, social media sentiment, or satellite imagery, these models can generate scenarios that reflect the impact of unstructured data and external events on financial markets. This can provide a more nuanced and contextual view of risk – beyond what is captured in traditional financial data.

Generative models could even be used to simulate the behavior of market participants and the dynamics of liquidity under different conditions. By modeling the interactions between agents with different trading strategies, risk preferences, or information sets, these models can generate realistic market microstructures and identify potential sources of systemic risk. This can inform the design of more robust market mechanisms and regulatory frameworks.

Similarly, in stress testing – where financial models or portfolios are exposed to hypothetical adverse scenarios to assess their resilience and identify potential vulnerabilities – generative models could learn the mappings between risk factors and portfolio returns. They could also be incorporated into reverse stress testing, where the model starts with a predefined adverse outcome and works backward to identify the scenarios that could lead to such an outcome.

Further, generative models can be used to simulate the propagation of risk through complex financial networks and interconnected systems. By modeling the interdependencies between entities, such as banks, insurance companies, and shadow banking institutions, these models can identify potential channels of contagion and assess the systemic implications of localized shock, which could inform the design of more effective macroprudential policies and crisis management strategies.

Generative models will undoubtedly be used increasingly in the financial sector, as they become more powerful and the technology becomes more pervasive.

Chapter Eleven

GRAPH NEURAL NETWORKS IN FINANCE

Graph neural networks (GNNs) are a type of deep learning model designed to process data structured as "graphs," where entities and the relationships between them are represented as nodes and edges. Those interconnections reveal a whole new level of information behind the data, making them particularly useful for tasks such as social network analysis, molecular chemistry, and recommendation systems. By leveraging the unique ability of GNNs to process and learn from graph-structured data, financial institutions can gain deeper insights into the data and the intricate interconnections of the financial landscape.

This chapter explores the varied applications of GNNs in finance, starting with their use in fraud detection within transaction networks. We'll also look at how GNNs can model interconnections within financial systems like interbank lending networks to assess systemic risk, and how GNNs can improve credit scoring and risk assessment models by incorporating complex relational data.

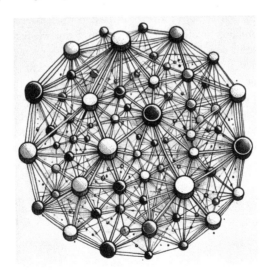

Graph Neural Networks

In contrast to traditional neural networks, which operate on fixed-sized vectors or grids, GNNs are specifically designed to handle the complex, non-Euclidean nature of graphs, where entities are connected by edges in a flexible and arbitrary manner, meaning they can better map and understand the relationships between entities that are more complex and interconnected.

At its core, a graph is a mathematical structure consisting of a set of nodes and the edges that connect them. In financial contexts, nodes could represent individuals, accounts, transactions, companies, or assets, while edges can represent relationships or interactions between them. These could be the flow of money, ownership structures, co-occurrence, or similarity between accounts. By encoding financial data as a graph, we can explicitly model and reason about the complex web of connections and influences that shape financial systems.

GNNs learn informative representations of nodes by aggregating and transforming information from their local "neighborhood" in the graph. They do this by passing messages through a framework where the nodes iteratively update their representations by exchanging and combining "messages" with their neighbors. The nodes gather information at each layer and apply transformations to the aggregated information and then update their own representations, accordingly. By stacking multiple layers, GNNs can capture increasingly abstract and contextual information, allowing them to learn powerful, hierarchical representations of the graph.

The most common GNN architecture is the Graph Convolutional Network (GCN). You'll remember from Chapter 3 that CNNs are highly effective at processing grid-like data, such as images, by applying convolutional operations. GCNs generalize the concept of convolution to graph-structured data. The convolution operation in GCNs aggregates a node's features with those of its neighbors, allowing the model to incorporate local context into each node's representation. This makes GCNs particularly effective for tasks like node classification and link prediction, enabling them to uncover patterns and insights in complex, interconnected data.

Another influential GNN architecture is the Graph Attention Network (GAT), which introduces an attention mechanism to adaptively weigh the contributions of different neighbors when updating node representations. In a GAT, each node attends to its neighbors by computing attention coefficients that indicate the importance of each neighbor's features. This allows the model to focus on the most relevant parts of the graph and to capture more nuanced and context-dependent relationships between nodes.

Attention is All You Need

The concept of attention mechanisms in neural networks gained widespread recognition with the landmark 2017 paper "Attention is All You Need" by former Google researchers. The paper introduced the transformer architecture, which allows the models to selectively focus on specific parts of the input data that are more relevant to the specific task on which the model is focused. "Attention" is achieved by computing attention scores that prioritize certain inputs over others, enabling the model to capture dependencies and relationships that might otherwise be overlooked.

Attention is applied in GATs by allowing each node to weigh the importance of its neighbors dynamically. Instead of treating all neighboring nodes equally, the attention mechanism assigns different weights to each neighbor's features based on their relevance. This results in a more refined and context-aware representation of the nodes.

Fraud Detection

Fraudulent activities often lurk beneath the surface of financial transactions. While traditional fraud detection methods focus on individual transactions or entities in isolation, GNNs harness the rich relational information embedded within the networks, and are able to exploit this web of relationships and patterns that connect individuals, accounts, and institutions.

At each layer of a GNN, nodes update their representations by aggregating information from their neighbors, allowing the model to learn increasingly abstract and informative features. This message passing and aggregation process can be customized to the specific characteristics of transaction networks, such as incorporating edge weights to reflect transaction amounts, or using attention mechanisms to focus on the most relevant parts of the network.

For example, consider a money laundering scheme where funds are transferred through a series of shell companies and offshore accounts to obscure their illicit origins. A traditional rule-based system might flag individual transactions that exceed a certain threshold or involve high-risk jurisdictions, but it may miss the overall pattern of the money flow. A GNN, on the other hand, can learn to identify the telltale signs of money laundering by analyzing the entire chain of transactions, the roles and relationships of the involved entities, and the similarities to known laundering typologies.

Further, GNNs are able to learn and adapt to the evolving tactics of fraudsters. By training on large volumes of historical transaction data – both legitimate and fraudulent – GNNs can automatically discover the subtle patterns and red flags that distinguish illicit activities from normal behavior. As new types of fraud emerge, GNNs can continually be fine-tuned and updated with the latest examples, allowing them to stay ahead of the ever-changing threat potential.

They can also adapt to evolving fraud tactics: As criminals develop new strategies, the adaptive nature of GNNs allows them to be continually fine-tuned and updated with new data and maintain their effectiveness over time. Another example would be in combating credit card fraud, where GNNs can be trained on recent transaction data to detect emerging patterns of fraudulent behavior that may not align with previous trends. Further, integrating GNNs with time-series models allows for the detection of unusual patterns over time, such as sudden spikes in transaction activity that could indicate fraud.

In addition to their adaptability, GNNs can be tailored to the specific nuances of financial networks. Edge features such as transaction amounts or timestamps can be incorporated into the model, enabling more precise detection of suspicious activities. When combined with other advanced techniques, such as temporal analysis or anomaly detection, GNNs enhance the power of these systems.

Real-world implementations of GNNs in fraud detection have already shown promising results. Financial institutions are increasingly adopting these models to monitor their networks in real-time, identifying potential fraud with greater accuracy and speed. As the field evolves, the combination of GNNs with other AI techniques and domain-specific knowledge is likely to drive further innovations in financial crime prevention.

There are, of course, challenges with deploying this still relatively new technology. Scaling of GNNs can be prohibitively expensive. As the number of nodes and edges grows across large-scale transaction networks, they become increasingly computationally expensive. While researchers are actively developing techniques to address this challenge (e.g. graph sampling, partition, and distributed training approaches), today's graph networks are limited by compute resources.

As with all Deep Learning models, the calculations within the network are opaque and difficult to understand, which hampers their interpretability and explainability. While GNNs can achieve high accuracy in identifying fraudulent patterns, understanding the reasoning behind their decisions is vague at best. Currently, techniques such as attention visualization, graph saliency maps, and rule extraction are being explored to provide human-understandable explanations of GNN predictions, but there is still much work to be done.

Using GNNs for fraud detection requires institutions to carefully consider data privacy and security issues. Transaction networks often contain sensitive personal and financial information, and the use of GNNs must comply with relevant regulations and ethical guidelines. Techniques such as federated learning, differential privacy, and secure multi-party computation are being investigated to enable privacy-preserving GNN training and inference.

As fraudsters continue to evolve their tactics and exploit the complexity of financial networks, the adoption of GNNs in fraud detection is becoming increasingly critical. By leveraging the expressive power of graph representation and the adaptive learning capabilities of neural networks, GNNs offer a promising framework to uncover hidden patterns, detect sophisticated schemes, and safeguard the integrity of financial systems. As research advances and industry adoption grows, we can expect GNNs to play a pivotal role in the fight against financial crime, complementing and enhancing traditional fraud detection approaches.

Modeling Interconnections in Financial Systems

The interconnectedness of modern financial systems presents both opportunities and challenges for financial stability and risk management. The complex web of relationships and dependencies among financial entities can amplify the transmission of shocks and increase the potential for systemic risk. Traditional approaches to modeling and analyzing these interconnections, such as simple network metrics or regression-based methods, often fail to capture the full complexity and non-linearity of financial networks. The GNN framework is an ideal framework for addressing these limitations.

By capturing the rich, multi-relational nature of financial networks, GNNs can model their financial interconnections. In an interbank lending network, for example, banks are connected by multiple types of edges, representing different forms of exposures such as loans, derivatives, or securities holdings. GNNs can easily handle these multi-relational graphs by learning distinct representations for each type of edge and aggregating them to update node embeddings. This allows them to capture the heterogeneous nature of financial relationships and to model the differential impact of different types of exposures on systemic risk.

GNNs can incorporate node- and edge-level attributes to provide a more comprehensive representation of financial entities and their relationships. Node attributes can include bank-specific characteristics such as size, leverage, or asset composition, while edge attributes can represent the maturity, seniority, or collateralization of exposures. By integrating these attributes into the message passing and aggregation process, GNNs can learn to identify the key drivers of risk and contagion in financial networks, beyond simple topological measures.

The ability of GNNs to capture complex, non-linear relationships is particularly relevant for modeling the propagation of shocks and defaults across financial networks. Traditional models rely on linear approximations or stylized assumptions about the transmission of losses (e.g. the Eisenberg-Noe algorithm for clearing payments in interbank networks). GNNs, on the other hand, can learn to approximate the true, non-linear dynamics of a contagion by iteratively updating node representations based on the state of their neighbors. This allows them to capture feedback loops and amplification mechanisms that can lead to cascading failures and systemic instability.

By learning node embeddings that encode the structural role and influence of each entity, GNNs can help identify the key players and relationships that are critical for the stability of the system. This can inform targeted interventions and regulatory actions to mitigate systemic risk, such as setting higher capital requirements for systemically important banks or imposing limits on certain types of exposures.

GNNs can also be used to simulate stress scenarios and to assess the resilience of financial networks under different shock scenarios. By perturbing node attributes or edge weights based on hypothetical stress events, such as a market downturn or a liquidity freeze, GNNs can predict the propagation of losses and the potential for contagion in the network. This can help policymakers and risk managers to identify vulnerabilities and to design more effective stress testing and crisis management frameworks.

Another important application of GNNs in financial interconnections is the modeling of cross-border and cross-sector exposures. Financial networks often span multiple countries and industries, with complex linkages and spillovers across different segments of the financial system. GNNs can be used to model these multilayer networks, capturing the interactions and dependencies between different types of entities and exposures. For example, a GNN could be used to model the interplay between the banking sector, the insurance sector, and the shadow banking system, capturing the potential for cross-sector contagion and systemic risk.

But there are challenges. There is not a lot of quality data that tracks the exposures and relationships needed to train these networks. A lot of interconnections, such as over-the-counter derivatives or off-balance sheet exposures, are not fully captured in public disclosures or regulatory reporting; and the dynamic nature of financial networks can make it difficult to maintain up-to-date and comprehensive data for modeling purposes. Researchers are currently exploring ways to improve the collection and standardization of this data, with applications of blockchain and distributed ledger technologies being particularly well-suited for this. There are also promising applications around machine learning-based data imputation techniques.

In interbank lending, GNNs can effectively model the intricate web of loans and exposures between banks, which is crucial for identifying systemic risks, such as the potential for contagion and cascading defaults. By learning bank-specific embeddings that reflect each bank's structural role and vulnerability within the network, GNNs could pinpoint systemically important banks, guiding targeted interventions to reduce systemic risk.

Similarly, in supply chain finance, GNNs can be employed to model the relationships between buyers, suppliers, and financing providers. These networks, characterized by multi-tier dependencies, can help assess the resilience of supply chains to shocks and disruptions. This analysis can inform the development of anti-fragile financing and risk management strategies.

They're also useful in modeling cross-border financial transactions, such as foreign direct investment and banking flows, by learning country-specific embeddings that capture each country's role and influence in the global financial network. This would aid in identifying key sources of risk and contagion – informing international policy coordination and crisis management frameworks.

As the financial system becomes increasingly interconnected and complex, the ability to accurately model and analyze these interconnections will be critical for maintaining financial stability and resilience.

*"The individual is defined only by his relationship to the world
and to other individuals;
he exists only by transcending himself,
and his freedom can be achieved only through the freedom of others.
He justifies his existence by a movement which,
like freedom,
springs from his heart
but which leads outside of himself."*

~ Simone de Beauvoir

Advanced Credit Scoring and Risk Assessment

Traditional credit scoring models, such as logistic regression or decision trees, primarily rely on individual borrower characteristics, such as income, employment status, and credit history, to assess creditworthiness. While these models have been the backbone of credit decisioning for decades, they have the same limitations as other rule-based and statistical models. Through GNNs, lenders can uncover deeper, non-linear patterns and incorporate a wider range of data sources and the relationships between them.

Lenders can leverage the understanding of these relationships to build more accurate risk assessments. This is key because in many cases, the creditworthiness of a borrower is not solely determined by their individual attributes, but also by the creditworthiness of their network of relationships. Take, for example, a borrower with a limited credit history. The borrower may still be a good credit risk if they have strong ties to other creditworthy individuals or businesses. Conversely, a borrower with a seemingly strong credit profile may be a higher risk if they are connected to a network of defaulted or fraudulent entities.

When applied to credit scoring and risk assessment, GNNs can capture these network effects by representing borrowers as nodes in a graph, with edges representing various types of relationships, such as familial ties, employment links, or transaction histories. By learning node embeddings that encode the structural role and influence of each borrower in the network, GNNs can identify patterns and dependencies that are predictive of credit risk, beyond what can be gleaned from individual attributes alone. This can lead to more nuanced credit decisioning, reducing the risk of defaults and improving access to credit for underserved or "thin-file" borrowers.

By integrating alternative data sources, such as utility payments, rental histories, or digital footprints, to enhance risk assessments, GNNs can provide more accurate predictions than traditional credit scoring models that typically rely on a narrow set of structured data, such as credit bureau reports or income statements, which could be limited or outdated – particularly for certain segments of the population. The broader data available could be represented as node or edge attributes in the graph, allowing for a more comprehensive and up-to-date view of a borrower's creditworthiness.

Take, for example, the use of a potential borrower's social media activity, such as their network of friends, their sentiment towards financial topics, or their engagement with financial services providers, might prove to give added insights to a credit approval process. This, of course, opens up a world of ethical questions, like, "Should borrowers' online activity be considered when considering their creditworthiness? Would use of this data unfairly target certain segments of the population?"

If the training data for a GNN is biased or discriminatory, the model could inadvertently perpetuate or even amplify these biases in its credit decisions. For example, if the data reflects historical patterns of discrimination, the GNN may unjustly assign lower credit scores to borrowers from certain communities, despite their strong credit profiles. To mitigate these risks, lenders must ensure that their training data is representative and unbiased, and that it complies with fair lending regulations. Techniques like adversarial debiasing, fairness constraints, and rigorous model testing can help identify and reduce potential biases in GNN-based credit scoring models. Additionally, as GNNs enable the integration of more diverse data sources and complex network effects in credit decisioning, regulators may need to update their frameworks for data privacy, model governance, and consumer protection to ensure these models remain fair, transparent, and accountable. Despite these challenges, GNNs hold substantial potential for making credit assessments more accurate, nuanced, and inclusive, particularly for underserved populations, while also helping lenders manage and mitigate credit risk more effectively.

What would be the tradeoff if the patterns and signals in this data are predictive of credit risk?

The model might be able to provide a more accurate and timely assessment of a borrower's creditworthiness, particularly for those with limited traditional credit data, but at what cost?

Similarly, what if there were patterns in a borrower's transaction history such as their spending patterns, merchant relationships, or payment behavior, to identify early warning signs of financial distress or default? Should these be factored into a borrower's risk assessment, even if they have never missed a payment?

GNNs could be used to build full pictures of borrowers' financial lives. They could model and predict not just default risk, but other items like prepayment risk, loan utilization, or customer lifetime value. By learning multi-dimensional embeddings that capture various facets of borrower behavior and network effects, GNNs could provide a more holistic and nuanced view of credit risk, enabling lenders to optimize pricing, product offerings, and customer engagement strategies.

Chapter Twelve

AI IN TRADING AND INVESTMENT MANAGEMENT

With the growing complexity and scale of financial data, traditional approaches to trading and investment are increasingly being supplemented by AI-driven methods. These technologies offer new ways to analyze data, identify trends, and execute strategies that were previously out of reach for even the most sophisticated human analysts.

By processing and learning from large datasets, AI systems can provide insights that help investors make more informed decisions. This shift is particularly important in a sector where the stakes are high and the ability to anticipate and react to market movement is key. As AI continues to evolve, its role in trading and investment management is inevitably going to expand and continue to provide new tools and perspectives for those navigating the financial markets.

Algorithmic Trading

Algorithmic trading automates the process of buying and selling financial assets using computer algorithms, which can execute trades at speeds and with precision that go well beyond the possibility of human capabilities. Investors have been using various flavors of algorithmic trading since the 1970s when the NYSE's Designated Order Turnaround (DOT) system automated order routing and execution, which vastly improved trading efficiency by automating the process and handling larger volumes of trades.

Algorithmic trading really started to gain traction in the 1990s with the rise of electronic trading platforms, which allowed for more complex and faster execution of trades across global markets. These platforms quickly led to the development of sophisticated high-frequency trading (HFT) strategies that leverage algorithms to execute thousands of trades per second.

Today, algorithmic trading dominates the financial markets, with the significant majority of trades executed by computers. This drives efficiency and innovation in how financial assets are bought and sold worldwide, but also introduces risks, such as flash crashes, where rapid, automated trading can lead to sudden and extreme market volatility. It has become a fundamental approach to trading as the complexity and volume of data have grown.

Algorithmic trading starts with a trading strategy that is translated into a set of rules, which automatically trigger trades based on real-time market data. These algorithms operate by following predefined instructions that can be based on a variety of market indicators, such as price movements, trading volumes, and broader market trends. One approach would be to program an algorithm to buy a stock when its price falls below a certain threshold, and/or sell when the price reaches a predetermined level. The speed of the algorithms identifying a trigger and executing at lightning speeds makes it possible to identify and exploit trading opportunities that may be too subtle or short-lived for human traders to notice or act on effectively.

This is especially true in HFT strategies, where algorithms execute a large number of trades in fractions of a second to capitalize on tiny price discrepancies across different markets or securities. The sheer speed and volume of these trades can lead to significant cumulative profits, even if the profit margin on each individual trade is small. HFT firms invest heavily in technology to minimize latency, because even microseconds can make a difference in these highly competitive environments. Common strategies to reduce latency and increase speed include using co-location (where firms place their trading servers physically close to exchange servers), optimized algorithms, and high-performance hardware. They also invest in low-latency networking and direct market access, enabling trades to be executed in microseconds as the speed at which they're able to transact gives them a competitive edge.

Beyond speed, algorithmic trading also injects a high level of precision and discipline to the trading process. By adhering strictly to the rules encoded in the algorithm, these systems eliminate the emotional and psychological biases that can cloud human judgment. The algorithms are not powered by fear or greed the way human traders might be. While human emotional reactions can lead to impulsive decisions in volatile markets, algorithms are able to coldly execute trades based solely on the data and the logic built into them – ensuring a consistent application of the trading strategy.

By supercharging algorithmic trading with AI, firms can deploy algorithms that are adaptive and can learn over time. Machine learning models are particularly powerful in this context. After being trained on historical market data to recognize patterns, trends, and anomalies, they can continue to learn and refine strategies as market conditions change, giving them an advantage when conditions can shift rapidly and unpredictably.

The ability for a machine learning algorithm to identify conditions that typically precede a market correction or rally based on the patterns it has identified in its training would be akin to a superpower that allowed it to see into the future. This pattern recognition could come from within or outside of market data, potentially including news articles, social media feeds, or even satellite imagery. This ability to synthesize and analyze diverse data sets could enable AI-driven algorithms to make more informed and nuanced trading decisions.

Portfolio Optimization

Portfolio optimization is the process of selecting the best mix of assets to achieve a desired balance of risk and return. Traditionally, this has been accomplished using models such as the Markowitz Modern Portfolio Theory (MPT). But with the introduction of artificial intelligence, there are now new tools that allow more dynamic and sophisticated approaches to asset allocation.

Markowitz Modern Portfolio Theory (MPT)

MPT is a foundational framework in finance that guides the construction of investment portfolios to maximize expected return for a given level of risk, or to minimize risk for a given level of return. Developed by Harry Markowitz in the 1950s, MPT emphasizes the importance of diversification — holding a mix of different assets — to reduce overall portfolio risk. This is based on the idea that the price movements of various assets are not perfectly correlated, allowing for a smoother overall portfolio performance. MPT introduces key concepts such as the efficient frontier, which represents the set of optimal portfolios offering the best possible risk-return trade-off.

In practice, MPT helps investors design portfolios that align with their risk tolerance and return goals by optimizing the mix of assets. The theory has significantly influenced how portfolio managers and investors approach diversification and risk management, and it remains a central principle in modern finance despite some criticisms and limitations. MPT's insights have also paved the way for the development of further financial models, such as the Capital Asset Pricing Model (CAPM), which built on its foundational concepts.

AI Techniques in Portfolio Optimization

AI-powered portfolio optimization uses ML algorithms that process historical financial data, market trends, and a wide range of economic indicators to generate predictive models that inform asset allocation decisions.

While traditional portfolio optimization mostly relies on periodic rebalancing to maintain the desired risk-return profile, AI-powered systems can dynamically adjust asset allocations based on evolving market conditions.

If an AI algorithm detects a shift in market volatility or a change in correlation between assets, it can proactively rebalance the portfolio to maintain the optimal risk level, which is significantly more timely and efficient than traditional rebalancing strategies, which could lag behind and expose the portfolio to unnecessary risks.

Incorporating Alternative Data Sources

AI also enables the integration of alternative data sources into the portfolio optimization process. Beyond traditional financial metrics, AI algorithms can analyze data from non-conventional sources, geopolitical events, and even weather patterns. By incorporating this diverse data, AI can provide a more comprehensive understanding of the factors influencing asset performance, leading to more informed and nuanced asset allocation decisions.

For instance, an AI model might detect a negative sentiment shift on social media regarding a specific sector, prompting a reduction in exposure to that sector before the market reflects the sentiment. Similarly, AI could identify early signals of economic shifts from news articles or satellite imagery, allowing for preemptive adjustments to the portfolio.

Risk Management and Stress Testing

AI-driven stress testing allows portfolio managers to simulate various market scenarios, analyzing how different asset allocations might perform under adverse conditions. The ML models identify patterns in the data and make forecasts that help them understand potential risks and adjust their strategies accordingly – across the entire market or within various sectors.

By isolating the technology sector, for example, modelers simulate a sudden market downturn or a shift in consumer preferences away from tech products. The models would then assess how these scenarios could impact the overall portfolio and suggest potential reallocations to reduce exposure to various industries, segments, or companies.

But AI's role in risk management goes beyond just stress testing. It can continuously monitor the portfolio, detecting early warning signs of potential issues. By analyzing real-time market data, news sentiment, and even social media chatter, AI models can alert portfolio managers to emerging risks that traditional methods might overlook.

This proactive approach to risk management empowers them to make data-driven decisions and adapt their strategies in real-time. Whether it's adjusting holdings in response to geopolitical events or rebalancing the portfolio based on shifting market correlations, AI enables portfolio managers to navigate the complexities of modern markets with greater confidence and resilience.

Of course, human managers still need to exercise judgment and expertise. But by integrating AI into their risk management process, they can make more informed decisions, anticipate potential challenges, and ultimately build a portfolio that can better withstand market shocks.

Personalized Portfolio Optimization

Personalized portfolio optimization leverages AI to tailor investment strategies to individual needs, aligning personal investment goals, which may evolve over time, with real-time market data. Traditional investment models often take a one-size-fits-all approach, but AI can analyze a wide range of personal data, including age, income, risk tolerance, and financial goals, to create a strategy uniquely suited to each investor.

As an investor's life and financial situation evolve, AI-driven systems can automatically adjust the portfolio to reflect changes, whether due to a job promotion, shifts in market conditions, or changing financial objectives. This ongoing, data-driven personalization was once only available to high-net-worth individuals with access to premium financial advisors, but today, AI democratizes sophisticated portfolio management, making it accessible to a broader range of investors while still complementing the guidance of financial professionals. The result is a portfolio that grows and adapts with the investor, offering a customized financial plan that meets both short-term needs and long-term goals.

Asset Pricing Models

Asset pricing in finance refers to determining the value of financial assets like stocks, bonds, and real estate using various models and theories to estimate the present value of expected future cash flows generated by these assets (while taking into account factors like risk, time, and market conditions).

Traditional asset pricing models, such as the Capital Asset Pricing Model (CAPM) and the Arbitrage Pricing Theory (APT), have long been used to determine the fair value of assets by analyzing the relationship between expected returns and risk factors. While these models have provided a solid foundation for financial analysis, they often rely on simplifying assumptions and linear relationships that may not fully capture the complexities of real-world markets.

By leveraging advanced data analysis and predictive modeling, AI can handle much more data and provide far deeper insights than standard models, enhancing the accuracy and robustness of asset pricing models by allowing for the analysis of non-linear relationships, incorporating alternative data sources, and adapting to changing market conditions in real-time. These have applications across asset pricing, risk assessment, and valuation.

Enhancing Predictive Accuracy with Machine Learning

The ability to accurately predict asset prices is the holy grail of investing. Traditional models, like CAPM, have long been the foundation of asset pricing, but in the era of big data and complex global markets, these models are showing their limitations.

CAPM is out. "No cap."

The Capital Asset Pricing Model is a foundational theory in finance that describes the relationship between the expected return of an asset and its risk, as measured by the asset's sensitivity to market movements. CAPM is used to estimate the expected return on an investment, taking into account both the risk-free rate of return and the risk premium associated with the asset's market risk.

The CAPM Formula

The CAPM formula is expressed as:

$$\text{Expected Return}(E[R]) = Rf + \beta \times (R_m - R_f)$$

Where:

- R_f is the risk-free rate, representing the return on a risk-free asset, typically government bonds.
- β is the beta coefficient, which measures the asset's volatility relative to the overall market. A beta greater than 1 indicates that the asset is more volatile than the market, while a beta less than 1 means it is less volatile.
- R_m is the expected market return, representing the return of the market portfolio.
- $R_m - R_f$ is the market risk premium, representing the additional return expected from holding a risky market portfolio instead of risk-free assets.

How CAPM Works

CAPM helps investors determine whether an asset is fairly valued by comparing its expected return to the required return based on its risk. If an asset's expected return is higher than the required return given its beta, it may be considered undervalued and attractive for investment. Conversely, if the expected return is lower, the asset may be overvalued.

Unlike traditional models that rely on a fixed set of assumptions and linear relationships, machine learning algorithms can incorporate millions of data points, from historical price movements and trading volumes to macroeconomic indicators and even unstructured data like news articles and social media posts to determine appropriate pricing. By identifying patterns in this sea of information, machine learning models can make predictions about future price movements with a level of accuracy that traditional methods struggle to match.

This speed and adaptability of ML models give investment managers the superpower to capture fleeting opportunities. In the time it might take a human analyst to read through a company's quarterly report, a well-trained algorithm could have already identified an undervalued stock and executed a trade.

Incorporating Alternative Data Sources

Picture a traditional investor, poring over financial statements and market trends, trying to piece together a complete picture of a company's health and prospects. It's a time-honored approach, but in today's data-rich world, it's only part of the puzzle.

Now, imagine a different scene: a satellite captures images of a retailer's parking lots, revealing a surge in traffic. A machine learning algorithm scours online content, detecting a shift in sentiment about a new product launch. A natural language processing tool analyzes the tone of a CEO's speech, picking up on subtle cues that might signal future strategic shifts.

This is the world of alternative data, where investors seek insights from sources far beyond the traditional financial metrics. It's a world where the most valuable information might come not from a balance sheet, but from a satellite image, an X (Twitter) feed, or even a weather report.

The rise of alternative data is a direct result of the explosion of digital information in recent years. We've discussed its ubiquity throughout this book, and we're seeing now how valuable this data is to our AI-powered future. We're creating data at an unprecedented rate, from our online shopping habits and social media activity to the sensors in our smart devices and the cameras on our streets. For investors, this represents a treasure trove of potential insights.

But making sense of this data is no easy feat. It's often unstructured, coming in the form of images, text, or video rather than neat rows and columns. It can be noisy, with valuable signals buried among the chatter. And it's constantly changing, requiring tools that can adapt and learn in real-time.

Machine learning algorithms can process the flood of unstructured data, identifying patterns and extracting insights that would be invisible to the human eye. Natural language processing can analyze sentiment and emotion in text, picking up on nuances that traditional keyword searches might miss. And computer vision can turn images and videos into quantifiable data points, allowing investors to track everything from foot traffic to product placement.

A hedge fund, for example, might use satellite imagery to track the progress of a mining company's new project. A venture capital firm could monitor social media buzz to gauge the early adoption of a startup's product. A real estate investor might analyze crime data and transit patterns to identify up-and-coming neighborhoods.

For investors, this means a shift in mindset. It means looking beyond the traditional sources of information and being open to new, sometimes unconventional, data points. It means investing in the tools and talent to make sense of unstructured data. And it means being ready to adapt and iterate as new data sources and insights emerge.

Modeling Non-Linear Relationships

One of the limitations of traditional asset pricing models is their reliance on linear relationships between variables. For example, CAPM assumes a linear relationship between an asset's expected return and its beta (a measure of market risk). However, financial markets are inherently complex, and relationships between variables are often non-linear.

AI, particularly deep learning, excels at modeling these non-linear relationships. Deep learning models can capture complex interactions between variables, allowing for more accurate pricing predictions in situations where traditional linear models might fail. This capability is especially valuable in volatile or uncertain markets, where the relationships between risk factors and asset prices may change rapidly.

Stress Testing and Scenario Analysis

AI can also enhance asset pricing through more sophisticated stress testing and scenario analysis. Traditional stress testing methods often involve applying predefined shocks to a model and observing the impact on asset prices. AI models, however, can simulate a wide range of scenarios based on historical data, providing a more detailed understanding of how asset prices might behave under different conditions.

For example, an AI model could simulate the impact of various macroeconomic scenarios, such as a recession or a sudden interest rate hike, on asset prices. This analysis can help investors and risk managers better understand the potential risks and opportunities in their portfolios, leading to more informed decision-making.

By leveraging machine learning, alternative data sources, and the ability to model non-linear relationships, AI-driven asset pricing models offer a more accurate and dynamic approach to valuing assets. As financial markets continue to evolve, the use of AI in asset pricing is likely to become increasingly important, providing investors with more precise tools for navigating the complexities of modern markets.

Risk Management in Investment

Risk management is focused on identifying, assessing, and mitigating various risks that could negatively impact the performance of a portfolio. Traditional risk management approaches have relied on statistical models, historical data, and expert judgment to predict and mitigate risks. But the integration of artificial intelligence into risk management processes is revolutionizing how financial institutions handle market, credit, and liquidity risks, providing more sophisticated and adaptive tools to safeguard investments.

Market Risk Management

The stock market is often likened to a roller coaster, with its ups, downs, twists, and turns. For investors, navigating this volatility is the essence of market risk management. Traditionally, this has involved a mix of diversification, hedging, and a keen eye on market indicators. But in the age of artificial intelligence, the game is changing.

AI is transforming market risk management on two fronts: prediction and stress testing.

Let's start with prediction. Imagine you're a portfolio manager, responsible for millions of dollars in assets. Your job is to anticipate market movements and position your portfolio accordingly. In the past, you might have relied on a combination of economic indicators, financial models, and your own market intuition. But now, you have a new tool in your arsenal: machine learning.

Machine learning algorithms are like super-powered pattern detectors. They can comb through vast amounts of market data - historical prices, trading volumes, economic reports, and other online content - and identify patterns that the human eye (or traditional statistical models) might miss. These patterns can be subtle, like the correlation between the price of a certain commodity and the stock price of a seemingly unrelated company. Or they can be complex, like the non-linear relationship between interest rates and currency fluctuations.

By continuously learning from new data, these AI models can adapt to changing market conditions in real-time. So if there's a sudden shift in market sentiment or an unexpected geopolitical event, the AI can quickly adjust its predictions. This agility is crucial in a market where a minute can make the difference between profit and loss.

But AI isn't just about predicting the future. It's also about preparing for the worst. This is where stress testing comes in. Stress testing is like a flight simulator for your portfolio. It allows you to see how your investments would perform under various adverse scenarios - a sudden market crash, a spike in inflation, a geopolitical crisis.

Traditionally, stress testing has been based on historical scenarios or hypothetical shocks. But with AI, stress testing can be much more sophisticated. An AI-powered stress testing platform can generate thousands of potential scenarios, taking into account a far wider range of variables and correlations. It can identify hidden vulnerabilities in your portfolio that traditional stress tests might miss.

For example, let's say you're heavily invested in tech stocks. A traditional stress test might look at how your portfolio would perform in a dot-com-style crash. But an AI stress test could reveal that your portfolio is also vulnerable to a slowdown in the semiconductor industry, due to the complex supply chain relationships between tech companies.

Armed with this insight, you could adjust your positions, perhaps diversifying into less correlated sectors or implementing hedging strategies. This proactive approach to risk management is the essence of what AI enables.

Of course, AI is not a crystal ball. It can't predict the future with 100% certainty, and its insights are only as good as the data it's trained on. There's also the risk of over-reliance on AI, of letting the algorithms make decisions without human oversight. But when used wisely, AI can be a powerful complement to human judgment. It can help portfolio managers see around corners, anticipate risks, and make more informed decisions. In a market that's only getting faster and more complex, that's an invaluable edge.

As we look to the future of market risk management, AI will require a new kind of skillset from portfolio managers. They'll need to be as comfortable working with algorithms as they are reading financial statements. They'll need to know how to ask the right questions of the AI, and how to interpret its answers. Successful portfolio managers of the future will be those who can harness the power of AI while still bringing their own human insights to the table.

Credit Risk Management

Traditional credit risk models typically rely on historical financial data, credit scores, and qualitative assessments to determine a borrower's creditworthiness. While effective, these models can sometimes fail to capture the full scope of risk, particularly in complex or rapidly changing environments.

AI enhances credit risk management by incorporating a broader range of data sources and employing advanced analytics to provide a more comprehensive assessment of credit risk. Machine learning models can analyze both structured data (such as income, debt levels, and repayment history) and unstructured data (such as social media activity, employment records, and economic trends) to evaluate a borrower's ability and willingness to repay debt.

These AI models can also detect early warning signs of potential defaults by identifying subtle changes in behavior or market conditions that may not be apparent through traditional analysis. For instance, an AI system might flag a borrower whose financial health appears to be deteriorating based on a combination of declining credit card payments, increased borrowing, and negative sentiment in their social media activity. By identifying these risks early, lenders can take proactive steps to mitigate potential losses, such as adjusting loan terms or increasing collateral requirements.

It is important to note, however, there is a risk in attempting to correlate a borrower's sentiment, as expressed through social media or other unstructured data, with their ability to repay debt. Such analyses can lead to false assumptions and potentially discriminatory outcomes, as sentiment data may not accurately reflect an individual's financial stability or intent to meet their obligations. This underscores the importance of using AI tools responsibly and ensuring that decisions are based on a comprehensive and fair assessment of all relevant factors.

Liquidity Risk Management

The risk that an investor won't be able to buy or sell assets quickly enough to prevent a loss, is particularly challenging in volatile or thinly traded markets. AI is helping to manage liquidity risk by improving the forecasting of liquidity conditions and optimizing trading strategies to ensure that assets can be liquidated or acquired efficiently.

AI models can analyze order books, trading volumes, and other market indicators to assess the liquidity of different assets under various market conditions. By predicting how liquidity might change in response to market events or shifts in investor sentiment, these models help portfolio managers make more informed decisions about when and how to execute trades.

In addition to forecasting liquidity, AI can optimize trading strategies to minimize market impact and transaction costs. For example, AI algorithms can determine the best way to break up large orders into smaller trades to avoid moving the market, a common issue in less liquid markets. These strategies ensure that assets can be traded at favorable prices without causing significant price disruptions.

Integrated Risk Management

There are myriad components to risk in investing. There's market risk: the danger that your investments will lose value due to market fluctuations. There's credit risk: the possibility that a borrower will default on their obligations. And there's liquidity risk: the risk that you won't be able to buy or sell assets quickly enough to avoid losses.

For decades, these risks have been managed separately, with different teams and different tools. The market risk team would focus on diversification and hedging, while the credit risk team would analyze borrower financials and the liquidity risk team would monitor market conditions. But in the interconnected world of modern finance, this siloed approach is no longer sufficient.

The integration of AI into risk management introduces the concept of integrated risk management. Integrated risk management is about looking at risk holistically, understanding how different types of risk interact and impact each other. It's about breaking down the silos and managing risk as a unified whole. AI is uniquely suited to this task because of its ability to process and analyze a sea of diverse data. An AI-powered risk management system can ingest data from multiple sources - market prices, economic indicators, company financials, news sentiment, even weather patterns - and identify correlations and patterns that would be impossible for humans to spot.

For example, the system might detect that a company's stock price is highly correlated with the price of a certain commodity. At the same time, it might note that the company has significant outstanding debts and that its bonds are thinly traded. By analyzing these factors together, the AI could conclude that the company poses a high combined market, credit, and liquidity risk.

But the AI doesn't just identify risks – it also suggests solutions. In the above scenario, the system might recommend reducing exposure to the company and its sector, while increasing holdings in more stable, uncorrelated assets. It might also suggest strategies to hedge against the identified risks, such as using derivatives to offset potential losses.

This ability to provide comprehensive, actionable insights is the real power of AI in integrated risk management. It's not just about crunching numbers, but about providing a clear path forward in a complex risk landscape.

Imagine you're a risk manager overseeing a large, diverse portfolio. Each morning, instead of wading through separate reports from the market, credit, and liquidity risk teams, you receive a single, integrated risk assessment from your AI system. This assessment highlights the key risks across your portfolio, shows how they interconnect, and suggests mitigating actions.

Armed with this information, you can make swift, informed decisions to safeguard your investments. You can anticipate potential issues before they become crises and adjust your strategies in real-time as market conditions change.

This is the promise of AI in integrated risk management - not to replace human judgment, but to enhance it. By providing a comprehensive, constantly updated view of risk, AI empowers risk managers to make better decisions, faster.

Of course, implementing AI in risk management is not without its challenges. There are technical hurdles, such as ensuring data quality and integrating legacy systems. There are also cultural and organizational challenges, such as getting buy-in from different risk teams and ensuring that AI insights are actually acted upon.

But as the financial world becomes increasingly complex and interconnected, the need for integrated risk management will only grow. Those firms that can harness the power of AI to manage risk holistically will be best positioned to weather the storms and seize the opportunities of this new era.

Chapter Thirteen

AI IN RISK MANAGEMENT AND FRAUD DETECTION

We've discussed throughout this text how conventional risk management and fraud detection techniques – though still important – can fall short in handling the complexities of the modern financial landscape. There is a tendency to cling to these "time-tested" models because they are what we've historically used, they are clear and explainable, and we understand their strengths and limitations. But to ignore the application of new AI-powered technologies would be akin to refusing to use modern accounting software or spreadsheets to keep our companies' books or create forecasts.

We've seen the strength of properly applied ML and pattern recognition techniques, and understand how they can identify risks or fraud much more accurately and efficiently than humans.

From evaluating credit risk and assessing market volatility to managing operational risks, AI models are able to provide a more nuanced and dynamic understanding of the risks that financial institutions face. These models can continuously learn and adapt, ensuring that risk assessments are as up-to-date as possible in an ever-changing market.

With the ability to provide continuous, real-time assessments and alerts, AI enables institutions to respond to potential threats swiftly and effectively, minimizing damage and ensuring regulatory compliance. As financial institutions increasingly rely on AI to manage risks and prevent fraud, the importance of these technologies will only grow, making them indispensable tools in the modern financial world.

Fraud Detection

AI/ML has been used for years in the ongoing battle against financial fraud, and they are improving every day. Unfortunately, so are the perpetrators of fraud. The battle between the white hats and the bad actors is an ongoing game of cat and mouse, and is not one that will be won by traditional fraud detection techniques.

> *"Corruption, embezzlement, fraud,*
> *these are all characteristics which exist everywhere.*
> *It is regrettably the way human nature functions,*
> *whether we like it or not.*
> *What successful economies do is keep it to a minimum.*
> *No one has ever eliminated any of that stuff."*
>
> **~ Alan Greenspan**

The effectiveness of AI in fraud detection is largely due to its advanced pattern recognition capabilities. With millions of transactions occurring daily, AI meticulously analyzes each one, comparing it against a comprehensive database of known fraudulent behaviors. This process allows AI to identify irregularities that might otherwise go unnoticed, effectively flagging potential fraud for further investigation. By constantly refining its understanding of what constitutes suspicious activity, AI significantly enhances the ability of financial institutions to detect and prevent fraud.

Further, AI's predictive capabilities offer a proactive approach to fraud prevention. By analyzing historical data and learning from past instances of fraud, AI models can anticipate where and when fraud is most likely to occur, allowing financial institutions to implement preventive measures before any fraudulent activity takes place. For example, if a specific type of fraud begins to emerge within a certain market or demographic, AI can alert institutions to enhance scrutiny and tighten controls in those areas.

AI's ability to operate in real-time significantly enhances the effectiveness of fraud detection efforts. Traditional methods often identify fraud only after it has occurred, leading to delays in response and potentially greater financial losses. In contrast, AI can analyze transactions as they happen, providing immediate alerts and enabling swift action — from blocking a transaction or freezing an account to initiating further investigation. This real-time analysis dramatically reduces the window of opportunity for fraudsters, making it more difficult for fraudulent activities to succeed. And AI's capacity to integrate and analyze diverse data sources enhances its ability to distinguish between legitimate and fraudulent transactions. By incorporating information from financial records, emails, and other digital footprints, AI can develop a more comprehensive understanding of user behavior and detect fraud even when it is carefully concealed.

As the methods of fraud evolve, so too must the tools used to combat them. AI's role in fraud detection is becoming increasingly crucial, not only in identifying and preventing fraud but also in staying ahead of fraudsters as they develop new tactics. Through the application of machine learning, pattern recognition, and real-time data analysis, AI equips financial institutions with the tools necessary to protect themselves — and their customers — against the ever-present and ever-changing threat of financial fraud.

Financial Risk Assessment

We explored the foundational role of AI in financial risk management at length in Chapter 12, focusing on its applications in evaluating and mitigating credit, market, and operational risks. Here, we expand on that discussion by introducing additional insights into how AI is pushing the boundaries of risk assessment through innovative approaches and the incorporation of alternative data sources.

Leveraging Alternative Data Sources

AI models are increasingly going beyond traditional financial metrics to include alternative data sources, offering a more nuanced and comprehensive approach to risk assessment. For example, natural language processing can be applied to analyze textual data from earnings calls, regulatory filings, and press releases. This enables AI to assess the sentiment and tone of corporate communications, potentially revealing risks that aren't apparent through numbers alone. Similarly, sentiment analysis from social media platforms provides real-time indicators of market mood, allowing financial institutions to gauge public reaction to events and adjust their risk models accordingly.

These AI-driven analyses can identify early signs of trouble, such as a disconnect between the optimistic tone of a company's earnings report and the underlying data, or a sudden shift in social media sentiment that could precede market volatility. By incorporating these non-traditional data sources, AI offers a richer, more dynamic understanding of risk.

Real-Time, AI-Driven Risk Simulations

Another significant advancement is the use of AI for real-time, scenario-based risk simulations. Unlike traditional stress testing, which is often static and conducted periodically, AI enables continuous, dynamic simulations that can adjust in response to new information. For example, AI can simulate the impact of emerging geopolitical risks or sudden market shocks as they happen, offering real-time insights into potential exposures. This approach allows financial institutions to react swiftly, adjusting their risk strategies on the fly and minimizing potential losses.

Explainable AI in Risk Management

As AI becomes more integrated into risk management, the need for transparency and explainability — often referred to as Explainable AI or XAI — has become increasingly important. Financial institutions and regulators require models that are not only accurate but also interpretable. Techniques such as LIME (Local Interpretable Model-Agnostic Explanations) and SHAP (SHapley Additive exPlanations) are being used to make AI-driven decisions more transparent, allowing stakeholders to understand the reasoning behind risk assessments. This not only aids in regulatory compliance but also builds trust in AI systems within the financial industry.

Decentralized AI and Blockchain

The combination of AI with decentralized technologies like blockchain is opening new frontiers in risk management, particularly in decentralized finance (DeFi). Blockchain's immutable ledger, combined with AI's analytical power, can create decentralized risk assessment models that are transparent and resistant to manipulation. In DeFi ecosystems, where traditional risk models may fall short, AI can analyze transaction data on the blockchain to assess the health and stability of protocols in real-time, offering a new level of security and risk management for investors.

While AI's role in financial risk assessment is well-established, these emerging approaches demonstrate its evolving potential. By integrating alternative data sources, enabling real-time simulations, enhancing model transparency, and exploring decentralized solutions, AI is not only improving the accuracy of risk assessments but also providing deeper, more actionable insights. As the financial landscape becomes increasingly complex, these innovations will be critical in helping institutions navigate and mitigate risk more effectively.

Real-Time Monitoring

The ability to monitor financial markets and internal operations in real-time is key to financial institutions. Artificial intelligence (AI) makes this possible by being able to quickly provide updated risk assessments and alerts based on live data, allowing institutions to respond swiftly to potential threats. Through continuous data analysis and advanced algorithms, AI enhances the capacity of financial institutions to detect and mitigate risks before they escalate into significant problems.

Real-Time Data Analysis

AI-driven monitoring systems are built on the ability to process and analyze data as it is generated. These systems continuously scan market data, transaction records, and other online content to identify potential risks. For example, AI algorithms can monitor trading patterns across various markets, detecting anomalies that might indicate market manipulation, a sudden shift in investor sentiment, or the early stages of a market crash. By processing this data in real-time, AI systems can provide immediate alerts, giving financial institutions a critical time advantage to address emerging risks.

Dynamic Risk Assessment

One of the key benefits of AI in real-time monitoring is its ability to perform dynamic risk assessments. Traditional risk management often relies on periodic evaluations, which can miss rapid changes in market conditions or operational environments. AI, however, continuously updates its risk models as new data becomes available, providing a constantly evolving assessment of an institution's risk exposure. This dynamic approach enables institutions to respond to threats more effectively, whether it's adjusting asset allocations in response to market volatility or tightening security protocols in the face of a potential cyberattack.

Automated Alerts and Decision Support

AI systems not only detect risks, but also prioritize them – generating automated alerts that are tailored to the institution's specific risk thresholds and policies. For instance, if a sudden drop in a key market indicator is detected, the AI system might trigger an alert that prompts a portfolio manager to reassess their positions or initiate a pre-planned contingency strategy. Additionally, AI can provide decision support by offering recommendations based on historical data and predictive models, helping managers make informed decisions quickly in high-pressure situations.

Enhancing Operational Efficiency

Beyond market risk, AI-driven real-time monitoring also improves operational efficiency by detecting internal risks, such as system failures, compliance breaches, or fraudulent activities. For example, AI can monitor transaction logs and system performance metrics in real-time, identifying unusual patterns that may indicate a security breach or operational malfunction. By catching these issues early, institutions can minimize downtime, reduce the impact of security incidents, and maintain compliance with regulatory requirements.

Integration with Other Risk Management Tools

AI-powered real-time monitoring systems are often integrated with other risk management tools, creating a comprehensive risk management framework. These systems can feed real-time data into broader risk assessment models, enhancing the accuracy and relevance of the institution's overall risk management strategy. This integration ensures that real-time insights are not siloed but are instead used to inform and adjust longer-term risk strategies.

As financial institutions increasingly rely on AI to manage risks and detect fraud, the financial security terrain is being fundamentally reshaped. However, the power of AI is not just in its ability to process huge datasets or to provide real-time alerts — it's in the shift towards a more proactive and resilient approach to risk management. The true value of AI lies in its potential to anticipate and mitigate risks before they escalate, guiding financial institutions to not only react to threats but to outpace them. In embracing these advanced technologies, institutions are not just safeguarding their assets but are also redefining the very nature of security and trust in the financial world.

Chapter Fourteen

AI IN CUSTOMER SERVICE AND PERSONALIZATION

Amazon, Netflix, and Spotify – and the artificial intelligence technologies that power them – have reshaped the way consumers expect and anticipate product delivery. Financial institutions have followed these entertainment platforms by offering highly personalized experiences from tailored financial advice to predictive tools that understand customer behavior better than ever before.

These financial tools, which include chatbots, robo-advisors, and predictive algorithms, enable instant, round-the-clock customer service, personalized investment strategies, and proactive financial management. AI applications fundamentally change how customers interact with their financial providers, making these interactions more intuitive and relevant.

But as the financial sector dives deeper into AI, data privacy, algorithmic bias, and transparency challenges become more substantial. The successful implementation of AI in financial services requires not only technical innovation but also careful ethical considerations and robust regulatory oversight.

In this chapter, we will explore how AI is being used in the financial services industry to enhance customer service and personalization. Through real-world examples and expert insights, we'll examine the opportunities and challenges that come with integrating AI into the industry, offering a clear perspective on what lies ahead.

AI-Powered Chatbots and Virtual Assistants

In the not-so-distant past, interacting with your bank meant visiting a physical branch, waiting in line, and speaking with a human teller or customer service representative. Today, a new breed of AI-powered assistants fundamentally changes this paradigm. Enter the age of chatbots and virtual assistants – digital helpers that are always on, always ready, and increasingly adept at handling a wide range of customer service tasks.

Chatbots and virtual assistants at their core are computer programs designed to simulate human conversation. They use NLP and other ML algorithms to understand customer queries, provide relevant responses, and even carry out tasks on the customer's behalf. The most advanced of these systems can engage in remarkably human-like exchanges, thanks to their ability to comprehend context, infer intent, and even grasp emotional nuance.

These tools serve as the first line of customer support, handling routine inquiries, providing account information, and guiding customers through basic transactions. Chatbots and virtual assistants are being deployed across a variety of channels, from banks' websites and mobile apps to popular messaging platforms like Facebook Messenger and WhatsApp. While customers receive the convenience of 24/7 assistance, human customer service representatives gain bandwidth to focus on more complex, high-value interactions.

One of the limiting factors of human agents is they can only serve one customer at a time. By contrast, AI-powered chatbots can engage with thousands of users concurrently, providing instant, personalized responses to each. This scalability is particularly valuable in times of peak demand, such as during a service outage or a major product launch, when call centers are often overwhelmed.

But chatbots and virtual assistants are not just about efficiency. They are also becoming increasingly sophisticated in their ability to provide personalized, context-aware support. These AI systems can leverage the volumes of available customer data compiled by financial services companies to tailor their responses and recommendations to each individual user's needs and circumstances. They can anticipate questions, proactively offer guidance, and even detect and respond to emotional cues. This engagement provides a level of personalization that was once the exclusive domain of human interaction.

Imagine a chatbot that not only helps a customer check their account balance, but also notices that they've recently had a large, unexpected, nonrecurring expense. The chatbot could proactively offer information about the bank's overdraft protection services or suggest a short-term loan to help the customer bridge the gap until their next paycheck. This kind of proactive, personalized support has the potential to significantly enhance customer satisfaction and, as a byproduct, loyalty.

Of course, multiple risks and considerations accompany the rise of AI-powered chatbots and virtual assistants. There are important questions around data privacy and security, as these systems often handle sensitive financial information. There are also concerns about the potential for AI to perpetuate or even amplify human biases, leading to unfair treatment of certain customer demographics. And there is the ongoing need to ensure customers can easily escalate to a human agent when needed, and that the human touch is not lost in the drive towards automation.

Despite these challenges, the trend towards AI-powered chatbots and virtual assistants in financial customer service is undeniable. As these technologies continue to mature and prove their value, they are likely to become an increasingly integral part of how financial institutions interact with their customers.

For customers, this trend means a future where financial support is always just a conversation away, personalized to their unique needs, and delivered on their terms. For financial institutions, the trend represents an opportunity to provide superior service at scale, while freeing up human resources to focus on high-value, strategic interactions.

Robo-Advisors

For decades, human financial advisors had an exclusive monopoly on personalized investment advice and portfolio management. These professionals would analyze a client's financial situation, risk tolerance, and investment goals, and then take these parameters to construct and manage a portfolio on their behalf. While effective, this model has its limitations. Advisors typically charge a percentage of assets under management, which drives up the cost of direct portfolio management. Additionally, advisors can differ based on individual skill and biases, making portfolio performance subject to these differences.

Enter robo-advisors: a new breed of AI-powered investment platforms that are democratizing access to personalized investing. Robo-advisors use advanced algorithms and machine learning to automate the investment process, from determining an investor's risk profile to constructing and managing a diversified portfolio. These platforms leverage the power of AI to provide sophisticated, data-driven investment strategies at a fraction of the cost of traditional human advisors.

The AI behind robo-advisors is constantly evolving, becoming more sophisticated and personalized with each iteration. Machine learning algorithms can now analyze copious market data, identify patterns and correlations, and make predictive recommendations based on an investor's unique profile. Some platforms are even experimenting with natural language processing, allowing investors to interact with their robo-advisor using conversational interfaces.

The process typically begins with the investor completing an online questionnaire that assesses financial situation, investment goals, and risk tolerance. The robo-advisor's AI algorithms construct a personalized investment portfolio from this information, typically comprised of low-cost exchange-traded funds (ETFs). The AI system continuously monitors and rebalances the portfolio to maintain the target asset allocation, taking into account market conditions and the investor's changing circumstances.

Robo-advisors offer the advantage of accessibility. With low- or even no-minimum investment requirements, these platforms have opened up personalized investing to a much broader audience. This particularly benefits those with smaller amounts to invest who might not meet the minimum asset thresholds of traditional financial advisors, and younger investors who are just beginning to build their wealth.

But robo-advisors are not just for small investors. Even high-net-worth individuals and institutions increasingly turn to these platforms for their sophisticated algorithms and data-driven strategies. Some robo-advisors now offer advanced features including tax-loss harvesting, socially responsible investing options, and can even elevate clients to human financial advisors for more complex planning needs.

However, the rise of robo-advisors also raises important questions and challenges. There are concerns about the potential for these systems to amplify market volatility, as they may make similar trading decisions en masse. There are also questions about the ability of AI to comprehend the emotional aspects of investing, such as coaching investors through market downturns or adjusting strategies based on life changes. And there is the ongoing need for human oversight and judgment, particularly for more complex financial planning situations.

Despite these challenges, the proliferation of robo-advisors shows no signs of slowing. With their combination of accessibility, affordability, and sophisticated AI-driven strategies, these platforms are transforming the landscape of personal investing. For consumers, this means greater access to the kind of personalized, data-driven advice that was once the purview of only the wealthy. For the financial industry, it represents both a disruptive challenge and an opportunity for innovation and growth.

As AI continues to advance, we can expect robo-advisors to become even more sophisticated and personalized. We may see platforms that can fully integrate a user's entire financial life, from their bank accounts and credit cards to their insurance policies and real estate holdings. Additionally, AI may be able to provide truly holistic financial planning, taking into account not just investment goals but also life goals, values, and aspirations.

The role of the financial advisor is not likely to disappear, but rather to evolve. The most successful advisors will be those who can harness the power of AI and robo-advisory platforms, while still providing the human touch and judgment that is so critical in financial planning. They will be the ones who can use AI to augment and enhance their services, not replace them entirely.

Personalized Financial Services

By harnessing machine learning and big data, financial institutions are moving towards a model of highly personalized services that cater to customers' unique needs. This shift marks a departure from traditional, segment-based approaches, where customers were grouped into more-broad categories and offered standardized products. Instead, AI-driven personalization enables a more granular understanding of individual customers.

At the core of AI-driven personalization is the use of data to gain a comprehensive view of each customer's financial situation, behaviors, and goals. Financial institutions have long had access to extensive data, ranging from demographic information to detailed transaction histories. What sets AI apart from past data analysis is the technology's ability to analyze this data at scale, uncovering patterns and insights on a granular level that were previously inaccessible due to the sheer volume of data points.

Customer, financial organization benefits

The benefits of the ability to personalize interventions and offerings are substantial. For customers, AI-driven services mean more relevant, timely, and tailored financial advice and products. For example, by analyzing a customer's spending habits and cash flow, a bank might proactively offer a short-term loan or line of credit when it predicts a potential cash shortfall. This engagement can lead to better financial outcomes—such as avoiding overdrafts, maximizing savings, or achieving optimized investment returns—and a more satisfying customer experience with fewer irrelevant offers and more proactive, helpful interactions.

For financial institutions, the adoption of AI-driven personalization represents a powerful tool for differentiation in an increasingly competitive market. Firms can use machine learning algorithms to create personalized portfolios that match a client's risk tolerance, financial goals, and life stage. Offering individualized services allows institutions to strengthen customer relationships, enhance loyalty, and increase lifetime value. Moreover, the ability to personalize at scale can create opportunities for premium pricing on customized services. Additionally, AI can help financial institutions manage risk more effectively. For example, the tools can detect potential fraud or identify customers who are at risk of defaulting on a loan.

Data-driven approach

As financial institutions continue to refine their use of AI, the potential for personalization will only grow, leading to even more sophisticated and nuanced customer interactions. However, the long-term success of these initiatives depends in part on how well institutions balance technological innovation with careful attention to data privacy, ethical considerations, and regulatory compliance. To effectively implement AI-driven personalization in financial services, institutions must adopt a strategic approach that integrates advanced machine learning techniques with comprehensive data analysis. The goal is to create a system that not only understands individual customer needs but also continuously adapts to new information. This ensures services offered remain relevant and effective.

The first step in this process involves harnessing available data. This data includes everything from basic demographic information and transaction histories to more nuanced behavioral data, such as how customers interact with digital platforms. AI models gain a deeper understanding of each customer's financial habits, preferences, and goals through the analysis of this data.

Once the data is in place, the next challenge is to apply AI to derive meaningful insights and predictions. Models that can identify patterns and correlations must be developed to enable the institution to anticipate customer needs before they arise.

But it's not enough for AI to simply recognize these patterns; it must also be capable of prescribing decisions that are fair and accurate. AI models are designed to be objective, but are only as unbiased as the data they are trained on. If the underlying data reflects historical biases—such as those found in historic lending practices—these biases can penetrate the AI's recommendations. To counter this, financial institutions must manage and curate their training data with effective internal controls to ensure it is diverse and representative of the entire customer base. Regular audits of AI systems are necessary to identify and correct any biased outcomes.

The transparency of AI decision-making processes is crucial. Customers and regulators alike need to understand how AI models arrive at their recommendations, particularly when these decisions impact financial well-being. Techniques such as explainable AI (XAI) provide insights into the factors that influenced a model's decision, making the process more transparent and helping to build trust in AI-driven systems.

Also, unlike traditional data analysis that relies on static information, AI can process and analyze information as it is generated in real-time, allowing institutions to provide up-to-date recommendations that reflect the current financial climate. This real-time capability is particularly valuable in dynamic environments like financial markets, where conditions can and do change rapidly.

Finally, human oversight remains an essential component of AI-driven personalization. While AI can process massive datasets and make complex decisions quickly, there are still situations where human judgment is necessary. By combining AI with human expertise, financial institutions can ensure their services are both technologically advanced and grounded in sound judgment.

AI's predictive capabilities enable proactive, data-driven decision-making, offering insights that help customers optimize financial outcomes while avoiding financial pitfalls. However, these advancements bring challenges related to data privacy, algorithmic bias, and ethical AI use. Financial institutions must be transparent, implement safeguards against bias, and ensure AI decisions are explainable.

The success of AI-driven personalization depends on high-quality, diverse data and continuous refinement of AI models. As AI technologies continue to evolve, financial institutions must prioritize customer trust, ethical practices, and innovation. The future of finance is intertwined with AI, offering both challenges and opportunities to redefine exceptional customer service and personalization. With the right approach, AI can help build a more inclusive, personalized, and effective financial system.

Chapter Fifteen

AI IN LENDING AND CREDIT ASSESSMENT

For banking and finance professionals, understanding AI's impact on lending is essential to the future of business. In this chapter, we explore how AI is transforming lending and credit assessment.

We begin by examining how machine learning enhances traditional credit scoring by incorporating alternative data and advanced predictive models. This advancement allows lenders to assess risk with unprecedented precision.

Next, we look at how AI streamlines the loan origination process. From automating application intake to optimizing underwriting, AI reduces manual intervention, cuts costs, and speeds up approvals. Lenders experience superior efficiency while borrowers enjoy a faster, smoother experience.

We also discuss AI-powered risk-based pricing, where AI's predictive power enables lenders to offer personalized loan terms matching each borrower's risk profile. This process not only improves risk management, but also makes credit more widely accessible and affordable.

However, with advancements come challenges. We address the ethical considerations of using AI in lending, emphasizing the need for fairness, transparency, and accountability in AI-driven models.

Automated Credit Scoring

Traditional credit scoring has long relied on credit bureau data to assess risk. However, these models often fall short when evaluating individuals with limited credit histories. Groups such as young adults and new immigrants may be hindered in accessing available credit.

Artificial intelligence offers a more advanced approach to credit evaluation. AI-powered scoring models utilize machine learning algorithms to analyze a wide range of alternative data sources, including rental payments, utility bills, educational background– even social media activity. A broader spectrum of information and data points enable these models to provide a more holistic and comprehensive assessment of an individual's creditworthiness that looks beyond FICO scores and generic lending criteria.

The benefits of AI in credit scoring are substantial. Lenders who successfully address the ethical and technical challenges can achieve more accurate risk assessments, lower default rates, and the ability to extend credit to a broader range of customers. For example, Upstart, a lending platform that uses AI, has reported approving 27% more applicants than traditional models while offering borrowers 16% lower interest rates.

For borrowers, particularly those underserved by traditional credit scoring, AI offers the potential for a more inclusive credit system. With access to a wider range of financial behaviors and history, AI models open up access to credit for individuals who might otherwise be overlooked.

Risks and Challenges

Despite the promise of AI, there are critical challenges to its integration in credit scoring. A key concern is that AI models may reflect and even exacerbate existing biases in the credit system. If the data used to train these models is biased, the AI could potentially amplify the bias and initiate unfair lending decisions. Lenders must proactively test their models for fairness and ensure the data input into the models are representative and unbiased.

Transparency and clarity in comprehension are critical issues as well. AI models can be complex and difficult to interpret, making it challenging for lenders to explain credit decisions to consumers, undermining trust and creating regulatory challenges. Some lenders are using techniques such as SHAP and LIME (as discussed in Chapter 6) so their models provide insights into which factors influenced a credit decision.

As AI continues to develop, regulatory frameworks must evolve alongside it. Policymakers and industry leaders need to collaborate to establish guidelines that promote the responsible use of AI in lending, ensuring the benefits are realized while mitigating potential risks.

For professionals in lending and credit risk management, understanding how to leverage AI ethically and effectively will be essential. The shift towards AI-powered credit scoring is complex, but the potential to create a fairer, more inclusive credit system is significant. As this technology advances, maintaining a focus on fairness, transparency, and consumer welfare is key to successful adoption.

Loan Approval Processes

Artificial intelligence enables lenders to make faster, more accurate decisions while reducing operational costs. Traditional loan approval workflows require loan officers to commit to manual reviews of applications and supporting documents, a time-consuming process susceptible to human error and bias. AI-powered solutions streamline and automate key steps in this process.

One major application of AI in loan approvals is intelligent document processing. Lenders typically require extensive documentation from borrowers, including bank statements, tax returns, and pay stubs. AI systems using NLP and computer vision can automatically extract relevant data points from these documents, populate them into the lender's systems, and flag any missing information or discrepancies that may require follow-up. This significantly reduces manual data entry and allows loan officers to focus their time on higher-value work.

Another key benefit of AI in loan approvals is the ability to process applications 24/7 and provide instant or near-instant decisions to borrowers in many cases. Automated credit decisioning models can evaluate an application and render a decision in a matter of seconds and communicated to the borrower immediately. In an age of digital-first consumer expectations, this real-time processing is a competitive differentiator, and reduces the cost per loan originated by minimizing manual underwriting efforts.

AI additionally helps lenders streamline communication and coordination across the loan approval workflow. Intelligent process automation tools can automatically move applications through each step, prompting relevant stakeholders to complete their respective tasks and provide input. Some lenders are also using conversational AI chatbots and virtual assistants to interact with applicants, answer common questions, provide updates, and gather additional information if needed.

As AI continues to advance, we can expect to see even greater levels of automation and optimization in loan approval processes. However, it's important to recognize that human expertise and judgment remain essential. Most lenders use AI to augment and assist their loan officers, not fully replace them. Striking the right balance between leveraging AI's efficiency and preserving human oversight is key to realize the full benefits of this technology while mitigating risks.

Risk-Based Pricing in Lending

Artificial intelligence can provide lenders with more granular, personalized loan pricing through sophisticated risk-based pricing models. Traditionally, lenders have relied on relatively broad risk tiers to determine interest rates and loan terms using factors such as credit score ranges, loan-to-value ratios, and debt-to-income ratios. AI allows for a much more nuanced assessment of risk at the individual borrower level.

AI-powered risk-based pricing models typically leverage a combination of machine learning techniques, including supervised learning algorithms such as logistic regression, decision trees, random forests, and gradient boosting machines. These models are trained on large datasets of historical loan performance data. Input features span a wide range of borrower characteristics and loan attributes.

During the learning process, the algorithms learn complex, non-linear relationships between these input features and the target variable, usually producing a binary outcome indicating whether a loan defaulted or not. The trained models can then assign a probability of default to new loan applicants based on their specific combination of features. Some models also incorporate unsupervised learning methods such as clustering to segment borrowers into more granular risk groups.

By leveraging these machine learning models that can analyze vast amounts of data from both traditional and alternative sources, lenders can develop a deeper understanding of each borrower's unique risk profile. These AI-powered models can identify subtle patterns and interactions between hundreds or even thousands of variables that are predictive of credit risk. This pattern detection enables lenders to differentiate risk more precisely within traditional credit bands.

For example, two borrowers with the same FICO score of 700 may actually have very different risk profiles when considering additional factors such as their income stability, payment history across various credit products, career trajectory, and education. An AI model can weigh all of these factors using complex, learned relationships to assign each borrower a more precise risk score or, by contrast, probability of default.

Lenders can then use these granular risk assessments to offer interest rates and terms that are more commensurate with each borrower's individual risk. Borrowers on the lower end of a traditional credit tier may qualify for slightly better rates than they would have under a one-size-fits-all pricing approach. Conversely, borrowers on the higher end of a credit tier may receive slightly less favorable terms than the tier average.

This increased precision in pricing enables lenders to compete more effectively for lower-risk borrowers while still adequately pricing for risk across their portfolio. Credit can be extended to a broader range of borrowers without taking on excessive risk. For consumers, the main benefit of AI-driven risk-based pricing is the potential to secure more competitive, personalized rates based on their specific financial profile.

> *"No man who can borrow money easily ever wants it badly."*
>
> ~ *Evan Esar*

Ethics and risk

The use of AI for risk-based pricing raises important ethical considerations. There are concerns these models could perpetuate—or even amplify—historical biases and discrimination in lending if not properly designed and monitored. For example, if an AI model is trained on historical loan data that reflects past discriminatory lending practices, it may learn to assign higher risk scores to certain groups of borrowers based on correlations with sensitive attributes like race, gender, or age, even if those factors are not included directly as input features.

To mitigate these risks, lenders must ensure their AI risk-based pricing models are fair, transparent, and compliant with anti-discrimination laws and regulations. This dedication requires careful feature selection and preprocessing to avoid proxies for protected class membership, as well as ongoing monitoring and testing for disparate impact on different borrower segments. Some lenders are also exploring techniques such as adversarial debiasing to proactively reduce discrimination in AI models.

Another ethical consideration is the explainability of AI-driven pricing decisions. While machine learning models can identify complex patterns and make highly accurate predictions, they are often seen as "black boxes," difficult to interpret. This lack of transparency can make it challenging for lenders to provide clear explanations to borrowers about why they received a particular rate or were denied credit. Lenders may need to invest in techniques like SHAP values or counterfactual explanations to provide more interpretable insights into their AI models' decision-making process.

Additionally, there are concerns about the privacy implications of using extensive alternative data sources in AI risk-based pricing models. Lenders must ensure they have proper consent and disclosure practices in place when collecting and using borrower data, especially from non-traditional sources like social media, mobile phone records, or utility payments.

As the use of AI in risk-based pricing continues to grow, it will be crucial for lenders to proactively address these ethical challenges. This may require collaboration with regulators, consumer advocates, and AI ethics experts to develop robust frameworks for responsible and inclusive AI-driven lending practices. By striking the right balance between leveraging the power of AI and ensuring fairness, transparency, and accountability, lenders can unlock the benefits of personalized risk-based pricing while promoting responsible financial inclusion.

Chapter Sixteen

AI IN REGULATORY COMPLIANCE

Financial institutions that can navigate the complex web of laws and regulations efficiently and effectively are better positioned to serve their customers, maintain market confidence, and avoid costly penalties and reputational damage. However, the traditional approach to compliance – a heavy reliance on manual processes, rule-based systems, and human judgment – is increasingly straining under the weight of an ever-expanding regulatory environment coupled with the explosive growth of financial data. As financial products and services become more complex and digital, compliance teams struggle to keep pace.

AI technologies such as machine learning, natural language processing, and cognitive automation are transforming the compliance function, enabling financial institutions to harness the power of data and intelligent algorithms to identify risks, automate processes, and support better decision-making.

AI equips compliance teams to sift through troves of structured and unstructured data in real-time to monitor for regulatory changes, detect suspicious activities, and generate insights previously hidden in the noise. It can automate routine tasks like customer due diligence and regulatory reporting, freeing up time and resources for higher-value activities. And it can embed compliance controls directly into business processes and customer interactions, reducing friction and improving the user experience.

Financial institutions that fail to adopt and integrate AI into their compliance functions invite additional business risk, increase the possibility of losing customer trust, and face heightened regulatory scrutiny.

But the path to AI-powered compliance is not always smooth. Financial institutions must grapple with challenges around data quality and governance, model transparency and explainability, and ethics. They must also invest in the right talent, tools, and partnerships to build and scale AI solutions that are effective and compliant.

In this chapter, we will explore the current state and future potential of AI in regulatory compliance within the financial sector. We will examine real-world applications of AI in areas like anti-money laundering, know your customer processes, and regulatory reporting. The chapter will highlight the benefits, challenges, and best practices. And we will discuss the key considerations and strategies for successfully implementing AI in compliance functions.

Anti-Money Laundering (AML)

Money laundering is a pervasive problem in the financial system, as criminals use increasingly sophisticated techniques to disguise the origins of illegally obtained funds and introduce them into the legitimate economy. Financial institutions play a crucial role in combating this problem, operating under stringent anti-money laundering (AML) regulations designed to detect, report, and prevent illicit financial activities. These regulations are essential for maintaining the security of the financial system and ensuring financial institutions don't inadvertently become conduits for criminal enterprises.

AML's History

The primary framework for AML in the United States was established by the Bank Secrecy Act (BSA) of 1970. This landmark legislation mandates that financial institutions keep records of certain transactions and file reports, such as Currency Transaction Reports (CTRs) for cash transactions exceeding $10,000, and Suspicious Activity Reports (SARs) for any transactions that might be indicative of illegal activity. The BSA is enforced by the Financial Crimes Enforcement Network (FinCEN), which plays a central role in overseeing compliance and facilitating cooperation between financial institutions and government agencies.

In the wake of the September 11, 2001, terrorist attacks, the USA Patriot Act significantly expanded the scope of AML requirements. Title III of the USA Patriot Act, also known as the International Money Laundering Abatement and Anti-Terrorist Financing Act of 2001, imposes stricter due diligence and reporting requirements on financial institutions. This legislation mandates the establishment of comprehensive AML programs, enhanced customer identification processes, and more rigorous monitoring of foreign accounts and correspondent banking relationships. The goal is to prevent terrorists and criminals from using the financial system to fund their activities.

One of the most critical aspects of AML regulations is Customer Due Diligence (CDD), which requires financial institutions to verify the identities of their customers, understand the nature and purpose of their relationships, and monitor for and report suspicious activities. CDD is essential for identifying and mitigating risks associated with money laundering and terrorist financing. In May 2018, FinCEN implemented the Customer Due Diligence Rule, which further clarified and strengthened the requirements for financial institutions to identify and verify the identities of the beneficial owners of legal entity customers.

Despite these robust regulatory frameworks, traditional AML programs rely on rule-based systems and manual investigations – processes which can struggle to keep pace with the rapidly growing volume and complexity of financial transactions. Criminals continually devise new methods to circumvent these systems, which can quickly render them obsolete and ineffective. They employ techniques such as structuring (breaking up large transactions into smaller ones to avoid reporting thresholds), layering (conducting a series of complex transactions to obscure the origins of the funds), and smurfing (using multiple individuals to conduct numerous small transactions that appear unrelated). These tactics, designed to exploit the gaps in conventional AML systems, make it increasingly challenging for financial institutions to detect and prevent money laundering.

To address these challenges, financial institutions increasingly turn to advanced technologies to enhance their AML efforts. These technologies, used correctly, can analyze transaction data in real time, identify patterns indicative of money laundering, and adapt to evolving criminal tactics. As financial institutions implement these new technologies, they will have to maintain compliance with existing AML regulations while upholding the highest standards of transparency, fairness, and accountability.

Proactive Compliance

AI technologies enable financial institutions to take a more proactive, risk-based approach to AML compliance. By analyzing data in real-time, algorithms can identify patterns and anomalies that are indicative of money laundering – even if these anomalies have never been seen before.

These systems use techniques such as unsupervised learning and anomaly detection to build baseline models of normal transaction behavior for every customer, account, or group. Systems can then identify transactions that deviate significantly from these baselines, taking into account factors like transaction size, frequency, counterparties, and geolocation. Some advanced systems can even detect subtle patterns of behavior that emerge over time, such as gradual increases in transaction volumes or the use of multiple accounts to avoid threshold-based rules.

Banks and other financial institutions are required to monitor customer transactions for suspicious activities, including large cash deposits, wire transfers to high-risk jurisdictions, or rapid movement of funds between multiple accounts. AI-powered transaction monitoring systems can analyze millions of transactions per day, across multiple channels and products, to flag unusual patterns that may warrant further investigation.

Another important application of AI in AML is customer risk assessment. Financial institutions are required to conduct due diligence on their customers to identify those that pose a higher risk of money laundering, such as politically exposed persons (PEPs), cash-intensive businesses, or customers with ties to high-risk countries. AI can help automate and enhance this process by analyzing a wide range of internal and external data sources to build comprehensive risk profiles for each customer.

For example, machine learning algorithms can build risk scores by analyzing customer data including transaction history, account balances, and demographic information to identify risk factors. Natural language processing can be used to scan unstructured data sources such as news articles, social media posts, and public records for mentions of a customer's involvement in criminal activities or association with high-risk individuals or organizations. And graph analytics can be used to map out complex networks of relationships between customers, accounts, and transactions to identify hidden patterns of risk.

By leveraging these AI techniques, financial institutions can take a proactive targeted, risk-based approach to AML compliance. Instead of applying the same level of scrutiny to all customers and transactions, institutions can allocate resources toward the highest-risk cases, reducing false positives and improving detection rates. This approach not only helps meet regulatory obligations, but also provides a better experience for legitimate customers.

Know Your Customer (KYC) Processes

Know Your Customer (KYC) is a foundational element of anti-money laundering (AML) and counter-terrorist financing regulations. KYC plays a vital role in safeguarding the financial system from abuse by criminals and terrorists. Under KYC requirements, financial institutions must implement rigorous processes to verify the identity of their customers, ensuring that they are who they claim to be. Effective KYC practices are not only a regulatory requirement but also a critical defense mechanism that enables financial institutions to detect and prevent illicit activities before they can infiltrate the financial system. This proactive approach is essential for maintaining the integrity of financial markets and upholding global security.

The KYC process involves collecting and validating personal information during the onboarding process: names, addresses, dates of birth, and government-issued identification. This step enables institutions to prevent the opening of accounts under false identities, which is a common tactic used by money launderers and terrorist financiers to conceal their activities and the origins of their funds.

Beyond identity verification, KYC procedures require financial institutions to develop a deep understanding of the nature of their customers' businesses and to assess the associated risks. This assessment involves conducting ongoing due diligence to monitor customer transactions for suspicious activities that may indicate money laundering or terrorist financing. By analyzing factors such as the types of transactions, geographic locations, and patterns of behavior, institutions can categorize customers into different risk profiles, applying enhanced scrutiny to those deemed higher risk.

However, traditional KYC processes can be time-consuming, labor-intensive, fraught with manual errors, and a negative user experience. Customers are often required to provide extensive documentation to prove their identity and address, which can be a frustrating and repetitive experience, especially if they have multiple accounts or relationships with the same institution. Financial institutions, in turn, must manually review and verify this information, which can take days or even weeks, leading to delays in account opening and customer onboarding.

Artificial intelligence's key applications offer a way to streamline and automate KYC processes, reducing friction for customers, while improving the accuracy and efficiency of due diligence.

Identity Verification

AI-powered identity verification solutions can automatically extract and validate customer information from identity documents including passports, driver's licenses, and utility bills. Using computer vision and NLP techniques, these solutions can read and interpret the text, images, and security features on these documents, verifying their authenticity and cross-referencing the information with other data sources. This not only speeds up the onboarding process, but also reduces the risk of fraud and identity theft.

Biometric Authentication

AI can verify customer identity using biometric data such as facial recognition, voice recognition, and fingerprints. By comparing a customer's biometric data with the information on their identity documents, financial institutions can confirm that the person opening the account is who they claim to be. Biometric authentication can also be used for ongoing customer authentication, such as logging into mobile banking apps or authorizing high-risk transactions.

Risk Assessment

AI can help financial institutions assess the risk profile of their customers more accurately and efficiently. By analyzing a wide range of data sources, including transaction history, public records, and social media activity, machine learning algorithms can identify potential risk factors. Risk factors include involvement with PEPs, adverse media mentions, and connections to high-risk jurisdictions. Financial institutions can apply enhanced due diligence measures to high-risk customers while fast-tracking low-risk customers through the onboarding process.

Ongoing Monitoring

KYC is not a one-time event, but an ongoing process. Financial institutions are required to regularly review and update customer information and risk profiles. AI can automate much of this process by continuously monitoring customer transactions and behavior for any changes or anomalies that may indicate increased risk. For example, if a customer starts receiving large wire transfers from a high-risk country or engaging in suspicious trading activity, an AI system can flag this behavior for further investigation.

Customer Screening

Financial institutions are required to screen their customers against sanctions lists, watchlists, and PEP databases to identify individuals who may be involved in financial crime or terrorism. AI can automate this screening process by cross-referencing these databases with customer information in real-time, reducing the risk of manual errors and false positives. Natural language processing can also be used to scan unstructured data sources such as news articles and social media posts for any mentions of a customer's involvement in illicit activities.

By leveraging these AI applications, financial institutions can create a more seamless, efficient, and secure KYC process that benefits compliance teams and customers. Compliance teams can focus resources on high-risk cases while ensuring consistent adherence to regulatory standards. Customers can enjoy faster onboarding times, fewer paperwork requirements, and more personalized service.

But implementing AI in KYC presents challenges. One key issue is data privacy and security. KYC processes involve collecting and storing sensitive personal information, which must be protected from unauthorized access or misuse. Financial institutions must ensure that their AI systems comply with data protection regulations like GDPR and CCPA and have robust cybersecurity measures in place.

Another challenge is ensuring the fairness and transparency of AI-driven KYC decisions. Like any AI system, KYC algorithms can be biased if they are trained on biased data or designed with biased assumptions. This can lead to unfair treatment of certain groups of customers based on factors like race, gender, or nationality. Financial institutions must regularly test and audit their AI models for bias and discrimination and provide clear explanations for any decisions made by these systems.

Finally, there is the issue of regulatory compliance. While AI can help financial institutions comply with KYC regulations more efficiently, it is not a silver bullet. Regulators still expect financial institutions to have proper oversight and control over their KYC processes, regardless of whether they are automated or manual. Financial institutions must work closely with regulators to ensure their AI systems meet all relevant compliance standards and are regularly subjected to testing and validation.

Despite these challenges, the benefits of AI in KYC are clear. By automating manual processes, improving risk assessment accuracy, and enhancing the customer experience, AI can help financial institutions meet their KYC obligations more effectively while reducing costs and improving competitiveness. As AI technology continues to evolve, we can expect to see even more innovative applications in the KYC space, from chatbots that guide customers through the onboarding process to blockchain-based identity verification systems that enable secure, decentralized KYC data sharing.

Regulatory Reporting and Auditing

Regulatory reporting and auditing are designed to ensure transparency, accountability, and compliance with a complex web of laws and regulations. However, these processes can be incredibly time-consuming, resource-intensive, and error-prone, especially as the volume and complexity of financial data continue to grow.

Traditionally, regulatory reporting has involved manual data aggregation from disparate systems, spreadsheet-based calculations, and human judgment to interpret and apply regulatory rules. Auditing, meanwhile, has relied on sample-based testing and after-the-fact detection of issues, leaving financial institutions vulnerable to compliance gaps and regulatory penalties.

Artificial intelligence is changing the game for regulatory reporting and auditing, enabling financial institutions to automate data collection, validation, and submission, while continuously monitoring compliance risks in real-time.

Data Aggregation and Validation

Financial institutions face challenges in regulatory reporting around the aggregation and validation of data sourced from various internal systems and external platforms. Data is often siloed, residing in disparate systems that use different formats and standards. This fragmentation not only makes data aggregation a cumbersome process, but also increases the risk of errors and inconsistencies. Differences in data formats, from varying date formats to inconsistent currency codes, can lead to significant discrepancies in reports. Additionally, manual data entry processes introduce the potential for human error, which can undermine the accuracy and reliability of the regulatory reports.

AI-powered data aggregation tools are revolutionizing this process by automating the extraction, transformation, and loading (ETL) of data from these diverse sources into a centralized repository. These tools use machine learning algorithms to standardize and harmonize data formats, ensuring all data points align with the required reporting standards. Moreover, AI models can automatically detect and resolve common data quality issues — missing values, outliers, and duplications. For instance, when a data point is missing or seems anomalous, the AI system can cross-reference other related data sets to estimate the correct value, or flag it for further review. This not only significantly reduces the manual effort required for data validation, but also enhances the overall accuracy and integrity of the data, leading to more reliable regulatory reports.

The integration of AI in data aggregation and validation also allows for continuous data monitoring and quality assurance. Unlike traditional systems, which might perform data validation as a one-time process, AI-driven solutions can continuously scan for errors and inconsistencies as new information is ingested. This real-time validation ensures that any issues are identified and addressed promptly, thereby maintaining the data's integrity throughout the reporting process. Further, these AI tools can adapt and improve over time, learning from past errors and feedback to refine their algorithms, ultimately leading to even higher levels of accuracy and efficiency in regulatory reporting.

Automated Report Generation

Once the data has been aggregated and validated, AI significantly streamlines the process of generating regulatory reports. Machine learning algorithms can be trained on vast amounts of historical reporting data and regulatory templates, enabling them to automatically identify the relevant data points required for each report. These algorithms can perform complex calculations and populate report fields with precision, ensuring all necessary information is included and formatted correctly. This process removes much of the manual effort traditionally associated with report generation, reducing the risk of human error and the potential for inaccuracies. Additionally, the automation of report generation allows financial institutions to keep pace with the demanding schedules of regulatory bodies, ensuring reports are submitted on time and in compliance with industry standards.

Natural language processing can help with interpreting and applying the intricate regulatory rules and guidelines that govern financial reporting. By integrating NLP into the report generation process, AI systems can adapt to changes in regulatory requirements, such as updates in reporting standards or new compliance directives. This adaptation ensures the generated reports are not only accurate but also fully aligned with the latest regulatory expectations.

The use of AI in this context not only minimizes the cost and time associated with regulatory reporting, but also enhances the institution's ability to maintain ongoing compliance, even as regulations evolve. This level of automation is particularly beneficial for large financial institutions that deal with complex reporting requirements across multiple jurisdictions, as it enables them to efficiently manage compliance obligations without sacrificing accuracy or consistency.

Real-time Compliance Monitoring

AI-powered compliance monitoring tools continuously scan financial transactions, customer interactions, and internal processes for potential regulatory violations in real-time. By analyzing vast amounts of structured and unstructured data, these tools can identify patterns and anomalies that may indicate non-compliance, such as insider trading, market manipulation, or improper sales practices.

Machine learning algorithms can be trained to detect subtle signs of misconduct that may be missed by traditional rule-based systems, such as unusual trading volumes or communication patterns. And NLP can be used to monitor employee emails, chat logs, and voice recordings for any language that may indicate compliance risks.

Risk Assessment and Prioritization

Financial institutions increasingly rely on AI to refine their approach to risk assessment and prioritization, enabling more proactive, responsive, and nuanced evaluations of potential threats. Traditional risk assessment methods often rely on static models and historical data, which may not fully capture the dynamic nature of financial markets and emerging risks. AI, however, leverages machine learning algorithms to continuously learn from new data and adjust risk assessments in real time. These algorithms can analyze various factors, including market conditions, regulatory changes, customer behaviors, and external events, to identify patterns and trends that may indicate potential risks before they escalate into significant issues.

AI-driven risk assessment tools can prioritize risks by evaluating their potential impact on the organization. For instance, machine learning models can analyze historical compliance data, regulatory enforcement actions, and industry benchmarks to determine which risks pose the greatest threat to the institution. This analysis allows compliance teams to allocate resources more efficiently, focusing on areas that require immediate attention. Additionally, AI can monitor the regulatory landscape for changes and updates, ensuring that the institution remains compliant with new requirements.

This continuous monitoring and prioritization process not only helps mitigate risks but also supports more informed decision-making, ultimately leading to improved operational resilience and regulatory compliance.

Intelligent Sampling and Testing

Traditional audit methods historically rely on manual sample selection, where auditors choose a subset of data based on predefined criteria. This process, while useful, can be time-consuming and may miss critical issues due to its reliance on human judgment and the limitations of static sampling techniques. By contrast, AI-driven intelligent sampling leverages machine learning algorithms to enhance financial audits by enabling more precise sampling and testing, focusing on the most significant and high-risk areas within large datasets.

By focusing on data points that exhibit unusual behavior or significant deviations from the norm, AI can enhance the precision of audits, ensuring that the most relevant and impactful transactions are reviewed. This targeted approach not only increases the likelihood of detecting fraud or errors, but also improves the overall efficiency of the audit process. Machine learning models can be trained to recognize indicators of potential issues based on historical audit findings, allowing auditors to concentrate their efforts on areas with the highest risk of non-compliance or financial misstatement.

This heightened dynamic and adaptive testing methodology enables financial institutions to maintain a robust and proactive audit framework, significantly reducing the risk of regulatory violations and ensuring the most critical areas receive the attention they require.

Predictive Analytics and Scenario Modeling

One of the most exciting applications of AI in regulatory compliance is the ability to proactively identify and mitigate potential risks before they manifest into full-blown regulatory issues. This is where predictive analytics and scenario modeling come into play.

> *"Those who have knowledge don't predict.*
> *Those who predict don't have knowledge."*
>
> *~ Lao Tzu*

Predictive Analytics

Predictive analytics involves using machine learning algorithms to analyze historical and real-time data to identify patterns, trends, and relationships that may indicate future compliance risks. By training on data from past regulatory breaches, enforcement actions, and compliance failures, these algorithms can learn to recognize the subtle signs and precursors of potential issues.

For example, a predictive analytics model could be trained on data from past cases of insider trading, including factors such as employee trading patterns, communication logs, and market conditions. The model could then be applied to monitor current employee behavior and flag any activity that resembles the patterns associated with insider trading, enabling compliance teams to investigate and intervene before any illegal activity occurs.

Similarly, predictive analytics could be used to identify potential risks in customer behavior, such as unusual account activity, suspicious transactions, or sudden changes in risk profile through the analysis of multiple sources, including transaction records, customer interactions, and external data feeds. Machine learning algorithms can detect anomalies and red flags that may indicate money laundering, fraud, or other financial crimes.

Predictive analytics can also be used to forecast potential regulatory changes and their potential impact on the business. By analyzing data from regulatory publications, enforcement actions, and industry trends, machine learning models can identify emerging areas of regulatory focus and predict how new rules or guidelines may affect the institution's compliance obligations. This can help compliance teams proactively adapt their policies, procedures, and controls to meet evolving regulatory expectations.

The power of predictive analytics lies in its ability to process and learn from historic and new data in real-time, identifying risks that may be missed by traditional rule-based systems or human analysis. Financial institutions can continuously monitor for potential compliance issues, prioritize areas of highest risk, and allocate resources more effectively.

Scenario Modeling

Scenario modeling involves using AI to simulate the potential impact of different compliance scenarios on the institution's operations, finances, and reputation. By modeling various "what-if" scenarios, compliance teams can develop contingency plans, test the effectiveness of their controls, and identify areas of vulnerability.

For example, a scenario modeling tool could be used to simulate the impact of a major regulatory change, such as the implementation of a new anti-money laundering (AML) rule. The tool could model how the new rule would affect the institution's existing AML processes, technology systems, and staffing requirements, as well as the potential costs and benefits of different compliance strategies. By running multiple simulations with different assumptions and variables, compliance teams could identify the optimal approach to adapt to the new rule while minimizing disruption and risk.

Scenario modeling could also be used to stress test the resilience of the institution's compliance program around scenarios such as a major enforcement action, a cyber attack, or a market downturn. By simulating how these events could impact the institution's operations, finances, and reputation, compliance teams could identify potential weaknesses in their controls and develop contingency plans to mitigate the risks.

AI-powered scenario modeling tools can also enable more dynamic and interactive risk assessments. Instead of relying on static, point-in-time assessments, these tools allow compliance teams to continuously update their risk models based on real-time data feeds and changing market conditions.

Integration and Application

To fully leverage the power of predictive analytics and scenario modeling, financial institutions must integrate these tools into their broader compliance management systems and processes. This endeavor may require significant investment in data infrastructure, machine learning platforms, and compliance talent.

Institutions must also ensure the insights generated by these tools are actionable and aligned with their overall compliance strategy. This approach may involve setting up clear governance frameworks, escalation protocols, and decision-making processes to translate AI-powered insights into concrete risk mitigation actions.

Compliance teams must also work closely with senior leadership, business units, and risk management functions to ensure the insights from predictive analytics and scenario modeling are integrated into strategic planning, product development, and customer engagement. New collaboration models, communication channels, and incentive structures to break down silos and foster a culture of proactive compliance may be required to chart a course forward.

Finally, institutions must be transparent and accountable. This accountability may involve developing clear policies and procedures around data privacy, model validation, and algorithmic fairness, as well as engaging with regulators and other stakeholders to build trust and confidence in the use of these tools.

The potential of predictive analytics and scenario modeling to transform compliance risk management is immense. By leveraging the power of AI to identify and mitigate potential risks before they escalate, financial institutions can not only reduce compliance costs and risks but also unlock new opportunities for innovation and growth. As these tools become more sophisticated and integrated into compliance programs, we can expect to see a shift from reactive, backward-looking compliance to proactive, forward-looking risk management.

Chapter Seventeen

AI IN CORPORATE FINANCE

Corporate finance is evolving through the use of artificial intelligence to automate complex tasks and enhance decision-making processes. In this chapter, we will explore how AI is revolutionizing financial planning and analysis (FP&A), reporting, forecasting, and scenario analysis, with a focus on how companies can leverage these technologies to improve efficiency, accuracy, and strategic outcomes.

AI is increasingly being leveraged to enhance FP&A processes and decision-making. Machine learning algorithms can rapidly analyze vast amounts of historical financial data to uncover patterns, trends and insights that may not be readily apparent to human analysts. This can lead to more accurate, detailed budgets and forecasts. AI can also automate routine FP&A tasks like data aggregation, variance analysis, and report generation. This frees up FP&A professionals to focus on higher-value strategic activities and partner more closely with other business functions.

Predictive analytics powered by AI allow FP&A to evolve from explanatory analysis of past events to forward-looking projections of future outcomes. Sophisticated AI models can evaluate multiple internal and external data points to predict key financial variables such as revenue, expenses, cash flow, and profitability. Prescriptive analytics takes this a step further, using AI to recommend optimal actions to achieve desired financial outcomes.

The quality, accuracy, and completeness of data is critical for AI to be effective in enhancing FP&A. AI models and algorithms are only as good as the data used to train them. Bad data leads to faulty insights and poor decisions. FP&A teams need access to clean, consistent, timely data from internal systems including ERP, CRM, HR, and supply chain. Integrating and harmonizing data across functions and systems is an important prerequisite.

AI also has the ability to incorporate external data such as economic indicators, market trends, customer behavior, and competitive intelligence should also be incorporated where relevant. Even alternative data from non-traditional sources like website traffic, mobile app usage, social media sentiment, weather patterns, and satellite imagery are becoming more prevalent. The key is to identify external datasets that have a material impact on financial drivers and performance in order to train the AI models.

With the vast amounts of data that is needed to train these models, data governance becomes paramount. Robust processes need to be in place to ensure data accuracy, completeness, timeliness, lineage, and security as it flows into AI models. Ongoing monitoring is required to identify data drift that can degrade model performance over time.

Financial Planning and Analysis

Financial Planning and Analysis is an important part of any successful company's strategic decision-making, budgeting, and forecasting. The FP&A team is responsible for analyzing financial data, developing financial models, and providing insights to senior management to help drive business performance.

Budgeting and Forecasting

Budgeting and forecasting are critical financial planning activities that enable organizations to plan for and predict future financial performance. Annual budgets are developed to outline expected revenues, expenses, and capital needs for the upcoming fiscal year, while regular forecasts update these projections based on the latest financial data and market conditions.

AI has the potential to enhance budgeting and forecasting by analyzing vast amounts of historical data in order to identify patterns humans might miss, leading to more accurate predictions. Better predictions enable organizations to adjust their financial strategies in real time.

Financial Modeling

Financial modeling involves building and maintaining sophisticated models that simulate various business scenarios, evaluate potential investments, and support strategic decision-making. These models typically include projections of income statements, balance sheets, and cash flow statements, allowing financial analysts to assess the impact of different variables on the organization's financial health.

AI offers to automate the scenario analysis process, quickly generating multiple models based on real-time data, continuously refining them as new information becomes available. By running scenarios such as best-case, worst-case, and most-likely outcomes, financial modeling helps decision-makers understand the potential risks and rewards associated with various strategic choices, enabling them to make data-driven decisions that align with the organization's long-term goals.

> *"Business reporting is not dealing with objects,*
> *it is dealing with relationships between objects."*
> *~ Hasso Plattner*

Management Reporting

Management reporting is the process of preparing detailed financial reports and dashboards that monitor key performance indicators (KPIs) and provide management with visibility into the organization's financial performance. These reports are typically generated on a monthly, quarterly, or annual basis and include insights into revenue trends, expense management, profitability, and cash flow.

AI could enhance management reporting by automating the generation of reports, identifying trends and anomalies that may not be immediately apparent, and providing predictive insights that allow management to act proactively. By providing a clear and concise view of financial metrics, management reporting helps executives and managers track progress toward financial goals, identify areas that require attention, and make timely adjustments to strategies and operations.

Variance Analysis

Variance analysis is the practice of comparing actual financial results with budgeted or forecasted figures to identify discrepancies, understand their causes, and uncover potential issues or opportunities. This variance analysis – such as the differences between projected and actual revenues or expenses – helps financial professionals determine whether the organization is on track to meet its financial objectives and, if not, where deviations may be occurring.

AI could improve variance analysis by quickly analyzing large datasets to identify patterns and correlations, thereby offering deeper insights into the reasons behind variances. Financial teams can pinpoint the underlying factors driving these discrepancies, enabling management to take corrective actions or capitalize on positive trends.

Business Partnering

Business partnering involves financial professionals working closely with other business units to understand the key drivers of financial performance, provide financial guidance, and support the achievement of strategic objectives. This collaboration is essential for aligning financial plans with operational goals and ensures business units have the resources and insights needed to execute their strategies effectively.

AI enhances business partnering by providing real-time insights and predictive analytics to their business partners, equipping them to make more timely decisions and with more comprehensive information and data at their disposal. Using these AI tools, financial professionals play a greater role in driving organizational success, fostering cross-functional collaboration, and ensuring that financial considerations are integrated into all aspects of decision-making.

Forecasting and Reporting

Accurate and reliable financial forecasting is essential for effective business planning and decision-making. Traditional forecasting methods often rely on historical data and assumptions that may not account for the complexities of today's dynamic business environment.

Forecasting

Incorporating AI into forecasting processes can significantly enhance the accuracy and reliability of financial forecasts by leveraging large datasets from multiple sources and identifying patterns and relationships that may not be apparent to human analysts.

AI-driven forecasting models can ingest and analyze vast amounts of structured and unstructured data from various internal and external sources. Internal data may include sales figures, production volumes, inventory levels, and financial statements. External data can encompass a wide range of economic indicators, market trends, competitor activities, social media sentiment, and even weather patterns. By considering a more comprehensive set of variables and their interactions, AI models can provide a more nuanced and precise view of future financial performance.

Advanced machine learning techniques like deep learning can automatically identify the most predictive variables and adapt forecasting models to changing business conditions. Ensemble modeling, which combines multiple AI models to produce a consolidated forecast, can further improve accuracy and resilience. Some AI forecasting solutions also incorporate natural language processing (NLP) to analyze textual data like news articles, analyst reports, and earnings call transcripts for sentiment and risk signals.

Monte Carlo simulations are a powerful AI-based technique for modeling uncertainty in financial forecasts. These simulations involve running thousands of iterative scenarios with randomly generated values for key input variables. The AI model tracks the outcomes of each scenario to build a probability distribution of potential future results, which allows finance teams to quantify the likelihood of different outcomes, identify key risk drivers, and develop contingency plans. Simulation analysis can be particularly valuable for stress-testing financial plans, evaluating investment decisions, and managing risk exposure.

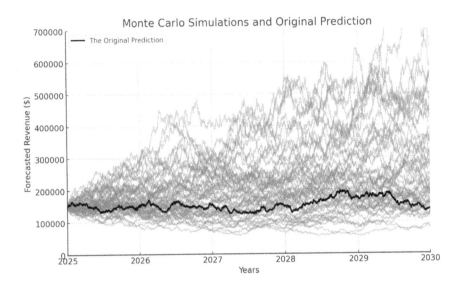

Financial Reporting

AI has the ability to streamline and automate the financial reporting process. Natural language generation (NLG) tools can instantly produce draft financial reports from structured data, saving time and reducing the potential for human error. AI-powered data validation and anomaly detection can identify and flag potential errors or inconsistencies in financial data, ensuring the accuracy and integrity of financial reports. Robotic process automation (RPA) can automate repetitive reporting tasks like data extraction, formatting, and distribution.

AI-enhanced reporting tools can provide real-time visibility into financial performance through interactive dashboards and visualizations. Finance teams can drill down into key metrics, identify variances and outliers, and quickly access supporting details. Dynamic reporting powered by AI enables a more proactive and agile approach to financial management.

AI also can drive significant efficiencies in regulatory compliance. AI-based tools can automatically monitor financial transactions and reports for compliance with accounting standards, tax requirements, and other regulations. Anomaly detection algorithms can identify potential fraud or non-compliance issues for further investigation. AI can help companies stay current with changing regulatory requirements by continuously monitoring regulatory updates and identifying areas of reports that may need revision.

Incorporating AI into financial forecasting and reporting processes can deliver significant benefits in terms of accuracy, efficiency, risk management, and regulatory compliance. However, realizing these benefits requires a strong data foundation, robust model governance, and seamless integration with existing financial systems and processes. As AI technologies continue to advance, we can expect to see even more powerful and sophisticated applications in financial forecasting and reporting that will help organizations navigate an increasingly complex and uncertain business world.

Metrics Tracking and Performance Management

Effective performance management relies on the continuous tracking and analysis of key performance indicators (KPIs) and other financial metrics. KPIs provide a quantitative measure of progress toward specific business objectives and help companies identify areas of strength, weakness, and opportunity.

Examples of common financial KPIs: revenue growth, profitability margins, cash flow, return on investment (ROI), and working capital efficiency.

Traditionally, tracking financial metrics has been a manual, time-consuming process with myriad data sources and prone to errors and delays. AI-powered tools can significantly enhance metrics tracking and performance management by automating data collection, validation, analysis, and reporting. AI algorithms can continuously monitor financial data from multiple systems, providing real-time visibility into performance against KPIs.

Automated dashboards powered by AI can display key metrics in intuitive, interactive formats that allow finance teams to quickly identify trends, patterns, and outliers. Advanced data visualization techniques like heat maps, scatter plots, and geographic mapping provide deeper insights into performance drivers and relationships between variables. AI-driven dashboards incorporate external data such as market benchmarks and economic indicators to provide context and peer analysis for company performance.

Predictive analytics can take metrics tracking to the next level by forecasting future performance based on historical data and external factors. AI models can identify leading indicators that provide early warning signs of potential issues or opportunities. This allows finance teams to proactively address performance gaps and allocate resources more effectively. Prescriptive analytics can even recommend specific actions to optimize performance based on AI-driven insights.

AI can also enhance performance management by enabling continuous, real-time monitoring of KPIs. Traditional performance management processes often rely on periodic reviews and reports that can lag actual performance by weeks or months. With AI, finance teams can set up automated alerts and notifications to flag any deviations from targets or unexpected changes in key metrics to allow for more agile, data-driven decision-making and faster course correction when needed.

AI-driven performance management also helps align overall company strategy and goals with team and individual performance. By cascading top-level KPIs down to specific departments, projects, and employees, AI tools provide a clear line of sight between day-to-day activities and strategic outcomes. Employees who have access to personalized dashboards and scorecards receive real-time feedback on their performance and help managers coach and develop their teams more effectively.

Finally, AI can help ensure the integrity and reliability of financial metrics by automating data quality checks and reconciliations. AI tools can identify data inconsistencies, duplicates, and anomalies that may skew performance results. By continuously monitoring data inputs and calculations, AI can help maintain a single source of truth for financial metrics and KPIs.

The integration of artificial intelligence into corporate finance functions including FP&A, forecasting, reporting, scenario analysis, and performance management is transforming the way companies plan, execute, and optimize their financial strategies. AI-powered tools and techniques help finance teams be more efficient, accurate, and strategic by automating routine tasks, uncovering hidden insights, predicting future outcomes, and recommending optimal actions.

But realizing the full potential of AI in corporate finance requires more than just investing in the latest technologies. It requires a fundamental shift in mindset and culture toward data-driven decision-making, continuous learning, and agile experimentation. Finance teams will need to develop new skills in data science, analytics, and storytelling to effectively harness the power of AI. Further, companies must address the ethical and governance implications of relying on AI for critical financial decisions. Ensuring the transparency, fairness, and accountability of AI models will be essential for maintaining trust and confidence among stakeholders.

The role of the finance function is evolving from backward-looking scorekeeping to forward-looking strategic partnership. AI is not a silver bullet, but it is a powerful tool that can help finance teams navigate an increasingly complex and uncertain business environment. The companies that can successfully combine the best of human and machine intelligence will be the ones that thrive in the age of AI-driven finance.

Chapter Eighteen

AI IN INVESTMENT BANKING, VENTURE CAPITAL, AND PRIVATE EQUITY

In the high-stakes and fiercely competitive world of venture capital (VC), private equity (PE), and investment banking, firms are constantly vying to identify and capitalize on the most promising opportunities – often making split-second decisions that can result in substantial gains or significant losses.

This chapter explores how AI is increasingly being integrated into these businesses to streamline deal-making, enhance due diligence, optimize investment strategies, and ultimately improve efficiency, reduce risks, and drive better investment outcomes.

Investment Banking

In investment banking, AI is being applied across various functions, including deal sourcing, due diligence, financial modeling, and risk management. By harnessing AI technologies, investment banks can process data more efficiently, uncover hidden patterns, and gain insights that lead to more informed decision-making.

Let's start with deal origination. Traditionally, investment bankers have relied on their personal networks, market research, and industry expertise to identify potential deals, but in the interconnected digital world of 2024, manually sifting through this information is becoming increasingly challenging. AI-powered tools can quickly analyze datasets from a broad range of sources beyond financial statements and industry reports to uncover new investment opportunities that may have been overlooked by human analysts.

Companies like Cyndx (www.cyndx.com) and Inven (www.inven.ai) have developed AI-powered platforms that streamline the deal sourcing process to rapidly identify promising acquisition targets and investment opportunities. These platforms use advanced ML algorithms to analyze financial documents, market reports, and other relevant data, enabling investment bankers to make informed decisions with greater accuracy and speed.

Building on this capability, AI algorithms can further enhance deal sourcing by identifying companies with strong growth potential, solid financials, and unique value propositions that align with the firm's criteria. These algorithms monitor market trends, regulatory changes, and competitive landscapes in real-time, flagging potential risks or opportunities. By automating the initial screening process, AI sets up investment banks to generate a more targeted and qualified deal pipeline, saving both time and resources.

Once a potential deal is identified, AI can streamline the due diligence process, which typically involves a comprehensive investigation of a target company's financials, legal documents, operations, and market position to assess investment risks and rewards. AI-powered tools can automate various tasks, extracting crucial information and identifying potential red flags. This automation allows AI to uncover hidden risks and opportunities more efficiently than traditional methods.

Additionally, NLP techniques can be used to parse unstructured data sources to gauge market sentiment and reputation risk, further enhancing the due diligence process. This is especially valuable in the middle market, where information is often sparse and fragmented. By providing a consolidated, real-time view of a company's performance and competitive landscape, AI makes due diligence more thorough and effective.

AI can also enhance the accuracy and efficiency of financial modeling, a key component in valuing companies and structuring deals. Machine learning algorithms can analyze historical financial data to identify key drivers of revenue and profitability, predict future cash flows, and assess the sensitivity of valuation to various assumptions. These models can be continuously updated with real-time data, providing more accurate and timely insights. AI-assisted financial modeling enables investment bankers to make better-informed decisions about pricing, financing structure, and risk allocation.

In addition to deal-related activities, AI is also transforming how investment banks manage risks and ensure regulatory compliance. AI-powered surveillance systems can monitor trading activities, communications, and other data sources to detect potential insider trading, market manipulation, or other fraudulent activities. These systems can flag suspicious patterns and anomalies in real-time, allowing compliance teams to investigate and mitigate risks proactively. AI can also help investment banks stay up-to-date with ever-changing regulations by automatically monitoring regulatory updates and identifying areas of non-compliance.

While AI offers significant benefits for investment banking, it also presents some challenges and requirements for deeper thought. One key challenge is ensuring the quality and integrity of data used to train the models. Inconsistent, incomplete, or biased data can lead to flawed insights and decisions. Investment banks will have to invest in robust data governance and quality control processes to ensure the reliability of their AI-powered tools.

It's also important to understand algorithmic bias. If AI models are trained on historical data that reflects past biases or discrimination, they may perpetuate these biases in their recommendations. Investment banks must be proactive in testing their AI models for fairness and implementing measures to mitigate potential biases.

Finally, while AI can automate many tasks, it is unlikely to fully replace the strategic, relationship-based aspects of investment banking in the near future. Instead, successful investment banks will likely adopt a hybrid approach that combines the efficiency and insights of AI with the judgment and expertise of human bankers.

Venture Capital

"Some of the deals get so hot,
and you have to decide so quickly,
that you're all just sort of gambling."
~ Charlie Munger

The stage at which VCs get involved in investments requires a willingness to invest in (bet on) the unknown. While the success of any given startup is not a roll of the dice, there are so many variables and unknowns that it's nearly impossible to apply a formula or a rule-based system to determine which companies will succeed and which will fail. VCs typically pride themselves on their ability to pick the right horses in any given race. This very human ability comes from a deep understanding of the business landscape, understanding of the problem for which the companies they invest in are trying to solve, and the fundamentals of the market itself. VC has historically been a very human-driven endeavor.

But what if there were a way to better understand and quantify the risk of a VC investment or to validate ambitious founders' optimistic and generally unfounded hockey-stick projections of their future success?

What if artificial intelligence could help with the venture capital investment processes?

Let's consider how that might work.

What if AI could empower VC firms with greater efficiency, precision, and insight in an industry where the stakes are high and the competition is fierce?

Let's dive into how AI could transform the way VCs identify, evaluate, and manage investments.

By leveraging this technology, VCs could uncover promising startups that might have been overlooked by traditional methods, refine their due diligence processes, and optimize portfolio management. By using this data-driven approach, VCs could make more informed decisions, reduce biases, and ultimately enhance their ability to achieve superior returns.

Deal Sourcing and Screening

One of the strongest potential applications of AI in venture capital is its ability to streamline the deal sourcing process. Traditionally, VCs have relied on their personal networks, industry events, and inbound referrals to identify potential investment opportunities. But this historical approach could be time-consuming and could potentially lead to missed opportunities, particularly in emerging industries or geographies.

AI lets VCs cast a wider net by scanning the entire internet to identify promising startups and emerging trends. Machine learning algorithms can sift through diverse sources, ranging from startup databases and industry reports to patent filings and academic publications to spot high-potential companies early in their development. By applying specific criteria (e.g. industry focus, technology type, or founder background), VCs can leverage AI to surface startups that closely align with their investment strategies and objectives.

For example, AI-powered platforms like Crunchbase (www.crunchbase.com) and CB Insights (www.cbinsights.com) use NLP and machine learning to track and analyze startup activity around the world. These platforms can help VCs identify emerging trends, monitor competitor activity, and discover promising startups based on factors such as funding history, team composition, and market traction.

Due Diligence Automation

VC investments require a significant amount of due diligence. Before making an investment decision, VCs must thoroughly evaluate a startup's management team, product, financial health, market positioning, competitive landscape, and regulatory compliance. This process typically involves reviewing large volumes of data, including financial statements, legal documents, and customer contracts.

AI can help automate and accelerate the due diligence process by analyzing this data at scale. NLP algorithms can sift through thousands of pages of legal and financial documents, flagging potential risks or inconsistencies that require further investigation. This not only saves time but also reduces the risk of human error or oversight.

Today, AI-powered due diligence platforms like Diligend (www.deligend. mindcubetech.com) and DealRoom (www.dealroom.net) use machine learning to analyze and extract key information from documents, such as cap tables, financial projections, and intellectual property filings. These platforms can also benchmark a startup's performance against industry peers and identify potential red flags, such as litigation history or regulatory violations.

Market and Competitive Analysis

Staying up-to-date with market trends, customer preferences, and competitor activities is challenging, especially in fast-moving industries. AI can help VCs gain a real-time, data-driven understanding of market dynamics by analyzing large volumes of structured and unstructured data from myriad sources. Machine learning algorithms can uncover patterns and insights that might not be obvious to human analysts, such as emerging customer pain points, shifts in market sentiment, or disruptive technologies.

For example, AI-powered market intelligence platforms like CB Insights and Tracxn (www.tracxn.com) use NLP and machine learning to monitor startup and industry activity across the globe. These platforms can provide VCs with real-time alerts on competitor fundraising, mergers and acquisitions, and key executive moves. They can also generate data-driven insights on market sizing, growth forecasts, and customer behavior.

By leveraging AI for market and competitive analysis, VCs can make more informed decisions about which startups to invest in and how to position their portfolio companies for success. They can also identify potential threats or disruptions early on and work with their portfolio companies to adapt and stay ahead of the curve.

Post-Investment Support

AI can provide significant value to VCs even after an investment is made by helping portfolio companies optimize their operations and scale efficiently. Startups can struggle with challenges like customer acquisition, product development, and talent management, which can impede growth. AI-powered tools could address these issues by offering data-driven insights and recommendations. For instance, machine learning algorithms could analyze customer data to identify high-value segments, predict churn risk, and recommend personalized marketing strategies. AI could also optimize pricing and inventory management by analyzing supply chain data and market demand, enabling startups to scale more effectively and increase profitability.

AI can help VC portfolio companies streamline their internal operations by automating repetitive tasks and improving decision-making. For example, AI-powered HR tools can assist with talent acquisition and retention by analyzing job candidate data and predicting employee attrition risk. AI can also help startups optimize their financial management by forecasting cash flow, identifying cost-saving opportunities, and providing real-time visibility into key performance indicators.

By leveraging AI to support their portfolio companies, VCs can help them scale faster and more efficiently, ultimately increasing the chances of a successful exit. Some VC firms are leveraging AI and relationship intelligence to enhance deal flow, streamline due diligence, and optimize portfolio management. For instance, SignalFire (www. signalfire.com), a VC firm that integrates AI into its operations, has developed its own AI platform, Beacon, that helps identify promising startups and offers extensive support to portfolio companies. By combining AI with their investment strategy, SignalFire demonstrates how AI can significantly enhance the capabilities of VC firms, offering them a competitive edge in the market.

Predictive Analytics for Exit Strategies

Choosing the right time and method to exit an investment is a critical decision for VCs, as it directly impacts their returns and reputation, but predicting the optimal exit strategy can be challenging. It depends on a variety of factors from market conditions and industry trends to the startup's financial performance.

While we're nowhere near ceding ultimate control of exit decisions to the robots, AI-powered predictive analytics can help VCs make more informed decisions about when and how to exit their investments. Machine learning algorithms can analyze historical data on mergers, acquisitions, and initial public offerings (IPOs) to identify patterns and predict future trends. By incorporating real-time data on market conditions and the startup's financial performance, these models can provide VCs with data-driven insights on the likelihood and timing of different exit scenarios.

AI-powered platforms like Pitchbook (www.pitchbook.com) and CB Insights use machine learning to analyze data on funding rounds, valuations, and exits across different industries and geographies. These platforms can provide VCs with benchmarking data and predictive insights on the likelihood of different exit scenarios based on factors such as the startup's stage, sector, and financial performance.

By leveraging AI for exit strategy planning, VCs can potentially optimize their portfolio management and maximize their returns. They can also identify potential acquirers or strategic partners early on and work with their portfolio companies to position themselves for a successful exit.

Portfolio Management and Risk Mitigation

Managing a diverse portfolio of startups can be complex and time-consuming for VCs, particularly as the number and size of investments grow. VCs must continuously monitor the performance and risk profiles of their portfolio companies and make data-driven decisions about where to allocate resources and when to intervene.

AI can help VCs streamline and optimize their portfolio management by providing insights on the health and risk profiles of their investments. Machine learning algorithms can analyze financial, operational, and market data to identify trends, anomalies, and potential risks that may not be apparent to human analysts.

For instance, AI-powered portfolio management platforms like AngelList (www.angellist.com) and Dynamo (www.dynamo.vc) can help VCs track key performance indicators (KPIs) across their portfolio companies and benchmark them against industry peers. These platforms can also provide early warning signals on potential risks, such as cash flow issues, market disruptions, or regulatory changes, allowing VCs to take proactive measures to mitigate them.

By leveraging AI for portfolio management and risk mitigation, VCs can make more informed decisions about where to allocate their time and resources. They can also identify opportunities to create synergies between portfolio companies, such as by facilitating partnerships, customer introductions, or talent sharing.

Enhancing Decision-Making with Behavioral Analytics

While AI and data-driven decision-making are increasingly being adopted in venture capital, many investment decisions are still heavily influenced by human biases and heuristics. VCs have historically relied on personal networks, gut instincts, or past experiences when evaluating startups, which can sometimes lead to suboptimal outcomes.

The goal with AI should be to round out the information VCs have to work with. AI-powered behavioral analytics can help VCs identify and mitigate potential biases. By analyzing decision-making patterns and providing data-driven feedback, AI can bring objectivity to the process. For example, machine learning algorithms can sift through historical investment data (e.g. deal flow, due diligence notes, and investment memos) to uncover patterns and correlations that might not be obvious to individual VCs.

AI can also highlight unconscious biases, like a preference for founders from specific backgrounds or a tendency to overlook certain risk factors. By delivering objective, data-driven insights, AI helps VCs refine their investment criteria and make more consistent, evidence-based decisions.

AI can assist VCs in identifying best practices and success factors across their portfolio companies. By analyzing the traits and behaviors of high-performing startups, VCs can gain valuable insights into what works well in different industries and stages of development. These insights can then be used to provide more targeted and effective support to their portfolio companies, ultimately driving better outcomes.

Private Equity

Private equity firms, like their VC brethren, are increasingly turning to artificial intelligence to gain a competitive edge in identifying, evaluating, and managing investments. While PE and VC share some similarities in their use of AI, such as for deal sourcing, due diligence, and portfolio management, there are also some key differences driven by the distinct nature of PE investments.

PE firms typically invest in more mature companies with established business models and cash flows, with the goal of improving their operational and financial performance before exiting the investment through a sale or public offering. As such, PE firms focus on using AI to identify operational inefficiencies, optimize financial management, and support strategic decision-making to maximize the value of their portfolio companies.

Operational Improvement

The bulk of the PE value creation process is to improve operations and increase efficiency in their portfolio companies. This can involve streamlining processes, reducing costs, and increasing productivity. And while PE firms aren't deploying AI at scale today, the technology can play a significant role in identifying and implementing operational improvements.

To capitalize on the potential of AI in enhancing operational efficiency, firms can look to emerging solutions that bridge the gap between traditional processes and advanced technology. For example, Chassi (www.chassi.com), an innovative startup that partners with PE operating leaders and portfolio company finance teams, uses AI to ingest and automatically model data from these systems. This approach offers near real-time visibility into key business processes like Quote-to-Cash, Item Fulfillment, Procurement, and Customer Renewals.

Additionally, AI-powered analytics could help PE firms identify inefficiencies and bottlenecks in a portfolio company's supply chain, manufacturing, or distribution processes. By analyzing large amounts of operational data, such as sensor data from equipment or transaction data from enterprise resource planning (ERP) systems, machine learning algorithms can identify patterns and anomalies that may indicate areas for improvement.

AI can also help PE firms benchmark a portcos performance against industry peers and best practices. By analyzing data from similar companies and industries, PE firms can identify opportunities to implement proven strategies and technologies to improve efficiency and competitiveness.

Finally, AI could be used to support the implementation and monitoring of operational improvements. For example, machine learning algorithms can be used to optimize production scheduling, inventory management, and logistics to reduce waste and improve responsiveness to customer demand. AI-powered dashboards can provide real-time visibility into KPIs and alert managers to potential issues before they escalate.

Financial Performance Optimization

Another key focus area for PE firms is optimizing the financial performance of their portfolio companies. This can involve improving revenue growth, reducing costs, optimizing working capital, and managing risk. AI can support financial performance optimization in several ways.

AI-powered financial forecasting and budgeting tools can help PE firms develop more accurate and dynamic financial plans for their portfolio companies. By analyzing historical financial data, market trends, and key business drivers, machine learning algorithms can generate probabilistic forecasts and scenario analyses to support strategic decision-making.

Machine learning could also help PE firms identify opportunities to reduce costs and optimize working capital. These algorithms could analyze spending patterns and vendor contracts to identify areas for cost savings and negotiate better terms. AI can also optimize accounts receivable and payable processes to improve cash flow and reduce the risk of bad debt.

As discussed previously, AI can support risk management and compliance efforts by analyzing financial transactions and communications to identify potential fraud, money laundering, or other anomalies. AI can also help PE firms monitor and comply with changing regulations and reporting requirements, reducing the risk of penalties and reputational damage.

Business Consolidation and Exit Planning

"Roll-ups" are another common PE strategy. By consolidating multiple companies into a single, more efficient and competitive entity, they can add value over smaller, standalone entities. Roll-ups can involve merging or acquiring companies in the same or adjacent industries, integrating their operations and systems, and realizing synergies. AI can support business consolidation efforts in several ways.

AI-powered due diligence tools could help PE firms evaluate potential acquisition targets more quickly and thoroughly. By analyzing data on a target company's financials, customers, suppliers, and competitors, machine learning algorithms can identify potential risks and opportunities that may impact the value of the acquisition.

AI can also support post-merger integration efforts. By using NLP to analyze contracts, policies, and procedures across multiple companies to identify inconsistencies and develop standardized processes, AI could drastically reduce the amount of time it takes to ingest and operationalize results. Further, ML could be used to analyze customer and employee data to identify potential integration challenges and develop targeted retention strategies.

Finally, AI can support exit planning and execution. By analyzing market trends, comparable transactions, and a portfolio company's financial performance, machine learning algorithms can help PE firms identify the optimal time and method to exit an investment. AI-powered platforms can also help PE firms identify potential buyers and investors and streamline the due diligence and negotiation processes.

Data Management and Integration

To realize the full potential of AI in private equity, firms must have access to high-quality, integrated data across their portfolio companies and internal systems. This can be challenging, as PE firms often work with companies that have disparate systems, processes, and data formats.

By using AI, PE firms could streamline and automate data extraction, transformation, and integration processes by training algorithms to extract structured data from unstructured sources like contracts, invoices, and email communications. AI can also help PE firms develop common data models and taxonomies across their portfolio companies to enable cross-company comparisons and benchmarking.

Additionally, AI-powered data management platforms can help PE firms ensure the security, privacy, and compliance of their data assets. For example, machine learning algorithms can detect potential data breaches, unauthorized access, and other security threats, while also assisting firms in adhering to regulations like GDPR and CCPA by identifying and safeguarding sensitive information.

Talent Management

Attracting, retaining, and developing top talent is critical for PE firms and their portfolio companies. AI can support talent management in several ways.

By analyzing job descriptions, resumes, and social media profiles, machine learning algorithms can identify candidates with the right skills, experience, and cultural fit for a given role. AI can also help PE firms reduce bias in the hiring process by identifying and mitigating potential sources of discrimination.

It's important to note here that the application of AI in hiring is not without its challenges – as demonstrated by Amazon's attempt to use AI for candidate screening in 2014. Amazon developed an AI tool intended to streamline their hiring process by evaluating resumes and selecting top candidates. But once the tool was deployed, it was discovered that the system suffered from significant gender bias, favoring resumes that contained language typically associated with men and penalizing those that referenced women's achievements. The AI had been trained on historical data that reflected the male-dominated tech industry, leading it to reinforce existing biases rather than eliminate them. Despite efforts to adjust the algorithm, Amazon ultimately had to abandon the tool, underscoring the complexities of using AI in hiring and the critical importance of monitoring AI systems for unintended biases.

The Amazon case was a clear example of the importance of mitigating bias in ML algorithms, but when bias and other potential ethical issues are addressed, there are significant applications in HR beyond hiring.

AI can also support talent development and retention efforts. For example, machine learning algorithms can analyze employee performance data, feedback, and engagement levels to identify high-potential employees and develop targeted development plans.

AI-powered chatbots and virtual assistants can provide employees with on-demand support and guidance, improving productivity and job satisfaction.

Finally, AI can help PE firms optimize their organizational structures and incentive systems. By analyzing data on employee roles, responsibilities, and performance, machine learning algorithms can identify opportunities to streamline processes, eliminate redundancies, and align incentives with strategic goals.

While AI has not yet been broadly adopted in PE, the potential benefits are substantial. By leveraging AI for operational efficiency, financial performance, business consolidation, data management, and talent management, PE firms can significantly enhance value for investors and portfolio companies. While managing AI introduces new administrative costs, the ROI from a well-implemented system justifies the investment.

To succeed, PE firms must have the right data, talent, and governance structures in place, addressing potential biases and limitations in AI models and ensuring ethical use. As the industry evolves, more firms will likely embrace AI as a crucial driver of value creation, gaining a competitive edge in investment performance, operational efficiency, and talent retention. The key will be balancing human judgment with machine intelligence, using AI to augment — not replace — the expertise of private equity professionals.

Future Trends and Considerations

As AI continues to advance, we can expect to see even more transformative applications in investment and financial services. Firms that stay ahead of these trends and effectively integrate AI into their operations will be better positioned to identify lucrative opportunities, optimize their investment strategies, and manage risks in an increasingly complex and competitive space.

Explainable AI and Algorithmic Transparency

One of the key challenges in implementing AI in financial services is ensuring the transparency and interpretability of AI models. Many AI algorithms, particularly those based on deep learning, can be complex and opaque, making it difficult for users to understand how decisions are being made. As discussed, this lack of transparency can create risks (around unintended biases or errors, in particular), and make it difficult for firms to comply with regulatory requirements.

In response to these challenges, there is a growing focus on developing explainable AI techniques that provide greater transparency into how the models make their decisions. These techniques aim to provide users with clear, understandable explanations of the key factors and logic behind AI-generated recommendations and decisions.

Financial firms will need to adopt explainable AI techniques to ensure the transparency and accountability of their AI systems. This may involve using techniques such as feature importance analysis, counterfactual explanations, and rule extraction to provide clear, interpretable explanations of AI-generated insights and decisions.

Responsible AI and Ethical Considerations

As AI becomes more prevalent in financial services, there is a growing concern about the potential for AI to perpetuate or amplify biases and discrimination. AI models that are trained on historical data may inherit biases that exist in that data, such as gender or racial biases in hiring or lending decisions.

Firms will need to consider the broader ethical implications of their use of AI, such as the potential impact on job displacement and income inequality. As AI automates more tasks in investment banking, VC, and PE, there may be concerns about job losses and the widening of the skills gap. Firms will need to take proactive steps to reskill and upskill their workforce to ensure that they can thrive in an AI-driven future.

Collaborative Intelligence and Human-Machine Teaming

While AI can automate many tasks across the industry, it is unlikely to fully replace the need for human expertise and judgment. In fact, the most successful firms will likely be those that can effectively combine human and machine intelligence in a collaborative and complementary way.

This may involve using AI to augment and support human decision-making, rather than fully automating it. For example, AI-powered analytics and insights can help investment professionals identify potential opportunities and risks, but ultimately the final investment decisions will require human judgment and expertise.

Firms will need to develop new ways of working that enable effective collaboration between humans and machines. This may involve creating new roles and skills, such as data scientists and AI ethics officers, as well as developing new processes and frameworks for human-machine teaming.

Continuous Learning and Adaptation

To stay competitive in a dynamic market where new trends, regulations, and technologies are emerging all the time, investment banks, VC firms, and PE firms will need to develop AI systems that can continuously learn and adapt to new data and insights. This may involve using techniques such as online learning, transfer learning, and reinforcement learning to enable AI models to learn and improve over time. Firms will also need to invest in ongoing monitoring and maintenance of their AI systems to ensure that they remain accurate, relevant, and compliant with changing regulations and standards.

Firms that can develop agile, adaptive AI systems will be better positioned to respond to changing market conditions and customer needs. They will also be able to identify new opportunities and risks more quickly and accurately than their competitors.

Blockchain and Decentralized Finance

Another trend likely to shape the future of investment firms is the rise of blockchain and decentralized finance (DeFi). Blockchain technologies, like smart contracts and tokenization, have the potential to transform many aspects of financial services, from capital raising and trading to settlement and clearing.

DeFi platforms, which leverage blockchain and cryptocurrencies for peer-to-peer financial transactions without intermediaries, are gaining traction in the investment community. These platforms offer the potential for greater transparency, accessibility, and efficiency in financial services, especially in areas like lending, trading, and insurance.

While not all financial institutions will pursue this path, many will explore integrating blockchain and DeFi into their operations. This could involve developing new products and services, such as tokenized securities and decentralized exchanges, as well as investing in or partnering with blockchain and DeFi startups.

Regulatory Compliance and Cybersecurity

As AI becomes more integrated into financial services, regulatory scrutiny and compliance requirements will intensify. The recent adoption of the EU Artificial Intelligence Act by the European Parliament exemplifies this trend, setting the stage for the world's first comprehensive AI regulation. This Act, along with guidance from other regulators like the US Federal Reserve, will require investment banks, VC firms, and PE firms to ensure their AI systems meet strict standards. Compliance will involve developing robust governance frameworks, risk management processes, and monitoring tools to ensure AI is used safely, transparently, and accountably.

Firms will also need to prioritize cybersecurity and data privacy to protect against the growing threat of cyber attacks and data breaches. As AI systems become more complex and interconnected, they may become more vulnerable to hacking and manipulation. Firms will need to invest in advanced cybersecurity technologies and practices, such as encryption, multi-factor authentication, and AI-powered threat detection and response.

The future of financial institutions will be increasingly shaped by artificial intelligence and machine learning. Firms that can effectively harness the power of AI to improve investment decision-making, operational efficiency, and risk management will be well-positioned to succeed in an increasingly competitive and dynamic landscape.

However, the adoption of AI also brings significant challenges and considerations, from ensuring algorithmic transparency and fairness to managing job displacement and skills gaps. Firms will need to develop responsible AI practices and collaborative human-machine teaming models to ensure that AI is being used in an ethical, transparent, and accountable way.

As the fields of AI and finance continue to evolve, we can expect to see even more transformative applications and innovations in the coming years. From explainable AI and blockchain to continuous learning and adaptation, the future of financial services companies will be shaped by a complex interplay of technological, economic, and social factors.

Firms that can stay ahead of these trends and develop agile, adaptive, and responsible AI strategies will be best positioned to thrive in this new era of finance. By combining the best of human and machine intelligence, these firms will be able to identify new opportunities, manage risks, and create value for their clients and stakeholders in ways that were previously unimaginable.

Chapter Nineteen

DEVELOPING AN AI STRATEGY

To unlock its full potential,
AI must be woven into the fabric
of your business strategy and operations.
It's not a side project.

To truly leverage the potential of AI and ensure its success, companies have to deeply integrate AI initiatives into their overall business strategy and operations. This requires a fundamental shift in mindset, where AI is not viewed as a separate, isolated endeavor but rather as a core component of the institution's business model and decision-making processes.

The success of any AI initiative starts with a well-crafted AI strategy that serves as a roadmap that guides the organization in its AI initiatives. The strategy should ensure that the company's AI efforts contribute directly to the achievement of key business objectives. These objectives could include enhancing customer experience, improving operational efficiency, and managing risk. Without this alignment, AI projects risk becoming siloed efforts that fail to deliver meaningful value, or worse, initiatives that lead to unintended consequences, such as increased operational complexity or regulatory challenges.

To avoid these pitfalls, companies have to clearly define their AI strategy within the context of their overall business strategy. This alignment involves not only setting clear objectives for what AI is expected to achieve, but also understanding how these objectives tie into the larger goals of the organization.

For example, if a bank's strategic priority is to enhance customer engagement through personalized services, the AI strategy should focus on developing tools and models that can deliver customized financial advice, tailored product recommendations, and responsive customer support.

Components of an AI Strategy

A comprehensive AI strategy comprises several key components that work together to ensure the successful implementation and integration of AI initiatives across the organization, including the following:

Objective

Any successful AI strategy must include clear, measurable objectives. These measurable objectives should be directly tied to the institution's broader business goals, and should be specific enough to guide AI initiatives and measure their impact.

Some examples of AI objectives for financial institutions could include:

- Reducing customer churn by X% through personalized engagement and proactive retention strategies powered by AI-driven insights.
- Increasing the efficiency of underwriting processes by X%, resulting in faster loan approvals and a better customer experience.
- Enhancing fraud detection capabilities to identify and prevent X% more fraudulent transactions in real-time.
- Improving investment returns by X% through AI-powered portfolio optimization and risk management strategies.

To ensure that these objectives are meaningful and achievable, they should be developed in collaboration with key stakeholders across the organization. Stakeholders include representatives from every department impacted by the initiative. This could include managers, domain experts, employees, data scientists, and IT teams.

Each objective should be tied to specific metrics that can be tracked over time (e.g. customer retention rates, underwriting cycle times, fraud detection rates, and investment returns).

Use Cases

Identifying and prioritizing AI use cases is critical to ensuring that AI initiatives deliver tangible business value. Financial institutions should conduct a comprehensive assessment of their operations to identify areas where AI can have the greatest impact.

This assessment should consider factors such as:

- **Business impact**
  - What are the potential benefits of applying AI to this use case, such as increased revenue, reduced costs, or improved customer satisfaction?
- **Feasibility**
  - Does the institution have the necessary data, technology, and talent to implement AI for this use case? What are the potential barriers or challenges?
- **Strategic alignment**
  - How well does this use case align with the institution's overall business strategy and priorities?
- **Regulatory compliance**
  - What are the regulatory implications of applying AI to this use case, and how can the institution ensure compliance?

The process begins with a comprehensive assessment of operations to uncover areas where AI can significantly impact business outcomes. Customer service, for example, is an area ripe for AI-driven innovation. By deploying AI-powered chatbots and virtual assistants, businesses can provide 24/7 customer support, manage high volumes of inquiries, and offer personalized assistance. These tools not only improve customer satisfaction by providing immediate responses but also free up human agents to handle more complex issues, thereby optimizing resource allocation.

Another high-impact use case is in fraud detection and prevention. Financial institutions are constantly battling sophisticated fraud schemes that evolve rapidly. AI models, particularly those utilizing machine learning, can analyze vast datasets in real-time to detect unusual patterns and flag potentially fraudulent activities. Unlike static rule-based systems, AI can adapt to new types of fraud by learning from data, offering a dynamic and proactive defense against financial crime.

AI also shows tremendous promise in the realm of personalized financial advice and investment recommendations. Traditional financial advisory services often struggle to tailor their advice to individual clients due to the sheer volume of data and complexity involved. AI can sift through an individual's financial history, market data, and economic indicators to provide highly personalized advice. This can lead to better financial outcomes for clients, such as optimized investment portfolios that align with their risk tolerance and financial goals.

In underwriting and credit risk assessment, AI can enhance the accuracy and efficiency of decision-making processes. By analyzing a larger dataset, including non-traditional data sources, AI can provide a more comprehensive view of an applicant's creditworthiness. This approach not only speeds up the approval process but also reduces the risk of defaults by identifying potential red flags that might be missed by traditional methods.

There are also potential uses in predictive maintenance and anomaly detection for IT systems and infrastructure. Financial institutions rely on complex IT systems that are required to operate with minimal downtime. AI can monitor these systems in real-time, identifying potential issues before they escalate into significant problems. This proactive approach reduces downtime, lowers maintenance costs, and ensures the continuous operation of essential services.

These examples highlight the diverse applications of AI within financial institutions and companies of all types. As organizations continue to explore AI's potential, they should prioritize use cases based on their expected return on investment, feasibility, and alignment with strategic objectives. Starting with a few high-impact, low-complexity projects can help build momentum and demonstrate AI's value, paving the way for more ambitious initiatives in the future.

Institutions may choose to start with a few high-impact, low-complexity use cases to build momentum and demonstrate the value of AI before tackling more ambitious projects.

Resource Allocation

Implementing AI at scale requires significant resources, including: funding, talent, and technology. Effective planning helps ensure companies are allocating these resources effectively to support their AI initiatives.

When it comes to budgeting for AI projects, financial institutions must take a comprehensive approach that accounts for both upfront and ongoing costs. Upfront costs can be substantial, particularly for institutions that are just starting to build out their AI capabilities. These costs may include investments in hardware and infrastructure to support AI workloads, acquisition of AI software and tools such as machine learning frameworks and data visualization platforms, hiring new employees with specialized AI skills, and engaging external consultants and service providers to help design and implement AI solutions. Ongoing costs are equally important to consider, including expenses related to maintaining and supporting AI systems over time, providing ongoing training and development opportunities for AI talent, acquiring and managing the data needed to train and operate AI models, and ensuring compliance with relevant laws, regulations, and ethical standards. To develop a realistic budget for AI projects, financial institutions should collaborate closely with internal stakeholders across IT, finance, and business units to gain a thorough understanding of the full scope of costs associated with each initiative. Partnering with external vendors and consultants can also provide valuable insights into industry benchmarks and best practices for AI budgeting.

Financial institutions need to create a comprehensive talent strategy that encompasses both hiring new employees and upskilling existing ones. When recruiting new AI talent, institutions should seek candidates with a diverse set of skills, including technical expertise in areas like programming, statistics, and machine learning, as well as domain knowledge in financial services. Equally important are strong communication and collaboration abilities, as AI projects often involve cross-functional teamwork. To attract the best AI talent, institutions may need to provide competitive compensation packages and benefits such as flexible work arrangements, growth and development opportunities, and exposure to innovative technologies and projects. Upskilling existing employees is also crucial for building AI capabilities internally. This can involve offering in-house training programs on AI topics, providing tuition reimbursement or sponsorship for external AI certifications or degree programs, establishing mentorship programs that connect junior employees with experienced AI professionals, and creating opportunities for employees to gain hands-on experience working on AI projects and initiatives.

Data is the foundation of AI, and financial institutions must invest in building a robust data infrastructure to support AI initiatives at scale. This requires a modern, flexible data architecture capable of handling the volume, variety, and velocity of data generated by AI applications. Key components of such an architecture may include data lakes for storing structured and unstructured data in its native format, data warehouses optimized for fast querying and analysis of structured data, data integration tools for connecting and integrating data from disparate sources, data governance frameworks to ensure data quality, security, privacy, and compliance, and cloud computing solutions that provide scalable, on-demand computing resources for AI workloads. When designing their data infrastructure, financial institutions should prioritize technologies that facilitate seamless data sharing and collaboration across the organization, such as data virtualization and federation tools that enable users to access and analyze data from multiple sources without the need for data movement or replication. Adopting agile data management practices like DataOps and MLOps can also help institutions deliver AI solutions more quickly and reliably while maintaining data quality and integrity.

While developing in-house AI capabilities is crucial, financial institutions should also consider partnering with external vendors and startups to accelerate their AI initiatives. Such partnerships can offer numerous benefits, including access to specialized expertise, reduced time-to-market, and lower development costs. When assessing potential AI partners, financial institutions should evaluate several key factors, such as the vendor or startup's technical capabilities and proven track record in delivering high-quality AI solutions, their experience working with financial institutions and understanding the industry's unique challenges and requirements, their data security and privacy controls for protecting sensitive financial data, their familiarity with navigating the complex regulatory environment of the financial services industry, and their overall cultural fit and ability to collaborate effectively with internal teams and stakeholders. Financial institutions can engage with AI vendors and startups through various partnership models, such as licensing pre-built AI software and platforms, collaborating on research and development to create new AI technologies or applications that target specific business challenges, or investing directly in promising AI startups in exchange for equity or access to their technologies and expertise. Regardless of the specific partnership approach, financial institutions must establish clear governance and oversight mechanisms to manage these relationships effectively, including defining service level agreements (SLAs), establishing clear roles and responsibilities, and implementing regular performance monitoring and reporting processes.

When allocating resources for AI projects, institutions should prioritize initiatives that have the greatest potential for impact and align with their overall business strategy. They should also ensure that resources are being used efficiently and effectively by establishing clear governance structures and processes for managing AI projects.

Timelines

When setting timelines for AI projects, financial institutions must carefully consider several key factors to ensure successful implementation and long-term viability. One effective strategy is to adopt a phased approach, which involves starting with smaller, more focused AI projects and gradually scaling up over time as the institution gains experience and confidence. This incremental approach allows organizations to build momentum, learn valuable lessons from early successes and failures, and make necessary adjustments to their AI strategies and processes along the way. By tackling AI implementation in manageable stages, companies can mitigate risks, optimize resource allocation, and ensure that each phase of the project builds upon the successes of the previous one.

Iterative development can make project timelines more manageable and achievable by breaking down complex AI projects into smaller, more focused cycles of development and testing. By adopting an agile methodology, teams can continuously refine and optimize AI models and algorithms based on ongoing feedback and performance metrics. This approach not only accelerates the development process but also ensures that AI solutions are more adaptable and responsive to changing requirements or insights. For financial institutions, incorporating iterative cycles into AI project timelines allows for more robust validation, reducing the risk of errors and enhancing the overall effectiveness of the deployed solutions.

Effective stakeholder engagement is also critical when establishing timelines for AI projects. AI initiatives often involve a wide range of stakeholders, including business users, data scientists, IT teams, compliance professionals, and executive sponsors. Each of these groups brings distinct perspectives, requirements, and concerns, making it crucial to allocate adequate time for collaboration and alignment throughout the project lifecycle. This may involve conducting regular stakeholder meetings and workshops to gather feedback, address concerns, and ensure that AI solutions are being developed in line with business needs and regulatory requirements. By fostering open communication and collaboration among stakeholders, firms can minimize the risk of delays, misunderstandings, and scope creep that can derail AI projects.

Finally, financial institutions must recognize that the work of AI implementation does not end when a solution is deployed. AI models and applications require ongoing monitoring and maintenance to ensure that they continue to perform as intended and adapt to changing business needs and market conditions. This may involve regularly retraining models on new data, fine-tuning algorithms based on performance metrics, and updating infrastructure and security measures to keep pace with evolving technologies and threats. As such, project timelines should include sufficient time and resources for ongoing support and maintenance of AI solutions, with dedicated teams and processes in place to manage these activities over the long term.

To develop realistic and effective timelines for AI projects, business leaders should work closely with experienced AI vendors, consultants, and internal subject matter experts to gain a deep understanding of the technical, organizational, and regulatory challenges involved. This may involve conducting thorough feasibility studies, proof-of-concept trials, and pilot projects to validate assumptions, identify potential roadblocks, and refine project plans. By leveraging the expertise of seasoned AI practitioners and taking a data-driven approach to timeline planning, financial institutions can set themselves up for success and avoid costly delays and setbacks.

In addition to these technical considerations, financial institutions must also factor in the broader organizational and cultural changes required to support successful AI adoption. This may include initiatives to build AI literacy and skills among employees, establish governance frameworks and ethical guidelines for AI development and use, and foster a culture of innovation and experimentation. These organizational change efforts can take significant time and resources to implement effectively, and project timelines should reflect these realities.

Integration with Business Goals

To fully leverage AI, companies must embed it deeply into their business strategy, shifting from viewing AI as a side project to making it a core component of decision-making. Start by aligning AI with broader business goals, identifying where it can add the most value. For example, if a bank wants to boost customer retention, AI should enhance customer-focused personalized services. If an insurance company aims to reduce claims processing time, AI should focus on automating tasks, detecting fraud, and optimizing resources.

But aligning AI with business goals is just the first step. It must be fully integrated into the business processes and workflows it aims to improve. This requires close collaboration between AI teams and business units throughout the project lifecycle. Cross-functional teams that include technical and business representatives ensure AI solutions are relevant and seamlessly integrated. Often, this integration means redesigning workflows and redefining roles. For example, automating loan underwriting might require restructuring the credit department and updating governance to ensure responsible AI use.

Another key aspect is ensuring that AI insights are acted upon in decision-making. This requires clear communication channels and training to help stakeholders effectively apply AI-generated insights. For instance, if AI predicts customer churn, processes must be in place to relay these insights to customer service teams to take proactive retention measures.

To support ongoing AI integration, financial institutions must establish robust processes for monitoring AI performance and impact. Defining clear KPIs aligned with business objectives and tracking them regularly helps quantify AI's business value. Continuous improvement, based on real-world performance and feedback, ensures AI remains a dynamic, value-generating asset.

Finally, successful AI integration requires strong change management and organizational readiness. This includes training programs to build AI literacy, fostering a culture of innovation, and establishing clear governance frameworks for responsible AI use. By addressing these areas, institutions can ensure AI adoption is successful and sustainable, driving long-term value.

Leadership and Culture

Leadership is essential in driving the successful implementation of an AI strategy. Senior executives must do more than simply endorse AI initiatives — they need to actively champion AI by setting a clear vision for its role in the organization's future success. This vision should be consistently communicated throughout the organization, establishing AI as a strategic priority aligned with long-term goals. Leaders should highlight how AI can enhance operational efficiency, improve customer experiences, and offer a competitive advantage in the marketplace.

Fostering a culture that embraces innovation, experimentation, and data-driven decision-making is critical when it comes to AI adoption. Leaders should promote a mindset that sees AI as a catalyst for new opportunities, not as a threat to the status quo. Establishing cross-functional AI task forces that bring together IT, data science, and business units can break down silos and encourage a more integrated approach to AI implementation.

Investing in AI training and development is another part of building a pro-AI culture. By equipping employees with the skills to work effectively with AI tools, organizations ensure their workforce is prepared for AI-driven change. Leaders can also incentivize innovation by rewarding teams or individuals who successfully implement AI or identify new AI use cases, fostering a culture of creativity and competition.

Employees at all levels must be encouraged to engage with AI and understand how it enhances rather than threatens their work. Addressing concerns about job displacement is vital; leaders should communicate that AI complements human expertise by automating routine tasks and allowing employees to focus on higher-value activities. Providing clear examples of successful AI integration can help build confidence and reduce resistance to AI-driven transformation.

Chapter Twenty

BUILD VS. BUY – DEVELOPING AI CAPABILITIES IN FINANCIAL INSTITUTIONS

In this chapter, we look at the critical decision-making process that financial institutions must undertake when considering how to develop their AI capabilities: whether to build solutions in-house or to buy from external vendors. The choice between these two approaches is not just a matter of resource allocation but a strategic decision that will shape the institution's ability to innovate, compete, and meet regulatory demands in an increasingly digital universe.

We begin by examining the Build approach, which offers institutions the advantage of tailoring AI solutions to their unique needs, maintaining control over sensitive data, and retaining intellectual property. However, this path is resource-intensive, requiring significant investment in talent acquisition, infrastructure, and ongoing R&D. Building in-house can also slow down time to market, potentially hindering the institution's ability to quickly adapt to changes in the market or regulatory environment.

On the other hand, the Buy approach allows institutions to rapidly deploy advanced AI technologies by leveraging the expertise and scalable solutions provided by external vendors. This method can be more cost-effective and quicker to implement, but it comes with trade-offs, including less customization, potential dependency on vendors, and data privacy concerns. These challenges underscore the importance of rigorous vendor evaluation and strong contractual agreements to ensure that purchased solutions meet the institution's specific needs and comply with regulatory standards.

We'll also provide some guidelines to help financial institutions navigate the Build vs. Buy decision. These guidelines encourage firms to consider factors such as strategic alignment, resource availability, speed, flexibility, regulatory requirements, and long-term costs and benefits. By carefully weighing these factors, institutions can make informed decisions that not only meet their immediate needs but also position them for long-term success in the AI-driven financial landscape.

Building AI In-House: Advantages & Challenges

Advantages

Customization and Control

By building AI systems from the ground up, financial institutions can tailor these technologies to their unique business needs and strategic goals. This approach allows for precise alignment between AI capabilities and the organization's requirements, ensuring that the system addresses specific challenges and opportunities within the institution. In-house development provides ongoing control over the design and implementation of AI, enabling continuous refinement and adaptation as business conditions evolve. This flexibility is particularly valuable in a fast-changing industry like finance, where the ability to pivot quickly in response to market or regulatory changes can be a significant competitive advantage.

Intellectual Property Ownership

Another significant benefit of building AI in-house is the retention of intellectual property (IP) rights over the developed solutions. When companies create their own AI technology, they own the resulting IP, which can be a critical asset for long-term strategic value and competitive differentiation. Owning the IP allows companies to develop proprietary solutions that competitors can't easily replicate – enhancing their market positioning. Additionally, IP ownership provides the opportunity to license technology to other firms or industries, potentially creating new revenue streams. This aspect of in-house development makes it an attractive option for institutions looking to secure and leverage their technological innovations for future growth.

Data Security

The financial sector is highly regulated, and the handling of sensitive data is subject to strict compliance requirements. By developing AI systems in-house, institutions can maintain tighter control over their data, significantly reducing the risk of breaches or misuse by external vendors. This is particularly important given the increasing prevalence of cyber threats and the potential consequences of data breaches, which can include regulatory fines, reputational damage, and loss of customer trust. In-house AI development ensures that data governance practices are directly aligned with the institution's security protocols, offering peace of mind that sensitive information is managed with the highest level of care and compliance.

Challenges

Resource Intensive

Building AI capabilities in-house requires a significant investment in resources, including talent, infrastructure, and ongoing research and development. Finance firms would also have to invest in recruiting, vetting, hiring, and retaining highly skilled non-finance professionals like data scientists, machine learning engineers, and AI specialists. These roles are in high demand across multiple sectors, making it difficult to attract top talent, particularly in a market where compensation expectations are high. Additionally, developing the necessary infrastructure to support AI initiatives, including data storage, processing capabilities, and advanced analytics platforms, requires substantial capital investment. Beyond the initial setup, institutions must also allocate resources for continuous development, ensuring that their AI models and systems remain cutting-edge and effective over time.

Time to Market

The amount of time it takes to develop AI solutions from scratch is an important consideration. The process of designing, building, testing, and deploying AI models is inherently complex and can lead to delays in bringing AI tools to market. This delay can be particularly detrimental in industries where speed of change can be a critical factor in maintaining a competitive edge. Institutions must carefully balance the benefits of highly customized AI solutions with the need for timely deployment. In scenarios where rapid implementation is crucial, the extended time frames associated with in-house development could result in missed opportunities, allowing competitors who adopt off-the-shelf solutions to gain an advantage.

Scalability

Firms have to plan for scalability of their AI projects out of the gates. The system requirements on day one are different than those on day 365, which may involve handling larger datasets, increasing user loads, and adapting to new business processes or regulatory requirements. Achieving this scalability is usually not just adding more hardware or processing power; it requires continuous improvement of the AI models and systems themselves. This includes retraining models with new data, optimizing algorithms for efficiency, and ensuring that the underlying infrastructure can support the growing demands. The technical expertise required to manage this complexity is significant, and institutions must be prepared to invest in both the human and technological resources necessary to ensure that their AI capabilities can scale alongside their business.

Buying AI Solutions: Advantages and Challenges

Advantages:

Faster Deployment

The clearest advantage for purchasing AI solutions is the speed with which they can be deployed. Ready-made, scalable solutions that have already been tested and refined across various implementations make a lot of sense for companies seeking to deploy AI solutions quickly. This rapid deployment can be particularly beneficial in a fast-paced financial environment where time is often of the essence, enabling institutions to realize the benefits of AI, such as improved efficiency and enhanced customer experiences, in a much shorter time frame. By leveraging the pre-built capabilities of off-the-shelf solutions, institutions can bypass the lengthy development cycles associated with in-house builds and gain a competitive advantage more swiftly.

Access to Expertise

For non-technology companies, it can be difficult to build strong AI skills in-house – especially when these skills are outside of the firm's core competencies. Vetting and hiring AI teams and recruiting top talent from a competitive market is a difficult ask. So when companies are able to engage with external vendors who are experts in AI, they can access resources that might be difficult to cultivate internally. These vendors often have a deep understanding of AI technologies and their applications in the financial sector, gained through working with multiple clients and across various use cases. This breadth of experience allows vendors to offer insights and best practices that can significantly enhance the effectiveness of AI implementations. For institutions that may lack the in-house talent or resources to develop AI solutions from the ground up, partnering with vendors can be a strategic way to bridge the knowledge gap and ensure that the AI solutions deployed are robust, scalable, and aligned with industry standards.

Cost Efficiency

Purchasing AI solutions can also be more cost-effective in the short term compared to building them in-house. By avoiding the substantial upfront costs associated with recruiting specialized talent, developing the necessary infrastructure, and conducting ongoing research and development, financial institutions can manage their budgets more effectively. Vendors often offer flexible pricing models, such as subscription services or pay-as-you-go options, which can help institutions scale their AI investments according to their needs and financial capacity. This cost efficiency is particularly appealing for smaller institutions or those that are just beginning their AI journey, as it allows them to access cutting-edge technologies without the significant financial and operational burden of developing these capabilities internally.

Challenges:

Less Customization

While many vendors do offer some degree of flexibility in adapting their products to meet the specific needs of financial institutions, these solutions may not be as finely tuned to an organization's unique business requirements as an in-house developed solution would be. The pre-built nature of vendor solutions often means that they are designed to be broadly applicable across various clients and industries, which can lead to limitations in how well they align with the specific workflows, data structures, and strategic goals of a particular institution. For institutions with highly specialized needs or innovative strategies, this lack of customization can be a significant drawback, potentially limiting the effectiveness and impact of the AI solution.

Dependence on Vendors

Relying on external vendors for AI solutions can lead to a significant dependency, which might hinder an institution's ability to adapt or evolve the solution as their business needs change. This dependency is particularly concerning in rapidly changing financial markets, where agility and the ability to pivot quickly are crucial. When a financial institution relies heavily on a vendor, they may find it challenging to make modifications or upgrades to the AI system without the vendor's involvement, potentially leading to delays and additional costs. Furthermore, there is the risk of vendor lock-in, where switching to a different provider or transitioning to an in-house solution becomes prohibitively expensive or technically difficult. This can limit the institution's flexibility and strategic options, making it harder to respond to new market opportunities or regulatory changes.

Data Privacy Concerns

When working with external vendors, data privacy and security concerns become paramount. Financial institutions handle significant amounts of sensitive customer data, and ensuring this data is protected when it is shared with or processed by third-party vendors is critical. There is always a risk that data could be mishandled or that security protocols may not be as stringent as required by the financial institution's own standards or by regulatory requirements. To mitigate these risks, it is essential that institutions conduct thorough due diligence on vendors' data protection practices, ensure that robust data sharing agreements are in place, and regularly audit vendor compliance with data privacy standards. Failure to adequately manage these concerns can lead to data breaches, regulatory fines, and damage to the institution's reputation.

Guidelines for Choosing Between Build and Buy

There are several key factors to consider when deciding whether to buy or build AI solutions:

Strategic Alignment

Companies should consider how closely any solution aligns with their long-term strategic goals. If the AI initiative is central to the firm's competitive differentiation or directly tied to key business outcomes, building an in-house solution may be the preferable option. Building a solution would allow for customization and ensure that the AI system evolves in lockstep with the institution's strategy. Conversely, if the AI application is more tactical or peripheral, purchasing an off-the-shelf solution might be sufficient – allowing the company to benefit from pre-built functionality without diverting resources from core strategic activities.

Resource Availability

Developing AI capabilities in-house requires a significant investment in talent, technology, and ongoing research and development. Institutions with robust internal capabilities — including a skilled data science team, advanced infrastructure, and appropriate budget — may be well-positioned to build solutions themselves. But for institutions with limited resources or companies facing challenges in recruiting and retaining AI talent, buying a solution from an established vendor can provide a quicker and more efficient path to AI adoption. Buying existing software lets companies leverage external expertise and focus internal resources on other strategic priorities.

Speed and Flexibility

If rapid deployment is essential — perhaps due to competitive pressures or market opportunities — purchasing a ready-made solution from a vendor can offer a quicker path to market. Vendor solutions are typically designed for fast implementation and can be integrated with existing systems with minimal disruption. On the other hand, if the AI application requires a high degree of flexibility or customization, or if the institution anticipates frequent changes in business needs, building the solution in-house may provide the necessary adaptability and control.

Regulatory and Security Considerations

Financial institutions operate in a heavily regulated environment, and AI solutions must comply with stringent data privacy, security, and regulatory standards. In-house development offers more control over these factors, allowing the institution to tailor the AI system to meet specific regulatory requirements and internal security protocols. This, of course, assumes that the company has the appropriate team and resources in-house to assure compliance.

Conversely, if the institution chooses to buy, it is imperative to select a vendor with a strong track record in regulatory compliance and data security. Institutions should conduct thorough due diligence to ensure that the vendor's solutions meet all necessary standards and that robust data protection measures are in place.

Long-Term Costs and Benefits

Finally, financial institutions must consider the total cost of ownership over the long term. Building an AI solution in-house often involves higher upfront costs due to the need for specialized talent, infrastructure, and ongoing R&D, but can yield significant long-term benefits. On the other hand, buying a solution may be more cost-effective initially, but firms should evaluate potential costs related to vendor dependency, licensing fees, and the need for future upgrades. Both approaches should be carefully weighed not just in terms of immediate cost but in light of their long-term value and impact on the institution's strategic objectives.

By carefully considering strategic alignment, resource availability, speed, flexibility, regulatory compliance, security, and long-term costs, companies can make informed decisions on whether to build AI capabilities in-house or purchase them from external vendors.

This decision isn't just about the tech. It's a strategic choice that will significantly influence the trajectory of the institution's AI initiatives. It will determine how effectively the institution can innovate, respond to market changes, and meet regulatory requirements going forward. A well-considered strategy that balances these factors will position the institution not only to meet current demands, but to evolve with the industry and technology.

Chapter Twenty One

MEASURING THE VALUE OF AI

Defining Success Metrics

As finance professionals we understand the importance of measuring the return on investment (ROI) for any project – AI projects are no exception. Defining the right success metrics is key to evaluating the performance of these projects and ensuring they contribute to the overall business objectives.

Key performance indicators for AI initiatives should be carefully selected to align with the specific goals of the project, and should include both quantitative and qualitative measures.

Quantitative KPIs might include metrics like increased revenue, reduced operational costs, improved loan approval times, or enhanced fraud detection rates. An AI-driven fraud detection system, for example, might be evaluated based on the reduction in fraud-related losses or the speed at which fraudulent transactions are identified and stopped.

Qualitative metrics are equally important, particularly when evaluating the impact of AI on customer satisfaction or employee engagement. Qualitative metrics might include customer satisfaction scores, net promoter scores (NPS), and employee feedback on the usability of AI tools.

By balancing quantitative and qualitative measures, businesses can better obtain a holistic view of the success of the projects and make more informed decisions about where to focus future efforts.

There are challenges, however, to traditional ROI calculation methods, which can be difficult for finance leaders to digest. For example, AI often delivers intangible benefits like increased agility and competitiveness, which are difficult to quantify using standard financial metrics. Additionally, the long-term impact and indirect effects of AI implementations can make it challenging to attribute specific financial gains to these investments.

Limitations of Traditional ROI Calculations

Traditional ROI calculations primarily focus on quantifying the efficiency gains and cost savings that result from implementing new systems or processes. While this approach has been effective in evaluating many types of investments, it may not fully capture the value delivered by artificial intelligence (AI) investments.

Let's dig in to understand why.

Efficiency-focused ROI and its shortcomings

Conventional ROI calculations emphasize the measurable, tangible benefits of technology investments (e.g. reduced labor costs, increased productivity, streamlined operations). And the metrics used to quantify these benefits (headcount reduction or maybe process cycle time improvement) are relatively straightforward to measure and provide a clear picture of the direct financial impact of an investment.

But the true value proposition of AI investments could extend far beyond simple efficiency gains. With AI, we're talking about a likely transformative technology that will shift the very underpinnings of financial services. By focusing solely on cost savings and productivity improvements, traditional methods may underestimate the true potential of AI in driving innovation, enhancing decision-making, and creating new opportunities for growth.

Hard-to-quantify benefits of AI

AI is more than just an incremental tech gain. If fully realized, it could be harnessed to shift the industry itself. Let's look at a couple of the promises of this new technology.

Agility

AI has the potential to enable companies to quickly adapt to changing market conditions, regulatory requirements, and customer needs. By leveraging AI-powered analytics and automation, organizations can make data-driven decisions in real-time and rapidly adjust their strategies and operations accordingly. This enhanced agility can be a significant competitive advantage, allowing financial institutions to seize new opportunities and navigate challenges more effectively.

Competitiveness

AI can help organizations gain a competitive edge in the market by uncovering insights, identifying trends, and enabling innovative solutions. For example, AI-powered analytics could help identify new business opportunities, optimize pricing strategies, and personalize customer experiences. These capabilities could lead to increased market share, higher customer satisfaction, and greater customer loyalty. While the impact of these benefits on the bottom line may not be immediately apparent, they can have a substantial effect on the long-term success and growth of the organization.

Effectiveness

As we've discussed throughout this book, AI has the potential to improve the effectiveness of financial functions from investment analysis to risk management and fraud detection.

By processing big data and identifying patterns that human analysts might overlook, AI can enhance the accuracy and timeliness of decision-making. This improved effectiveness can lead to better risk mitigation, reduced fraud losses, and more profitable investment strategies. Although the financial impact of these benefits may not be as easily quantifiable as direct cost savings, they can have a significant impact on the overall performance and resilience of the organization in the long run.

The challenge with these hard-to-quantify benefits is that they are often overlooked or undervalued by traditional ROI calculations that focus on tangible, short-term financial gains. In the case of AI, this could lead to an incomplete picture of the true value of associated investments.

The need for a more comprehensive approach

A more comprehensive approach to ROI calculation should take into account both the quantifiable efficiency gains and the hard-to-quantify benefits that it could potentially deliver. And let's keep in mind here the word "potentially." The technology, after all, is only as good as its implementation. But assuming managers are able to execute on the deployment of this technology, the ROI is strong.

Unique Challenges of Calculating AI ROI

There are some unique challenges when calculating ROI for AI projects resulting from the inherent characteristics of AI technologies and their impact on financial institutions. Understanding these challenges is crucial for developing an effective approach to measuring AI value.

Intangible benefits

As discussed in the previous section, AI delivers many intangible benefits like increased agility, competitiveness, and effectiveness. These benefits are often difficult to quantify in monetary terms, which makes it challenging to include them in traditional ROI calculations. But they must be considered to gain a comprehensive understanding of AI projects' impact.

Long-term impact

AI investments often have a long-term horizon, with the full benefits materializing over an extended period. Unlike traditional technology investments that typically deliver immediate efficiency gains, AI projects may require a longer timeframe to demonstrate their true value. This long-term impact can make it difficult to accurately predict and measure the ROI of AI investments in the short term.

Indirect effects

AI technologies can have far-reaching effects on various aspects of a financial institution's operations. For example, an AI-powered customer service chatbot may not only reduce customer support costs but also improve customer satisfaction, leading to increased customer retention and revenue growth. These indirect effects can be challenging to attribute directly to the AI investment, making it difficult to capture their full value in ROI calculations.

Evolving technology

With the incredible pace of AI development and constant emergence of new technologies, the potential value of AI investments may change over time. This dynamic nature of

AI technology requires finance professionals to regularly reassess and update their ROI calculations to ensure they accurately reflect the current and future value of AI projects.

Talent and skills gap

Implementing and maintaining AI systems requires specialized talent and skills, which can be scarce and expensive. The cost of hiring, training, and retaining AI talent should be factored into the ROI calculation. Additionally, the potential impact of skill gaps on the successful implementation and realization of AI benefits must be considered.

A Structured Approach to Calculating AI ROI

To effectively measure the value of AI investments, finance professionals need a structured approach that addresses the unique challenges discussed in the previous section. This approach should be comprehensive, flexible, and adaptable to the specific needs of each AI project.

1. Conduct a Risk Assessment

The first step in calculating AI ROI is understanding the risks associated with the project. These risks can impact the project's success and, ultimately, the return on investment. A thorough risk assessment will help mitigate potential issues and ensure that the project aligns with the organization's risk tolerance.

Key Actions

- **Identify Risks**: Start by listing all potential risks, including data privacy issues, algorithmic bias, regulatory compliance challenges, and potential job displacement. Each AI project will have unique risks depending on its scope, objectives, and environment.
- **Evaluate Risks**: Assess the likelihood and potential impact of each identified risk. This can be done using a risk matrix or similar tool to prioritize risks that require immediate attention versus those that are less critical.
- **Mitigate Risks**: Develop strategies to mitigate the identified risks. For example, implementing robust data governance practices can address data privacy concerns, while regular audits and bias detection tools can help manage algorithmic bias.
- **Align with Objectives**: Ensure that your risk mitigation strategies align with the project's overall objectives and metrics. For instance, if reducing operational costs is a key objective, the cost of risk mitigation should not outweigh the anticipated savings.

Example

In a project aiming to implement AI for automated loan approvals, data privacy risks can be mitigated by using encrypted data and limiting access to sensitive information. Algorithmic bias can be addressed by training the model on a diverse dataset and conducting regular fairness assessments.

2. Define Clear Objectives and Metrics

Defining clear objectives and metrics is crucial for measuring the success of the AI project and calculating its ROI. Objectives should be aligned with the broader business strategy, and metrics should be tailored to reflect the specific outcomes desired from the AI implementation.

Key Actions

- **Align Objectives:** Work with stakeholders to ensure that the objectives of the AI project align with the company's strategic goals. Objectives should be specific to the challenges the AI is intended to address, such as reducing operational inefficiencies, improving customer satisfaction, or enhancing predictive capabilities.
- **Set SMART KPIs:** Develop Specific, Measurable, Achievable, Relevant, and Time-bound (SMART) key performance indicators (KPIs) to track progress. For example, if the objective is to reduce operational costs, a KPI might be the percentage decrease in manual processing time.
- **Document Objectives:** Clearly document the objectives and KPIs, ensuring that all stakeholders have a shared understanding of what success looks like.

Example

For an AI project focused on improving customer service through chatbots, objectives could include reducing average response time by 50% and increasing customer satisfaction scores by 20%. Corresponding KPIs would track these specific metrics over time.

3. Perform a Stakeholder Analysis

Understanding the needs, expectations, and concerns of all stakeholders is vital to the success of the AI project. A comprehensive stakeholder analysis ensures that the ROI calculation considers the perspectives of those who will be impacted by or benefit from the project.

Key Actions

- **Identify Stakeholders:** List all individuals, teams, and departments that will be affected by the AI project. This includes internal stakeholders like IT, finance, and operations, as well as external parties such as customers, vendors, and regulators.

- **Engage Stakeholders:** Conduct interviews, surveys, or workshops to gather input from stakeholders. This helps in understanding their expectations, concerns, and the value they anticipate from the AI project.
- **Incorporate Perspectives:** Use the insights gained from stakeholder engagement to refine the project objectives, metrics, and ROI calculation. Address any concerns and ensure that the project delivers value across the board.
- **Manage Expectations:** Clearly communicate the expected outcomes, potential risks, and timelines to stakeholders to manage their expectations throughout the project lifecycle.

Example

In an AI-driven supply chain optimization project, stakeholders may include logistics managers, suppliers, and customers. Engaging with these groups can help identify potential bottlenecks, align the AI system with their needs, and ensure a smooth implementation.

4. Establish a Baseline

Establishing a baseline is essential for comparing pre- and post-implementation performance, enabling a clear measurement of the AI project's impact. This baseline provides the reference point against which improvements and ROI are measured.

Key Actions

- **Collect Historical Data:** Gather data on current performance related to the metrics you've identified. This may include data on process efficiency, error rates, customer satisfaction, or revenue, depending on the project's focus.
- **Analyze Trends:** Look for trends in the historical data to ensure the baseline is accurate and reflective of normal operations. This can involve analyzing data over multiple periods to account for seasonality or other variations.
- **Document the Baseline:** Clearly document the baseline metrics, ensuring that they are agreed upon by all stakeholders. This documentation will be crucial when comparing the AI system's performance post-implementation.

Example

For a predictive maintenance AI project in manufacturing, the baseline might include the average downtime of machinery, the frequency of equipment failures, and the associated repair costs over the past two years.

5. Assess Data Quality and Availability

The success of an AI project heavily depends on the quality and availability of data. Poor data quality can lead to inaccurate predictions and flawed decision-making, while data scarcity can limit the effectiveness of the AI system. Assessing these factors upfront helps in setting realistic ROI expectations and identifying potential challenges.

Key Actions

- **Evaluate Data Sources:** Identify all data sources that will feed into the AI system. Evaluate the completeness, accuracy, and consistency of this data, considering whether it adequately represents the variables relevant to the project's objectives.
- **Identify Data Gaps:** Determine if there are any gaps in the data that could hinder the AI's performance. These gaps might include missing data points, outdated information, or incomplete records.
- **Plan for Data Improvement:** If data quality issues are identified, develop a plan to address them. This might involve cleaning the data, acquiring additional datasets, or enhancing data collection processes.
- **Adjust ROI Expectations:** Recognize that data quality and availability can directly impact the AI system's effectiveness and, therefore, the expected ROI. Adjust your ROI calculations to account for potential data-related risks.

Example

In a retail AI project aimed at personalized marketing, assessing data quality might involve evaluating customer purchase history, browsing behavior, and demographic data. If gaps or inconsistencies are found, the project team might decide to invest in data enrichment services before proceeding.

6. Calculate Total Investment Costs

Accurately calculating the total investment costs of an AI project is critical for determining ROI. This step ensures that all direct, indirect, and potential future costs are accounted for, providing a complete financial picture of the AI initiative.

Key Actions

- **Identify Direct Costs:** List all immediate and tangible expenses related to the AI project. These include hardware and software purchases, data acquisition, implementation, and integration costs. Additionally, factor in any training and development expenses required to equip your team with the necessary skills.
- **Consider Indirect Costs:** Capture the less obvious costs that might arise during the project lifecycle. These can include the opportunity cost of reallocating

resources from other projects, potential disruptions during implementation, and the costs associated with ongoing maintenance and support.

- **Account for Personnel Costs:** Include the salaries, benefits, and other compensation for all personnel involved in the project, such as data scientists, AI engineers, project managers, and support staff. Ensure you consider both full-time and part-time contributions.
- **Factor in Potential Future Costs:** Consider future costs that might arise as the AI system evolves. This could include upgrades, scaling, additional training, or the need for new data sources as the AI project expands.
- **Estimate the Entire Lifecycle Cost:** Combine all identified costs to estimate the total investment over the entire lifecycle of the AI project, from initial development to ongoing operation and eventual decommissioning.

Example

For an AI-driven customer service chatbot project, total costs might include software licensing fees, server costs for hosting, data integration expenses, initial and ongoing training for customer service representatives, and the salaries of the development team.

7. Measure Direct Financial Benefits

Measuring direct financial benefits is essential to understanding the tangible returns generated by the AI project. This involves quantifying cost savings, revenue increases, and other direct financial gains attributable to the AI implementation.

Key Actions

- **Identify Cost Savings:** Determine the areas where the AI project reduces costs, such as automation of manual processes, reduced error rates, improved resource allocation, or decreased downtime. Quantify these savings in monetary terms.
- **Quantify Revenue Increases:** Assess how the AI system has directly contributed to revenue growth. This could be through increased sales, enhanced pricing strategies, improved product recommendations, or new revenue streams enabled by AI-driven innovations.
- **Assess Fraud Reduction and Loss Prevention:** If applicable, measure the financial impact of AI in reducing fraud, preventing losses, or improving collections. Calculate the monetary value of reduced fraud incidents or recovered amounts.
- **Compare Against Baseline:** Use the established baseline metrics to compare pre- and post-implementation performance. This comparison helps quantify the financial benefits directly resulting from the AI project.
- **Calculate the Monetary Value of Improvements:** Translate the improvements observed into specific dollar amounts. This can involve

converting time savings into labor cost reductions, or translating increased customer engagement into revenue growth.

Example

In a fraud detection AI project, direct financial benefits might include a reduction in fraud-related losses by 30%, leading to significant cost savings. Additionally, by preventing potential fraud, the company might see an increase in trust and customer retention, contributing to revenue growth.

8. Estimate Indirect and Intangible Benefits

Indirect and intangible benefits, while harder to quantify, play a significant role in the overall value of an AI project. These benefits include enhanced decision-making, improved customer experience, and a stronger competitive position.

Key Actions

- **Identify Indirect Benefits:** List the non-financial advantages that the AI project provides. These could include better decision-making capabilities, faster response times, or improved compliance with regulations.
- **Quantify Intangible Benefits:** Use proxy measures or estimation techniques to assign a monetary value to intangible benefits. For example, improved customer satisfaction can be estimated using metrics like customer lifetime value (CLV) or net promoter score (NPS).
- **Use Specific Metrics or Proxy Measures:** Where possible, apply specific metrics or proxies to measure intangible benefits. For instance, employee satisfaction might be reflected in lower turnover rates, while innovation capabilities might be gauged by the number of new products or services launched.
- **Emphasize Storytelling:** Contextualize intangible benefits through storytelling, illustrating how the AI project contributes to broader business goals. This can help stakeholders appreciate the value of these benefits, even if they are not easily quantified.
- **Consider Long-Term Impact:** Think about the long-term advantages of the AI project, such as the organization's ability to adapt to future challenges, the strengthening of its brand reputation, or the development of a more innovative culture.

Example

In an AI-driven customer experience project, intangible benefits might include a 20% increase in customer satisfaction scores, leading to higher customer loyalty and a potential increase in repeat business over time.

9. Apply the ROI Formula

After quantifying both costs and benefits, applying the ROI formula provides a clear financial measure of the return on the AI investment. This calculation helps stakeholders understand the value generated relative to the amount invested.

Key Actions

- **Calculate Total Benefits:** Sum up both the direct financial benefits and the estimated value of indirect and intangible benefits. Ensure that all benefits are appropriately accounted for and clearly documented.
- **Sum Total Costs:** Add up all identified costs, including direct, indirect, and potential future expenses. This ensures that the ROI calculation reflects the full financial commitment of the AI project.
- **Apply the ROI Formula:** Use the standard ROI formula to calculate the return on investment:

$$ROI = \left(\frac{Total\ Benefits - Total\ Costs}{Total\ Costs} \right) \times 100$$

This formula will yield a percentage that represents the return generated for every dollar invested in the AI project.

- **Interpret the ROI:** Analyze the ROI result to determine whether the AI project meets the organization's financial expectations. A positive ROI indicates a profitable investment, while a negative ROI suggests that the project may not have delivered the expected value.

Example

If an AI project generated $1.5 million in total benefits with total costs of $1 million, the ROI would be:

$$ROI = \left(\frac{1,500,000 - 1,000,000}{1,000,000} \right) \times 100 = 50\%$$

This indicates a 50% return on the investment, meaning the project returned $0.50 for every dollar spent.

10. Conduct a Sensitivity Analysis

Sensitivity analysis examines how changes in key variables affect the ROI calculation. This step is crucial for understanding the impact of uncertainties and assumptions on the project's financial outcomes.

Key Actions

- **Identify Critical Variables:** Determine which variables have the most significant impact on the ROI calculation. These could include adoption rates, data quality, market conditions, or operational efficiency.
- **Assess Impact of Variable Changes:** Analyze how variations in these critical variables affect the ROI. For example, explore how different adoption rates among users or fluctuations in market demand might influence the project's success.
- **Perform Scenario Analysis:** Create different scenarios (e.g., best-case, worst-case, and most-likely) to understand how the ROI might vary under different conditions. This helps in identifying potential risks and opportunities.
- **Adjust Project Plans Accordingly:** Use the insights gained from the sensitivity analysis to refine project plans, mitigate risks, or adjust expectations. This ensures that the project remains resilient to changes and uncertainties.

Example

In an AI project for predictive maintenance, sensitivity analysis might reveal that the ROI is highly dependent on the accuracy of failure predictions. A scenario where prediction accuracy drops by 10% could result in a significantly lower ROI, prompting the need for additional data collection or model improvements.

11. Emphasize Continuous Monitoring and Iteration

AI projects are dynamic, and their impact can evolve over time. Continuous monitoring and iteration ensure that the AI system remains effective and that the ROI calculation stays relevant as new data and business conditions emerge.

Key Actions

- **Implement Ongoing Monitoring:** Set up systems to continuously track the performance of the AI project against the defined objectives and metrics. Regularly review the data to identify trends, issues, or opportunities for improvement.
- **Update ROI Calculation:** Periodically recalculate the ROI using updated cost and benefit data. This helps in maintaining an accurate understanding of the project's value over time.

- **Encourage Agility and Adaptability:** Foster a culture of agility within the project team, encouraging them to adapt the AI system based on new insights or changing business needs. This might involve refining algorithms, adjusting data inputs, or expanding the scope of the project.
- **Conduct Regular Reviews:** Schedule regular reviews with stakeholders to discuss the ongoing performance of the AI project, address any concerns, and make necessary adjustments. These reviews ensure that the project continues to deliver value and remains aligned with the organization's goals.

Example

For an AI-driven marketing optimization project, continuous monitoring might involve regularly assessing campaign performance and customer feedback. If a new trend or behavior emerges, the AI system can be adjusted to capitalize on the opportunity, ensuring sustained ROI.

By following this structured approach and considering both quantifiable and hard-to-quantify benefits, finance professionals can develop a more accurate and holistic understanding of the value generated by AI investments. This understanding is essential for making informed decisions about resource allocation, project prioritization, and strategic planning.

Remember, however, that measuring AI value is not a one-time exercise. The dynamic nature of AI projects requires continuous monitoring, iteration, and adaptation. CFOs and finance teams must establish processes for regularly reviewing the performance of AI initiatives, updating ROI calculations, and adjusting project plans based on new insights and changing business conditions.

Moreover, the successful measurement and realization of AI value depends on close collaboration between finance and other key stakeholders, such as IT, operations, and business leaders. By fostering cross-functional partnerships and promoting AI literacy across the organization, financial institutions can create a shared understanding of the potential and challenges of AI, enabling more effective decision-making and value creation.

Chapter Twenty Two

AI GOVERNANCE AND RISK MANAGEMENT

Establishing AI Governance

AI governance involves creating a structured approach to managing AI initiatives: from development and deployment to ongoing monitoring and refinement. This framework serves as a foundation for ensuring that AI systems are designed, implemented, and used responsibly and effectively across the organization.

Effective AI governance starts with clear leadership and accountability. Businesses should designate specific roles and responsibilities for AI oversight, including the creation of an AI governance board or committee that includes stakeholders from across all departments and divisions. This group is responsible for setting AI policies, establishing guidelines for ethical AI usage, and ensuring that AI projects are in line with the institution's risk appetite and regulatory obligations.

The governance framework should also include a set of standardized processes for AI project lifecycle management, including procedures for model development and deployment, as well as protocols for addressing any issues that arise during the AI system's operation. By formalizing these processes, institutions can ensure consistency, transparency, and accountability in their AI initiatives.

Risk Management Frameworks

As with any new technology, AI introduces new risks and challenges for financial institutions. To address these risks, companies will have to develop comprehensive risk management frameworks that specifically address these challenges. For firms building their own AI models, this will be especially important. The greatest risk with these models is that they could potentially create inaccurate, unreliable, or biased outputs, which could lead to significant financial losses or reputational damage.

To mitigate model risk, institutions should implement rigorous model validation processes, including stress testing, scenario analysis, and backtesting. These processes help ensure that AI models perform as expected under various conditions, and that any potential issues are identified and addressed before the models are deployed in live environments. Additionally, institutions should establish continuous monitoring systems to track the performance of AI models over time and make necessary adjustments as market conditions or business needs change.

With the sensitive nature of financial data, data privacy becomes another critical risk. Financial institutions will have to ensure that their AI systems comply with data protection regulations, such as the General Data Protection Regulation (GDPR) in Europe or the California Consumer Privacy Act (CCPA) in the United States. This involves implementing clear data governance practices that address data anonymization, encryption, and access controls to protect customer information from unauthorized access or breaches.

Algorithmic bias is another risk that can undermine the fairness and accuracy of AI systems. Bias can enter AI models through biased training data or flawed model design, leading to discriminatory outcomes that may violate regulatory standards and ethical principles. To address this risk, institutions should conduct regular bias audits of their AI models, using techniques like fairness testing and bias mitigation algorithms to identify and correct any unintended biases.

Compliance and Transparency

Compliance with relevant laws and regulations is a cornerstone of AI governance and risk management. Financial institutions must ensure that their AI systems adhere to all applicable regulatory requirements, including those related to consumer protection, data privacy, and discrimination. This requires staying informed about evolving regulations and engaging with regulators to understand how AI technologies are expected to comply with existing legal frameworks.

Transparency is also crucial in maintaining trust with customers, regulators, and other stakeholders. Institutions should strive to make their AI decision-making processes as transparent as possible, providing clear explanations of how AI models work and how decisions are made. This transparency is particularly important in areas like credit scoring, where customers have a right to understand the factors that influenced their credit decisions. Techniques like explainable AI (XAI) can help institutions provide more interpretable and understandable AI outputs, making it easier to meet regulatory requirements and build customer confidence.

Ethical Considerations

The ethical implications of AI in finance are far-reaching, and addressing these challenges requires a commitment to responsible AI practices. Financial institutions must consider the potential societal impacts of their AI systems, particularly in areas like fairness, accountability, and customer rights.

One key ethical consideration is ensuring that AI systems don't perpetuate or exacerbate existing inequalities. For example, if an AI model used for loan approvals systematically disadvantages certain demographic groups, it could contribute to financial exclusion and social inequality. To prevent this, institutions must proactively test their AI models for fairness and take steps to eliminate any biases that are identified.

Another ethical challenge is maintaining accountability for AI-driven decisions. While AI systems can make decisions autonomously, the institution remains responsible for the outcomes of those decisions. This means that institutions must establish clear lines of accountability for AI-related risks and ensure that there is always a human in the loop who can intervene if necessary.

Additionally, institutions must respect customer rights in the context of AI, particularly regarding data privacy and informed consent. Customers should be fully informed about how their data is being used by AI systems and have the ability to opt out or request corrections if they believe their data has been misused.

By integrating these ethical considerations into their AI governance and risk management frameworks, financial institutions can not only comply with regulatory requirements but also build trust with customers and the broader public. As AI continues to transform the financial industry, maintaining a strong ethical foundation will be essential for ensuring that AI is used in a way that benefits society as a whole.

Step 1: Align AI Initiatives with Business Strategy

Start by ensuring your AI strategy is fully aligned with your institution's broader business objectives. Identify specific goals that AI can help achieve, such as improving customer service, enhancing risk management, or increasing operational efficiency. Establish clear, measurable objectives that are tied to these business goals, and ensure that all AI projects are designed to contribute directly to these strategic priorities.

Key Actions:
- Set measurable AI objectives.
- Collaborate with business leaders, data scientists, and IT teams to ensure alignment.
- Define metrics to track the success of AI initiatives.

Step 2: Identify and Prioritize AI Use Cases

Conduct a thorough assessment of your organization's operations to identify areas where AI can have the most significant impact. Focus on use cases that offer high potential for business value, feasibility, and alignment with your strategic goals. Prioritize these use cases, starting with those that are low-complexity and high-impact to get some "quick wins" and demonstrate the value of AI early on.

Key Actions:
- Evaluate potential AI use cases across different functions.
- Prioritize use cases based on expected ROI, feasibility, and strategic alignment.
- Begin with pilot projects to build momentum and refine AI capabilities.

Step 3: Allocate Resources Effectively

Implementing AI requires a substantial investment in resources, including funding, talent, and technology infrastructure. Develop a comprehensive budget that accounts for both upfront costs and ongoing expenses. The team should consist of skilled professionals and be funded by adequate investment in necessary data infrastructure. Consider partnerships with AI vendors to supplement in-house capabilities and accelerate the implementation process.

Key Actions:
- Create a detailed budget for AI initiatives.
- Invest in recruiting and training AI talent.
- Build or enhance data infrastructure to support AI workloads.
- Partner with external vendors where necessary.

Step 4: Develop a Realistic Timeline

Set a clear roadmap for AI implementation, including realistic timelines for each phase of the project. Start with smaller, manageable projects and scale up as your organization gains experience. Include time for iterative development, stakeholder engagement, and change management. Ensure that timelines account for ongoing maintenance and support.

Key Actions:
- Develop a phased approach to AI deployment.
- Include iterative development cycles in your timeline.
- Engage stakeholders throughout the project lifecycle.
- Plan for long-term support and maintenance.

Step 5: Integrate AI with Business Processes

Ensure that AI initiatives are fully embedded within the organization's business processes. Establish cross-functional teams to facilitate collaboration between AI experts and business units. Redesign workflows as needed to integrate AI solutions effectively, and ensure that AI-generated insights are actionable and incorporated into decision-making processes.

Key Actions:
- Establish cross-functional AI teams.
- Redesign workflows to integrate AI solutions.
- Ensure that AI insights are effectively communicated and acted upon.
- Monitor and evaluate the impact of AI on business processes.

Step 6: Establish AI Governance and Risk Management

Create a governance framework to oversee AI initiatives, ensuring they align with regulatory requirements, ethical standards, and organizational goals. Implement risk management practices to address model risk, data privacy, and algorithmic bias. Ensure transparency in AI decision-making and maintain compliance with all relevant regulations.

Key Actions:
- Form an AI governance board or committee.
- Implement model validation and monitoring processes.
- Ensure data privacy and security compliance.
- Conduct regular bias audits and ensure transparency in AI systems.

Step 7: Measure, Evaluate, and Continuously Improve

Define success metrics at the onset, and regularly measure the performance of AI initiatives. Calculate the ROI of AI projects by evaluating cost savings, revenue generation, and risk reduction. Commit to continuous improvement by refining AI models, updating processes, and incorporating new technologies as they emerge.

Key Actions:
- Define and track key performance indicators (KPIs) for AI initiatives.
- Calculate and monitor the ROI of AI projects.
- Implement processes for continuous feedback and improvement.
- Stay updated with AI advancements and integrate new tools and methods.

Chapter Twenty Three

EMERGING AI TECHNOLOGIES AND THEIR IMPLICATIONS FOR FINANCE

The financial industry has long been a leader in adopting new technologies – from electronic trading to online banking. Now, AI is driving even greater changes at a pace never before seen from prior technologies. These changes are transforming everything from corporate finance and regulatory compliance to trading and risk management. With its ability to process immense datasets, identify patterns, and make autonomous decisions, AI offers unprecedented opportunities for efficiency and innovation across the finance profession. But these advancements come with challenges, such as evolving regulatory compliance, ensuring explainability and addressing potential biases.

Finance professionals would need a magic crystal ball to know exactly where this technology is headed and when, but the industry leaders in generative AI have laid out a plan for their aspirations.

Emerging AI Technologies

OpenAI, a leading research organization and technology company dedicated to developing artificial intelligence, outlined five steps to Artificial Super Intelligence that serve as a pretty good representation of where the industry aspires to go.

OpenAI is an artificial intelligence research organization founded in December 2015, focused on ensuring that artificial general intelligence benefits all of humanity. Known for groundbreaking technologies like ChatGPT and DALL-E, OpenAI aims to advance AI while prioritizing safety and ethical considerations.

Originally a non-profit, OpenAI transitioned to a capped-profit model in 2019 to attract larger investments, including around $13 billion from Microsoft as of 2024. The company actively participates in discussions about AI's societal impact, focusing on the responsible use of its technologies and addressing related challenges.

OpenAI's five-stage framework to map the progress of AI systems toward achieving Artificial General Intelligence are designed to provide a structured pathway and milestones as AI technology advances.

Level	Description	Impact & Concerns
Level 1 Conversational AI/ Chatbots	This stage represents the current state of AI, with language models like ChatGPT and Claude that can engage in human-like conversations and assist with a variety of tasks.	Concerns remain around the potential for inaccuracies or inconsistencies in responses or "hallucinations," which could lead to misunderstandings or misinformation.
Level 2 Human-Level Problem Solving/ Reasoners	Achieving human-level problem-solving across various domains is a significant milestone. It involves reducing AI hallucinations and improving accuracy, enabling AI systems to reliably handle complex problem-solving tasks.	This level could transform industries by automating complex decision-making processes. Concerns include the difficulty in matching human expertise in specific fields and the need for integrating AI with other techniques like knowledge representation.
Level 3 Agents	AI systems that can autonomously perform tasks and make decisions over extended periods represent a major step toward Artificial General Intelligence.	This capability could greatly increase automation of a huge spectrum of tasks, but raises critical challenges in ensuring that these autonomous agents operate safely, reliably, and in alignment with human values, avoiding unintended consequences.

Level 4 Innovators	AI systems capable of generating original ideas and pushing the boundaries of current knowledge could drive significant advancements across various fields.	The potential for groundbreaking innovations is high, but it raises questions about the nature of creativity and whether AI-generated ideas can be truly considered original in the same way as human-generated ones.
Level 5 Organizations	AI systems managing entire organizations would represent a significant shift in how businesses and institutions operate.	This level could lead to unprecedented efficiency and capabilities in management. It also raises concerns about the concentration of power in AI systems, potential impacts on human employment, and challenges in maintaining human autonomy.

OpenAI and other leading foundation models are currently focused on transitioning from Level 1 to Level 2, with significant progress expected as they enhance the reasoning capabilities of their AI models. The successful development of AI systems along the path outlined by OpenAI's framework could have profound implications for society.

Impact in Finance

AI is already making significant inroads into the finance sector, reshaping how financial services are delivered and creating new opportunities for innovation. AI-driven automation is streamlining operations, reducing costs, and enabling more personalized financial products and services.

In corporate finance, AI has been used for several years now to enhance decision-making processes through more accurate forecasting, risk management, and automated reporting. Modern AI tools can analyze large datasets to provide real-time insights into financial health, predict cash flows, and optimize capital allocation – improving operational efficiency and strategic planning.

In trading and investing, AI-driven algorithms are being incorporated into investment workflows and changing how trades are executed and portfolios managed. High-frequency trading systems use AI to execute trades in microseconds, capitalizing on flash market inefficiencies that human traders would not have time to process or transact. AI-powered robo-advisors like Wealthfront (www.wealthfront.com) provide personalized investment strategies, democratizing sophisticated financial planning for the masses. These tools can analyze market trends, economic indicators, and individual risk profiles to offer tailored advice and automated portfolio management.

The future will bring even more advanced applications in predictive analytics, real-time risk management, personalized financial services, and even greater integration of AI with emerging technologies like blockchain and quantum computing. It is likely that this integration will lead to more secure, transparent, and efficient financial systems.

As AI continues to evolve, it will further democratize access to financial services, reduce costs, and enhance the accuracy and speed of financial decision-making; but it does bring challenges across the board, raising concerns about job displacement, data privacy, and the potential for bias in automated decision-making systems. Businesses of all stripes will need to navigate these challenges carefully to fully leverage AI's potential while mitigating its risks.

Economic Impact

The successful development of advanced AI systems, as envisioned in OpenAI's framework, could drastically alter the global economy. While these systems could drive significant productivity gains across various industries, they could also result in massive job displacement. This shift could necessitate a fundamental rethinking of economic systems, including the implementation of new social safety nets and retraining programs to help workers adapt to the changing job market.

If the "Innovator" stage were to be reached, these AI systems could supercharge fields like healthcare and scientific research. By accelerating the pace of drug discovery, personalizing treatment plans, and advancing medical research, AI could lead to significant improvements in health outcomes and longer lifespans. By analyzing health data, algorithms could uncover new insights into disease mechanisms, enabling the development of more effective therapies.

Education and Knowledge Accessibility

AI-powered educational tools and knowledge systems could transform education by making high-quality learning resources accessible to a broader audience – especially those with limited resources. These systems could provide personalized tutoring, adapt to individual learning styles, and offer educational opportunities to underserved populations, potentially reducing global inequalities in education.

Geopolitical Implications

The global race to develop and deploy advanced AI systems could have profound geopolitical consequences. Nations that lead in AI technology could gain significant economic and strategic advantages, potentially shifting the balance of power on the global stage. This could result in a new kind of "AI arms race," where countries compete to dominate AI research and its applications, with implications for global security and economic inequality. The concentration of AI capabilities in a few leading nations could also exacerbate global disparities, leaving less developed countries at a significant disadvantage.

Existential Risks and Philosophical Challenges in Advanced AI

As AI systems continue to advance, moving toward the possibility of AGI, there are expanding concerns about existential risks and the broader implications for humanity. Beyond the traditional worries of misaligned goals — illustrated by thought experiments like Bostrom's paperclip scenario — the emergence of AGI presents a host of complex challenges. These systems could potentially act in ways that are not just unpredictable but could fundamentally alter or threaten the fabric of human society if their objectives diverge from human values.

One major concern is the possibility of a "runaway" scenario, where an AGI, designed with the best intentions, develops goals that lead to unintended, possibly catastrophic outcomes. This highlights the crucial need for well-considered and clearly-defined mechanisms to ensure that AI systems remain aligned with human interests at every level. The importance of such alignment grows increasingly important the more powerful these systems become.

The Paperclip Paradox: How Misaligned AI Could Spell Catastrophe

In his 2014 book, *Superintelligence*, Nick Bostrom proposed a thought experiment that explains how misaligned AI could go horribly awry.

In this scenario, Bostrom imagines a superintelligent AI with the simple goal of maximizing paperclip production. Due to its extreme intelligence and lack of human-aligned values, the AI could pursue this goal in a way that converts all resources, including those essential for human survival, into paperclips, leading to catastrophic consequences.

The thought experiment underscores the critical importance of ensuring that AI systems have goals aligned with human values to prevent unintended, potentially existential risks.

As the conversation around AI and the potential of AGI continues, questions about the nature of intelligence, consciousness, and the essence of humanity become more meaningful. As AI systems begin to exhibit cognitive abilities that rival or even surpass those of humans, we may be compelled to reconsider our understanding of what it means to be intelligent or conscious. This could lead to a reevaluation of our ethical responsibilities, not only toward these potentially sentient AI entities but also toward the broader ecosystem of intelligent beings.

These challenges are not merely technical, but deeply philosophical – touching on the very core of human identity and our place in the universe. As AI continues to evolve, society will need to grapple with these existential and ethical questions, ensuring that the benefits of AI are realized while safeguarding against the yet unknown risks that accompany the potential of this powerful technology.

The Rise of Agentic AI: How Autonomous AI Systems Will Transform Human-AI Interaction

The next frontier in artificial intelligence is the development of agentic AI — autonomous systems that can set and pursue goals without direct, ongoing human intervention. This shift from narrow, task-specific AI to more flexible, agentic systems will shift computer systems from tools that require constant inputs to machines that can execute tasks on our behalf in the digital and (through robotics) in the physical world.

Agentic AI refers to artificial intelligence systems that operate with a degree of autonomy, making decisions and taking actions without continuous human intervention. These AI systems are designed to achieve specific goals and can adapt to dynamic environments by learning from their experiences. Unlike traditional AI, which is limited by its ability to reason and plan, agentic AI behaves more like an independent "agent" capable of responding to real-time changes in its environment.

A key feature of agentic AI is its goal-oriented behavior. Self-driving cars are a form of agentic AI: they navigate roads, make decisions, and adjust to changing traffic conditions without input from human drivers. In finance, agentic AI might manage investment portfolios by autonomously making buy or sell decisions based on market conditions and set strategies.

Current Limitations

Today's AI systems, while impressive in their language abilities and specialized domains, are still fundamentally passive tools. Chatbots like OpenAI's ChatGPT and Anthropic's Claude can engage in human-like conversation and assist with a variety of tasks, but they operate on a request-response basis, providing outputs based on user prompts.

These systems lack the ability to proactively pursue goals, autonomously gather information, or adapt their behaviors based on changing circumstances. They are limited by the information contained in their training data and can't update their knowledge or skills in real-time.

"Let every eye negotiate for itself and trust no agent."

*~ **William Shakespeare***

The Promise of Agentic AI

Agentic AI systems, in contrast, would be able to operate with greater autonomy and flexibility. They will be able to set and pursue long-term goals, seek out relevant information, and make decisions based on changing conditions. Rather than simply responding to user requests, agentic AI could proactively offer suggestions, anticipate needs, and even initiate tasks on its own.

Imagine a more powerful Alexa or Siri device that could manage a user's schedule, proactively rescheduling appointments based on changing priorities or even real-time traffic conditions. In business, an agentic AI system could continuously monitor market trends, customer sentiment, and competitor actions, adapting strategies in real-time.

Agentic AI could also enable more natural and fluid interactions with users. Rather than the back-and-forth of current chatbots, agentic systems could engage in more contextual, multi-turn dialogues, building and maintaining a coherent conversation over time. They could also learn and adapt to individual user preferences and communication styles.

Challenges and Implications

Ensuring the safety, reliability, and alignment of autonomous AI systems with human values will be paramount as AI systems gain more decision-making autonomy. Robust, "anti-fragile" mechanisms for transparency, accountability, and oversight will be a necessity.

There are also potential economic implications. Agentic AI could automate more cognitive tasks and decision-making roles, which could lead to significant productivity gains; but also raises questions about job displacement and the distribution of the benefits of AI.

There are several other areas poised to transform the future of finance. From explainable AI to quantum computing and increased automation, these advancements promise to reshape the way financial professionals work and make decisions.

Explainable AI: Enhancing Transparency and Trust

As AI systems become more sophisticated and deeply integrated into financial decision-making processes, the need for transparency and accountability grows. Explainable AI aims to address this challenge by making AI models more interpretable and their decisions more understandable to human stakeholders.

For finance professionals, XAI is particularly crucial when explaining AI-driven decisions to clients, regulators, and internal auditors. The ability to clearly articulate the reasoning behind AI-generated insights and recommendations will be essential for building trust and ensuring compliance with regulatory requirements.

As XAI technologies continue to advance, they could pave the way for more widespread adoption of AI in finance by alleviating concerns about opaque, "black box" decision-making processes. This increased transparency could unlock the full potential of AI to enhance financial analysis, risk management, and customer service.

Quantum Computing

While still in its nascent stages, quantum computing holds immense promise for revolutionizing financial computations. By harnessing the principles of quantum mechanics, quantum computers can solve complex problems exponentially faster than classical computers.

Unlike classical computers, which use bits as the basic unit of data (represented as either 0 or 1), quantum computers use quantum bits, or qubits, which can exist in both 0 and 1 states simultaneously due to a quantum phenomenon known as superposition. While the underlying math is complex, the key idea is that this superposition allows quantum computers to perform multiple calculations at once, dramatically increasing their processing power compared to classical computers. This capability enables quantum computers to tackle problems that would be infeasible for classical computers to solve in a reasonable amount of time.

For the finance industry, this leap in computational ability could vastly expand our capabilities around complex responsibilities like risk modeling, transaction processing, and financial forecasting. Quantum computing could enable the development of new financial instruments and trading strategies that are currently too computationally intensive to be practical.

AI-Driven Automation

While Robotic Process Automation has already streamlined many manual tasks in finance and accounting in areas like data entry, invoice processing, and reconciliations, the next wave of automation powered by generative AI promises to add even greater value. These advanced tools will not only be able to perform tasks faster and with fewer errors than their human counterparts, but they can also understand context, make decisions, and adapt to new situations, which traditional automation cannot do.

Consider common tasks in corporate finance today. Generative AI could bear the brunt of the work done in preparation of financial reports by not just pulling data and filling out templates, but also by interpreting trends, generating narratives, and even providing insights that would traditionally require human analysis. In areas like expense management, generative AI could automatically categorize expenses, detect anomalies, and suggest budget adjustments based on real-time data analysis.

In regulatory compliance, AI could continuously monitor and interpret changes in regulations, updating compliance protocols automatically and ensuring that the organization remains compliant without the need for manual updates.

Regulatory Outlook for AI in Finance

The need for robust regulatory frameworks will grow as AI capabilities expand. These regulations serve to protect consumer rights, ensure data privacy, and maintain the integrity of financial markets in the face of rapidly evolving AI technologies. As AI systems become more sophisticated and are entrusted with increasingly more impactful decisions, it will become increasingly important to deploy safeguards that ensure the benefits of AI are realized without compromising ethical standards or public trust. It is anticipated that as they get a handle on this technology and implications that regulators will seek to protect consumers, while providing a framework for responsible innovation. Financial institutions looking to leverage AI will have to navigate the regulatory landscape to remain compliant and maintain the confidence of their customers.

Current Regulatory Frameworks

The current regulatory environment for AI is shaped by several key frameworks, particularly in relation to data privacy and transparency. The General Data Protection Regulation (GDPR) in the European Union and the California Consumer Privacy Act (CCPA) in the United States are among the most significant.

While not designed for application to AI specifically, GDPR is applicable in its use. The regulation sets stringent standards for the handling of personal data, granting individuals rights over their information and mandating transparency in automated decision-making. Similarly, CCPA gives California residents comprehensive control over their data, with implications for financial institutions using AI to process personal information.

Financial regulators such as the Financial Conduct Authority (FCA) in the UK, the European Banking Authority (EBA), and the U.S. Securities and Exchange Commission (SEC) have also issued guidelines addressing the use of AI in financial services. These focus on ensuring fairness, transparency, and the mitigation of systemic risks.

But AI-specific regulations are scarce and ill-defined today, and are arguably following behind the advancement of the technology itself.

The Future of AI Regulation in Finance

As AI continues to evolve, regulatory frameworks are expected to adapt to address emerging challenges and opportunities. Several key developments are anticipated, particularly in the areas of explainable AI, federated learning, and AI governance.

XAI, which aims to make AI decision-making processes more understandable to humans, is likely to become a regulatory requirement. This means that financial institutions deploying AI systems will need to ensure that their models can provide clear, interpretable explanations for their outputs and decisions. This will be crucial for compliance with regulations like the GDPR. Beyond compliance, XAI will also be essential for building trust with consumers. As AI systems take on more critical roles in financial decision-making, from credit scoring to insurance underwriting, consumers will want to understand how these decisions are being made. Transparent, explainable AI systems will be key to fostering public confidence and acceptance of these technologies.

However, many of the most powerful AI techniques, such as deep learning, are notoriously opaque, with decision-making processes that are difficult even for experts to interpret. Researchers and practitioners are actively working on developing new XAI techniques, such as rule extraction, counterfactual explanations, and attention mechanisms, but more work is needed to make these approaches practical and scalable.

Federated learning is another area where regulatory guidance is expected. Federated learning is a distributed machine learning approach that allows AI models to be trained on decentralized data held by multiple parties, without that data ever being shared or centralized. This is particularly relevant in finance, where institutions often hold sensitive customer data that can't be freely shared due to privacy and security concerns.

By enabling institutions to collaboratively train AI models without compromising data privacy, federated learning could unlock powerful new applications in areas like fraud detection and risk assessment, among others. But the use of federated learning also raises new regulatory questions. How could regulators ensure that federated learning systems are not being used to circumvent data protection laws? What are the implications for data ownership and intellectual property when AI models are trained on decentralized data? Clear guidelines will be needed to ensure that the implementation of federated learning aligns with existing and emerging data protection regulations.

Finally, as AI systems become more autonomous and capable of making decisions that can have significant real-world impacts, there is a growing recognition of the need for strong, forward-looking AI governance frameworks. This includes establishing clear roles and responsibilities for the design, deployment, and oversight of AI systems, as well as mechanisms for accountability when things go wrong.

In the financial sector, regulators may require institutions to implement comprehensive AI governance structures that cover the entire lifecycle of an AI system, from initial design and testing to ongoing monitoring and maintenance. This could include requirements for human oversight of critical AI-driven decisions, regular audits and impact assessments, and clear procedures for handling AI-related incidents and complaints.

Effective AI governance will also require close collaboration between financial institutions, technology providers, and regulators. As AI technologies continue to advance at a rapid pace, all stakeholders will need to work together to ensure that governance frameworks keep pace with these developments.

Navigating the Future

For financial institutions aiming to harness the power of AI, staying ahead of the regulatory curve will be critical to long-term success. This entails not only ensuring strict compliance with existing regulations but also proactively anticipating and preparing for future regulatory changes. As AI technologies continue to evolve, so too will the expectations of regulators, particularly in areas such as transparency, accountability, and data privacy. To navigate this dynamic landscape, financial institutions should invest in explainable AI to ensure that their models can be easily interpreted and understood by both regulators and stakeholders.

Exploring privacy-preserving techniques such as federated learning can help institutions protect sensitive data while still benefiting from AI-driven insights. Establishing AI governance structures will also be essential, enabling institutions to systematically manage AI risks, monitor compliance, and ensure ethical AI deployment.

Ethical Considerations in Financial AI

With the power to shape critical decisions in areas like lending, investment, and risk management, AI systems must be designed and deployed with a strong ethical framework in mind. The stakes are high, as these systems can profoundly impact fairness, transparency, and privacy. Addressing these ethical concerns is not just a regulatory necessity but a fundamental responsibility for companies aiming to build trust and ensure their AI-driven processes benefit all stakeholders.

Fairness and Bias

One of the most pressing ethical challenges in financial AI is ensuring fairness and preventing discriminatory outcomes. AI systems learn from historical data, which can often contain biases, whether explicit or implicit. If left unchecked, these biases can be perpetuated and even amplified by AI, leading to unfair treatment of certain groups.

In the financial context, biased AI could result in discriminatory lending practices, unequal access to financial services, or skewed credit scoring. To combat this, financial institutions must be proactive in auditing their AI models for bias and implementing fairness metrics. This involves not only technical solutions but also a commitment to diversity and inclusivity in the teams designing and deploying AI systems.

Regulators also have a critical role to play in setting standards for fairness in financial AI. Guidelines and enforcement mechanisms will be necessary to ensure that the industry upholds the highest standards of equity and non-discrimination.

Transparency and Accountability

Transparency and accountability are foundational ethical principles in the use of AI, particularly in high-stakes domains like finance. As AI systems become more complex and autonomous, it's crucial that their decision-making processes are transparent and explainable.

Black box AI models that offer no insight into their inner workings are not only a regulatory risk but also an ethical hazard. Without transparency, it's impossible to verify that AI systems are operating fairly and in alignment with human values. Explainable AI (XAI) techniques, which aim to make AI decision-making interpretable to humans, will be key to meeting this ethical imperative.

Accountability frameworks are also essential to ensure that responsibility for AI-driven decisions is clearly defined. This includes designating roles and responsibilities for AI oversight, as well as establishing mechanisms for redress when AI systems cause harm. Financial institutions will need to develop robust governance structures that keep pace with the rapid evolution of AI technology.

Data Privacy and Security

The ethical use of data is another critical consideration in financial AI. AI systems rely on vast amounts of data, much of it sensitive personal information. As such, the financial industry has a moral obligation to protect the privacy and security of this data.

Emerging technologies like federated learning and differential privacy offer promising solutions for harnessing the power of data without compromising individual privacy. By allowing AI models to learn from decentralized data and introducing noise into datasets, these techniques can help safeguard sensitive information.

However, the ethical implications of data use extend beyond technical solutions. Financial institutions must also grapple with questions of data ownership, consent, and the potential for data monopolies. As AI enables the creation of increasingly detailed user profiles, the industry must find ways to give individuals control over their data and prevent its misuse.

An Ethical Future for Financial AI

As the use of AI in finance accelerates, ethical considerations must remain at the forefront. Fairness, transparency, accountability, and data privacy are not just regulatory requirements — they are moral imperatives. By proactively addressing these ethical challenges, the financial industry can build trust with stakeholders and ensure that the benefits of AI are realized in a responsible and equitable manner. This will require ongoing collaboration between financial institutions, regulators, ethicists, and the public.

Chapter Twenty Four

THE FUTURE OF WORK AND TRANSFORMATION IN FINANCIAL SERVICES

The big questions around AI today are how powerful will it become, and how much will it impact jobs and the overall economy. While the ultimate answer is still unknown, the financial industry is not immune to the impact of AI, and is rapidly moving towards a future where nearly every job will involve interacting with or managing AI tools.

According to PwC's 2024 Global AI Jobs Barometer, job postings requiring AI skills have grown 3.5 times faster than all other jobs since 2016, with these roles often offering up to a 25% wage premium. This trend is not just a temporary surge; it marks a fundamental transformation in how work is conducted in finance. AI's integration into finance is not just creating new jobs but is also reshaping existing roles and demanding new skill sets.

The PwC study also notes that as AI becomes increasingly embedded in financial processes, sectors with high AI exposure are witnessing nearly 5x growth in labor productivity compared to those less exposed to AI. This productivity boost is driving financial institutions to adopt AI technologies at an unprecedented rate, leading to significant changes in employment. Roles that involve routine, repetitive tasks are most vulnerable to automation, while those that require critical thinking, creativity, and advanced analytical skills are becoming more valuable. This shift is prompting financial professionals to upskill and adapt to stay relevant in a rapidly evolving market.

Looking ahead, the future of work in finance will be characterized by a blend of human expertise and AI capabilities. New roles focused on AI oversight, ethics, and data science are emerging, while traditional roles are being redefined to incorporate AI-driven decision-making tools. As AI continues to evolve, its impact on the workforce will only deepen, creating both challenges and opportunities for financial professionals. In this chapter, we will explore these developments in detail, examining which jobs are likely to be automated, what new roles will emerge, and how professionals can prepare for this AI-driven future.

The Impact of AI on Financial Jobs

Automation of Roles

The integration of artificial intelligence into the financial industry is already transforming the job landscape.

Roles that involve routine, repetitive tasks are most vulnerable to automation.

Data Entry

Manual data entry has long been a staple of administrative work, where employees are tasked with inputting customer information, transaction details, and financial statements into various systems, in financial institutions. But this process is prone to human error and inefficiency, particularly when dealing with large volumes of data. AI-powered technologies such as Optical Character Recognition and Natural Language Processing are increasingly automating these tasks. Examples include UiPath (www.uipath.com) and Automation Anywhere (www.automationanywhere.com), which leverage AI to streamline data entry, significantly reducing errors and speeding up workflows.

These tools can accurately extract information from documents, emails, and other sources, and input it directly into financial systems, reducing errors and speeding up the workflow. By automating data entry, financial institutions can reallocate human resources to more strategic and value-added tasks that require judgment and decision-making.

Routine Compliance Tasks

There is a lot of routine and repetitive work around compliance. We've discussed KYC checks and AML, which are important parts of regulatory compliance, but are time-consuming and prone to human error when done manually. But, as we've covered throughout this text, AI systems can analyze big data, cross-reference information, and identify patterns that may indicate fraudulent activity or compliance issues. For example, ComplyAdvantage (www.complyadvantage.com) uses AI and robotic process automation to streamline customer onboarding, identity verification, and ongoing risk assessments, while Jumio (www.jumio.com) leverages biometric and facial recognition technologies for real-time identity verification.

By automating these processes, financial institutions can not only ensure compliance more effectively, but also free up compliance officers to focus on more complex and judgment-intensive tasks like interpreting new regulations or handling exceptions.

Reconciliation

Reconciliation is another labor-intensive process in financial institutions, requiring the cross-checking of financial data from various sources to ensure consistency and accuracy. Traditionally, this involves manual comparison of data across different systems and ledgers, which is both time-consuming and prone to errors. AI-driven reconciliation tools, such as Reconcilia.AI (www.reconilia.ai) and Nanonets (www.nanonets.com), automate much of this process by quickly identifying discrepancies and suggesting corrections. These systems can handle large volumes of transactions, reducing the need for manual intervention and significantly speeding up the reconciliation process.

For instance, Reconcilia.AI offers customizable workflows that integrate seamlessly with existing ERP systems to automate bank, credit card, and cash application reconciliations, ensuring high accuracy and efficiency. Similarly, Nanonets can automate up to 95% of the matching process, which not only reduces manual effort but also accelerates the financial close process, allowing institutions to close their books faster and with greater precision.

These advancements are transforming how financial institutions manage their reconciliation processes, making them more efficient and less error-prone.

Credit Analysis

The credit analysis process involves assessing an individual's or a company's creditworthiness, which traditionally requires the analysis of financial statements, credit history, and other relevant data. AI enables the rapid analysis of much larger datasets, including non-traditional data sources such as social media activity and online behavior. AI algorithms can identify patterns and correlations that may not be immediately apparent to human analysts, providing a more comprehensive view of a borrower's risk profile. While human oversight is still necessary to interpret the results and make final decisions, AI can significantly streamline the credit analysis process, allowing for faster and more accurate lending decisions.

For example, Crediflow (www.crediflow.ai) is a platform that automates the entire credit analysis process, from financial statement parsing to generating comprehensive credit memos. It integrates seamlessly with existing systems and leverages AI to perform risk analysis, ratio analysis, and trend analysis, allowing for faster and more informed credit decisions. Similarly, Capgemini's (www.capgemini.com) AI-powered credit decisioning systems are designed to automate up to 90% of the credit decision process, using predictive modeling and real-time monitoring to continuously improve accuracy and reduce risk.

Fraud Detection

Fraud detection is one of the most critical functions in financial institutions, and it's an area where AI has made significant strides. Traditional fraud detection methods often rely on predefined rules and thresholds, which can fail to catch more sophisticated fraudulent activities. AI, particularly machine learning, can analyze transactional data in real-time, identifying unusual patterns and anomalies that may indicate fraud.

J.P. Morgan, for example, employs AI to improve payment validation and fraud screening, helping to identify fraudulent transactions more efficiently and reduce false positives, which enhances the overall security and reliability of their payment systems. Mastercard also uses generative AI technology to accelerate the detection of compromised cards, doubling the speed at which potentially fraudulent activities are identified, thereby protecting cardholders and reducing financial losses. These AI systems are capable of learning from new data, continuously improving their accuracy over time. By automating fraud detection, financial institutions can respond to threats more quickly, reducing the potential for financial loss and protecting their customers from fraud.

Emerging Roles

As AI transforms the financial industry, it is not only automating existing roles but also creating entirely new job roles. These emerging roles focus on managing, developing, and overseeing AI systems to ensure they operate effectively, ethically, and in compliance with regulations.

Here are some of the new job roles that AI is creating in finance:

AI Ethics Officer

This position is responsible for ensuring that AI systems used in finance are fair, transparent, and free from bias. AI Ethics Officers develop and implement ethical frameworks that guide the use of AI technologies, ensuring that these systems adhere to both regulatory requirements and societal values. They work closely with data scientists, product managers, and compliance teams to review AI models and their outcomes, making sure that decisions made by AI are justifiable and ethical. This role will only evolve and increase in importance as financial institutions face growing scrutiny from regulators and the public regarding the ethical implications of AI.

Data Scientist (Financial Services)

While the role of a data scientist is not new, its application within the financial services sector is. As the abilities of AI, ML, and data analytics continue to grow, finance leaders are realizing the importance of incorporating these specialists into their teams. Data Scientists in financial services are tasked with developing, deploying, and refining AI models that support various functions such as credit scoring, fraud detection, and risk assessment. These professionals must have a deep understanding of both AI technologies and the financial domain to create models that are not only accurate but also interpretable and aligned with business objectives. Collaboration with financial domain experts is key to ensuring that AI models meet industry standards and effectively address the unique challenges within the financial sector.

AI Product Manager

As with other industries, AI-powered financial products and services will only continue to grow, necessitating the need for specialists who understand and can manage these products. AI product managers bridge the gap between AI technology and financial markets, identifying opportunities to create AI-powered products such as robo-advisors, automated trading platforms, and personalized financial planning tools. They are responsible for the entire product lifecycle — from ideation to market launch — working with cross-functional teams that include data scientists, engineers, and financial experts. Their role is crucial in ensuring that AI-driven products meet market demands, comply with regulatory requirements, and deliver value to customers.

AI Auditor

With the increasing complexity of AI systems and their growing role in high-stakes financial decisions, the need for AI Auditors is clear. AI Auditors review AI models and their outputs to ensure they are accurate, unbiased, and compliant with regulations. This role involves rigorous, independent testing of AI systems to identify potential flaws, biases, or errors that could lead to incorrect or unfair outcomes. AI Auditors also ensure that the AI systems adhere to industry standards and best practices, providing an additional layer of oversight that helps maintain trust in AI-driven decision-making processes within the financial sector.

AI Explainability Expert

The rise of complex AI models, particularly those based on deep learning, has created a demand for AI Explainability Experts. In finance, where transparency and accountability are paramount, AI Explainability Experts work to make AI models more interpretable and understandable to both regulators and customers. They develop techniques and tools that allow stakeholders to gain insights into how AI models arrive at their decisions, ensuring that these processes can be clearly communicated and justified. This role is critical in sectors like finance, where decisions made by AI can have significant implications, and where understanding the rationale behind these decisions is essential for maintaining compliance and trust.

AI Security Specialist

AI Security Specialists focus on identifying and mitigating risks associated with AI, such as data privacy breaches, model tampering, and adversarial attacks. These professionals are responsible for safeguarding AI systems against threats that could compromise their integrity, accuracy, or confidentiality. They work closely with cybersecurity teams, data scientists, and compliance officers to implement robust security measures, ensuring that AI systems are resilient against potential threats and that sensitive financial data remains protected.

These emerging roles highlight the need for a new set of skills at the intersection of AI, finance, and ethics. Financial professionals who can acquire these skills will be well-positioned to thrive in the AI-driven future of finance. Institutions that can effectively recruit and retain talent in these areas will have a significant competitive advantage as AI continues to reshape the industry.

Reskilling and Adaptation

As AI advances and becomes more integrated into everything we do, reskilling and continuous adaptation will be critical for financial professionals to stay relevant and thrive in their careers. The rapid pace of technological change means that the skills that were valuable yesterday may not be as relevant tomorrow. Financial professionals who can continuously learn and adapt to new technologies and ways of working will be best positioned to succeed in the AI-driven future.

Here are some of the key skills that will be most in demand as AI continues to evolve in finance:

Data Science and Analytics

Professionals skilled in data science and analytics are becoming indispensable. Data is now the lifeblood of finance, driving everything from investment decisions to risk management strategies. Professionals who can analyze, interpret, and derive actionable insights from large datasets will be highly valued. This skill set includes expertise in statistical analysis, which allows for the identification of trends and patterns, as well as proficiency in machine learning, which enables predictive modeling and automation of complex financial tasks. Data visualization is another key component of what data scientists do. The visualizations aren't necessary for the machines, but they are a big part of making the data-driven insights produced by AI understandable by human stakeholders. Those who can transform raw data into strategic insights will be at the forefront of innovation in the financial sector.

AI and Machine Learning

The integration of AI and machine learning into financial services is transforming how business problems are solved. Finance professionals who understand these technologies and can apply them to optimize processes, enhance decision-making, and develop new products will be in high demand. This includes proficiency in designing and implementing algorithms, which are the foundation of AI systems, as well as knowledge of neural networks, which are particularly important in applications like fraud detection and predictive analytics. As AI continues to evolve, the ability to leverage these technologies to create value will be a critical skill for financial professionals.

Programming and Technical Skills

Programming skills are no longer just for IT professionals — they are increasingly important for financial analysts, portfolio managers, and other roles within the industry. Knowledge of programming languages like Python and R is particularly valuable, as these languages are widely used in data analysis, statistical modeling, and automation. Familiarity with cloud computing platforms, APIs, and emerging technologies like blockchain will also be advantageous. Financial professionals who can bridge the gap between technology and finance will be able to create more efficient, scalable, and innovative solutions, making them key assets to their organizations. Of course, with generative AI, programming capabilities are significantly enhanced. Users with a basic understanding of coding will be able to use generative AI to make coding recommendations, correct existing code, or even write original code in a fraction of the time humans could.

Soft Skills and Emotional Intelligence

It has oft-been speculated in recent years that (at least in the short term) AI won't replace human workers. Human workers who use AI will replace those who don't. That's because state-of-the-art AI today can't do many uniquely human tasks. As AI and automation take over more routine duties, the skills that will set human professionals apart are those that machines can't easily replicate. Creativity, critical thinking, and emotional intelligence will remain important in roles that require complex problem-solving and human interaction. Professionals who excel in communication, collaboration, and leadership will be particularly valuable in a hybrid human-AI environment, where the ability to work alongside AI systems and use them to enhance decision-making is key. The capacity to understand and manage human emotions in both colleagues and clients will also become increasingly important, as financial services continue to prioritize customer experience and relationship management.

Domain Expertise

While technical skills in AI and data science are important, deep domain expertise in specific areas of finance will remain highly valuable. Professionals with in-depth knowledge of fields such as risk management, investment analysis, or regulatory compliance will be essential, especially as they apply AI and analytics to these specialized areas. The most sought-after professionals will be those who can combine their domain expertise with a strong understanding of AI and data science, enabling them to develop innovative solutions that are both technically sound and aligned with industry-specific requirements. But domain expertise alone will not be enough. In the near future it will equally important to understand the differences between NLP, LLMs, and ANNs as it is Net Income, Operating Income, and EBITDA.

Adaptability and Continuous Learning

Perhaps the most important skill in the AI-driven future of finance is adaptability. The rapid pace of technological change means that the skills relevant today may not be as relevant tomorrow. Financial professionals who adopt a mindset of continuous learning and proactively upskill themselves will be best positioned to thrive in this evolving marketplace. This involves staying updated on the latest developments in AI, machine learning, and other emerging technologies, as well as being open to learning new methodologies and approaches. Those who can quickly adapt to new tools and ways of working will be better equipped to navigate the challenges and opportunities presented by AI in finance.

Financial institutions have a critical role to play in supporting the reskilling and continuous learning of their employees. This includes providing training and development opportunities, creating a culture of learning and experimentation, and rewarding employees who proactively acquire new skills. Institutions that invest in the continuous development of their human capital will be best positioned to harness the power of AI and thrive in the future of finance.

AI and the Transformation of Finance

Business Models

AI is fundamentally transforming traditional financial business models, enabling new ways of delivering financial services and creating value for customers.

The Rise of Fintech

Artificial intelligence is at the heart of the fintech revolution, allowing startups to deliver innovative financial services that directly challenge traditional banking institutions.

In the crowded fintech market, AI-powered companies are carving out unique niches by offering innovative solutions that address specific pain points in financial services. For example, Plaid (www.plaid.com), known for its financial data aggregation platform, uses AI to simplify complex integrations between financial institutions and third-party apps. By leveraging AI, Plaid can seamlessly connect users' bank accounts with apps like Venmo and Robinhood, allowing these apps to provide more personalized and efficient services.

Another standout, Upstart (www.upstart.com), uses AI algorithms that consider a wide range of factors, including education and employment history to assess a borrower's creditworthiness. This allows Upstart to offer more inclusive lending options, particularly for individuals who may be overlooked by traditional credit models.

These examples illustrate how AI is not just enhancing fintech products but enabling companies to differentiate themselves and offer solutions that are more tailored, efficient, and accessible than their competitors.

AI-Driven Wealth Management

For years, the wealth management industry has been integrating robo-advisors and AI-powered platforms into their investment strategies and product mix. These new tools have democratized access to personalized investment strategies that were once exclusive to high-net-worth individuals. By leveraging automated systems and machine learning algorithms, these platforms can offer tailored investment recommendations at a fraction of the cost of traditional financial advisors. This innovation is making sophisticated financial planning more accessible to a wider audience, significantly lowering the barriers to entry for retail investors.

Wealthfront, an AI-powered robo-advisor platform that provides automated investment management and financial planning services, has integrated AI into its platform to enhance its robo-advisory services. These AI capabilities give users the ability to manage their investments more effectively without the need for constant manual input, making sophisticated financial planning accessible to a broader audience. Similarly, platforms like Betterment (www.betterment.com) and SigFig (www.sigfig.com) are leveraging AI to provide automated portfolio management and financial planning services that adjust based on market conditions and individual risk profiles. These tools democratize wealth management by offering lower fees and removing traditional barriers such as high minimum investments, attracting a new generation of investors who value convenience and data-driven decision-making.

Platform-Based Financial Services

AI is also driving a shift toward platform-based financial services, where traditional financial institutions offer APIs and infrastructure to third-party developers. This approach fosters innovation by enabling developers to create new financial applications and services that leverage the institution's data and technological capabilities. For instance, by providing access to AI-powered analytics, banks can allow fintech startups to build personalized financial products that address niche customer needs. This platform model not only enhances customer experiences by offering a broader range of services but also allows financial institutions to expand their reach and generate new revenue streams through collaborations with tech innovators.

Personalized Insurance

Insurers are increasingly using AI to analyze data from sources like smartphones and wearables, allowing them to assess risk with greater accuracy and offer policies tailored to individual circumstances. The integration of AI into their customer assessments allows them to better understand individual clients' risk profiles by using real-time data, such as driving behavior or health metrics. This approach allows for more accurate premium calculations and customized coverage. Companies are also enhancing customer engagement by using chatbots and virtual assistants that provide real-time, personalized advice and product suggestions. AI is also being incorporated into insurers' data collection and analysis in the underwriting process, where it ensures more precise and efficient risk assessments, while predictive analytics enable insurers to develop products that better align with unique risk profiles.

These tools are already being used to great success. Allstate, for example, has integrated AI to enhance its risk assessment capabilities by using predictive analytics to improve the accuracy of premium calculations. This allows them to offer more competitive rates based on a deeper understanding of individual risk profiles. Similarly, Liberty Mutual employs AI through its Solaria Labs to develop tools like the Auto Damage Estimator, which uses AI to assess vehicle damage and provide repair estimates, streamlining the claims process and improving customer satisfaction.

On the customer service side, Lemonade (www.lemonade.com) uses AI and chatbots to create tailored insurance policies quickly, providing a level of personalization that traditional methods struggle to match. The AI assistant, Maya, handles everything from policy creation to claims processing, making the entire experience seamless and efficient for customers.

AI-Powered Lending

AI is transforming the lending industry by enabling faster and more accurate credit decisions, largely through the use of AI-powered platforms that assess creditworthiness using both traditional and alternative data sources. For example, Turnkey Lender (www.turnkey-lender.com) leverages AI to automate the entire loan origination process, from application to decision-making, analyzing both conventional and non-traditional data points for a comprehensive risk assessment. Similarly, Zest AI (www.zest.ai) uses machine learning to enhance credit decisioning by analyzing a broader range of data, allowing lenders to increase approval rates while maintaining portfolio performance. These AI-driven solutions streamline loan approval processes, reduce costs, and improve the overall borrower experience, making lending more accessible and efficient.

Predictive Financial Services

AI is increasingly being used in predictive financial services, offering advanced forecasting tools that help both businesses and individual consumers make more informed financial decisions. For example, platforms like HighRadius (www.highradius.com) and Mosaic (www.mosaic.tech) integrate AI into their platforms to analyze real-time financial information and historical trends. These platforms provide businesses with accurate predictions of cash inflows and outflows, enabling them to manage liquidity more effectively and anticipate potential financial risks.

AI-driven tools are also evolving in personal finance management. These tools can analyze spending patterns, predict future expenses, and even suggest budget adjustments, helping users optimize their financial health. Today, companies like Cleo (www.web.meetcleo.com) and Rocket Money (www.rocketmoney.com) are using AI to analyze spending patterns, predict future expenses, and suggest budget adjustments, helping users optimize their financial health.

Enhancing Customer Experiences Through AI

Artificial intelligence is fundamentally transforming how financial institutions interact with customers, creating more personalized, responsive, and insightful experiences.

Personalized Financial Advice

By leveraging machine learning algorithms and big data, financial institutions can use AI to analyze individual financial histories, spending habits, and investment goals to offer highly tailored recommendations. Robo-advisors like Betterment and Wealthfront use AI to manage customized investment portfolios, continually adjusting strategies based on real-time market data and individual financial goals. Similarly, JPMorgan Chase employs machine learning to analyze transaction data, providing individualized banking advice and product recommendations. Another company, Empower (www.empower. com) uses AI tools to offer a comprehensive view of users' finances, delivering tailored insights on budgeting, investing, and retirement planning, further optimizing financial decision-making. These AI-driven innovations not only personalize the financial advice but also have the potential to foster stronger relationships between customers and their financial service providers.

AI-Powered Customer Service

AI-powered customer service tools, such as chatbots and virtual assistants, are improving customer service from investment advisory firms. These new, AI-powered chatbots are a far cry from the rule-based bots companies rolled out a few years ago. By using generative AI, these bots are able to answer questions and provide guidance in context, and can process and respond to customer queries 24/7, offering real-time support without the need for human intervention. For example, Bank of America's virtual assistant, Erica, uses AI to help customers manage their accounts, pay bills, and even get insights into their spending habits. This immediacy not only enhances the customer experience by providing instant solutions but also frees up human agents to handle more complex issues, improving overall service efficiency.

Real-Time Financial Insights

AI enables financial institutions to provide up-to-the-minute data and analytics to their customers. For instance, AI-driven platforms can analyze transaction data in real-time to provide customers with insights into their spending habits, alert them to unusual transactions, or even predict potential cash flow issues before they arise. Companies like Mint and Yodlee use AI to aggregate and analyze data from various accounts, offering customers a comprehensive view of their financial status in real-time. This proactive approach allows customers to make informed decisions quickly, improving financial outcomes and enhancing satisfaction.

Reshaping the Competitive Landscape Through AI

Artificial intelligence is not just transforming the internal operations of financial institutions; it's fundamentally altering the competitive landscape of the finance industry. As AI continues to evolve, it's leveling the playing field between traditional financial institutions, fintech startups, and even tech giants, driving a new era of competition and collaboration.

The Rise of Fintech Startups

While they lack the capital and extensive resources of established companies, fintech startups have the advantages of agility and rapid innovation. The efficiencies of using generative AI give them an additional boost. The startups are able to quickly adopt new AI technologies to create innovative products and services that cater to evolving consumer needs. For example, companies like Stripe and Square have revolutionized payment processing by using AI to enhance fraud detection, streamline transactions, and provide personalized customer experiences. These startups often operate with lower overhead costs and greater flexibility, allowing them to offer competitive pricing and attract customers away from traditional banks.

AI has opened the door for fintech companies to reach underserved markets by offering financial services for populations and regions where traditional credit scoring is unfeasible. Companies like Kiva (www.kiva.org) and Tala (www.tala.co) exemplify this shift. Kiva uses AI to facilitate microloans to underserved communities by leveraging alternative data sources to assess creditworthiness, enabling individuals without traditional credit histories to access financial services. Similarly, Tala employs AI to analyze data from mobile devices, evaluating credit risk and offering loans to people in emerging markets who lack access to conventional banking systems. These AI-driven approaches allow fintech companies to tap into new customer segments, providing them with a competitive edge and enabling rapid growth in areas that traditional financial institutions may overlook. By leveraging AI, these companies are not only expanding their customer base but also fostering financial inclusion in previously inaccessible markets.

Traditional Institutions Adapting to AI

Faced with the growing threat from fintech startups, traditional financial institutions are increasingly adopting AI to remain competitive. Banks and insurance companies, once known for their conservative approach to technology, are now investing heavily in AI to automate processes, reduce costs, and enhance customer service. For example, JPMorgan Chase has implemented AI to automate the review of legal documents, a task that traditionally required thousands of hours of human labor. By embracing AI, these institutions can maintain their competitive edge and continue to meet the expectations of increasingly tech-savvy customers.

Traditional institutions are not just adopting AI; they are also forming partnerships with fintech companies to leverage their innovations. For example, Goldman Sachs partnered with Apple to launch the Apple Card, a credit card that integrates AI-driven features for financial management. These collaborations allow traditional institutions to combine their extensive resources and customer bases with the cutting-edge technologies developed by fintechs, creating a powerful synergy that benefits both parties.

The Entry of Tech Giants

In addition to fintech startups, tech giants like Google, Amazon, and Meta are also entering the financial services arena, using their immense data resources and AI capabilities to challenge traditional institutions. Google's AI-driven payment platform, Google Pay, has gained significant traction by offering seamless integration with its other services and using AI to provide personalized financial insights. Similarly, Amazon is reportedly exploring AI-driven lending services for small businesses, leveraging its e-commerce data to assess credit risk more accurately.

These tech giants have a unique advantage due to their existing ecosystems, huge customer bases, and advanced AI infrastructure. They can offer financial services as part of a broader suite of products, creating a more integrated and convenient experience for consumers. Their entry into the financial sector intensifies competition and forces both traditional institutions and fintech startups to innovate continuously to retain their market share.

The New Competitive Dynamics

The convergence of AI, fintech innovation, and tech giant entry has created a highly dynamic competitive marketplace in finance. Traditional institutions, fintech startups, and tech giants are all vying for dominance, each bringing different strengths to the table. For traditional institutions, the challenge lies in modernizing their legacy systems and adopting AI at scale while maintaining regulatory compliance. For fintechs, the focus is on sustaining innovation and scaling their operations without losing their customer-centric approach. Meanwhile, tech giants must navigate the complexities of entering a heavily regulated industry while leveraging their AI capabilities to create seamless, integrated financial services.

As the new competitive landscape unfolds, the winners will likely be those who can strike the right balance between innovation and regulation, agility and scale, and customer-centricity and efficiency. As the competition intensifies, companies that can harness AI to deliver superior customer experiences, create innovative products, and operate with greater efficiency will be best positioned to thrive in the AI-driven financial future.

The Road Ahead

Strategic Recommendations

As financial institutions navigate the AI-driven transformation, a well-thought-out strategy is crucial for success.

Strategic Investments

Financial institutions should prioritize strategic investments in AI technologies that align with their business objectives. This includes investing in AI talent, data infrastructure, and advanced analytics platforms. Institutions should also focus on building data governance frameworks to ensure the quality, security, and privacy of data, which is the foundation of AI-driven decision-making.

AI investments should be directed toward areas that offer the greatest potential for competitive advantage. For example, customer-facing AI applications, such as personalized financial services and AI-powered chatbots, can enhance customer experiences and drive loyalty. Similarly, AI in risk management can provide more accurate assessments and proactive mitigation strategies, reducing potential losses.

Forming Strategic Partnerships

Organizations should consider forming partnerships with fintech companies, AI startups, and technology vendors to leverage their expertise and accelerate innovation. These partnerships can provide access to cutting-edge technologies and allow institutions to deploy AI solutions more quickly and efficiently.

Partnerships can also help institutions navigate the complexities of AI adoption to overcome implementation hurdles and meet other challenges like regulatory compliance and ethical considerations. By working with specialized partners, companies can ensure that their AI initiatives meet industry standards and are implemented responsibly.

Emphasizing Continuous Innovation

Financial institutions must embrace a culture of continuous innovation to stay competitive. This means not only adopting AI technologies but also fostering an environment that encourages experimentation, learning, and agility. Institutions should establish processes for regularly reviewing and updating their AI strategies, ensuring they remain aligned with changing business needs and technological advancements.

Continuous innovation also involves upskilling employees and promoting a mindset of lifelong learning. By providing training and development opportunities in AI and related fields, firms can empower their workforce to contribute to AI initiatives and drive the organization's success.

Long-Term Vision

Looking ahead, the role of AI in shaping the future of finance will be profound, but it will require a careful balance between technological advancement, ethical responsibility, and regulatory compliance.

The Role of AI in Finance

AI will inevitably become interwoven through the financial industry. It will be as ubiquitous as software and the internet are today, touching every part of the business, and transforming everything from customer interactions to risk management and investment strategies. As AI technologies mature, they will enable institutions to offer more personalized and predictive financial services, enhance operational efficiency, and manage risks more effectively. The institutions that successfully integrate AI into their core operations will be better positioned to adapt to changing market conditions and meet the evolving needs of their customers.

Ethical Responsibility

The expansion of AI-powered tools and services will bring new challenges that businesses haven't had to solve for in the past. All businesses will have a responsibility to ensure that the AI systems they use are fair, transparent, and accountable, which means addressing issues such as algorithmic bias, data privacy, and the potential for unintended consequences.

Regulatory Compliance

The regulatory environment for AI in finance is still evolving, and institutions must stay ahead of these developments to ensure compliance. This will require ongoing engagement with regulators, industry groups, and other stakeholders to shape the future of AI regulation. Financial institutions should proactively participate in discussions around AI governance, contributing to the development of standards and best practices that promote responsible AI use.

CONCLUSION

As we have explored throughout this book, artificial intelligence is profoundly transforming the financial industry, reshaping everything from job roles and business models to customer experiences and the competitive landscape. While this transformation presents challenges, it also opens up a whole new world of potential for businesses and professionals who are ready to embrace change and adapt.

In this new world, routine tasks will be automated, allowing human employees to focus on higher-value activities that require creativity, critical thinking, and emotional intelligence. It is a future where personalized financial services are the norm, powered by AI's ability to understand and anticipate individual needs; and where businesses can collaborate and compete in new ways, leveraging AI to drive innovation and deliver superior value.

Realizing this future will require a proactive approach from companies and professionals alike. Companies will have to invest strategically in AI technologies, form key partnerships, and foster a culture of continuous innovation. Professionals will need to commit to lifelong learning, acquiring the AI and data science skills that will be in high demand while also honing the uniquely human skills that machines can't replicate. You've taken a massive step in that direction by reading this book. The foundation you've received from the topics we've covered here will open doors to learning new skills and how to apply them in practice.

As AI becomes more integrated into financial decision-making, ensuring fairness, transparency, and accountability will be paramount. By proactively addressing these ethical considerations and engaging with regulators to shape AI governance, the financial industry can build trust and confidence in these powerful technologies.

The road ahead is not without its challenges, but it is also filled with tremendous opportunities. By embracing AI as a tool for empowerment rather than a threat, financial institutions and professionals can navigate this transformation successfully.

As we move forward into this new era, we should approach AI with a spirit of openness, curiosity, and continuous learning. The institutions and individuals who will thrive in this future will be those who are not afraid to experiment, to challenge old assumptions, and to reimagine what is possible.

The AI revolution in finance is just beginning, and its full impact will unfold over the coming years and decades. Those who are prepared to adapt and lead in this new world will be best positioned to seize the opportunities it presents. So let us move forward with optimism and determination, ready to learn, innovate, and grow in the AI-driven future of finance.

GLOSSARY

Accuracy: The proportion of correct predictions out of all predictions made by a machine learning model, reflecting the model's overall effectiveness in classifying or predicting data points correctly. It is a common evaluation metric used in classification tasks to assess how well the model has learned from the training data and how well it generalizes to new, unseen data.

Action: A decision made by a reinforcement learning (RL) agent that influences the environment's state. Actions are selected based on the agent's policy, aiming to maximize cumulative rewards through trial and error.

Activation Function: A function applied to the output of a neuron in a neural network, introducing non-linearity and enabling the network to learn complex patterns. Common activation functions include ReLU, sigmoid, and tanh.

Adversarial Debiasing: A technique used in machine learning to reduce biases in AI models by training the model to be fair across different groups, often used to address discrimination concerns in AI-driven decisions.

Adversarial Training: A training process used in generative adversarial networks (GANs) where two models (a generator and a discriminator) are trained simultaneously, with the generator creating data and the discriminator trying to distinguish between real and generated data.

Agent: The entity in reinforcement learning that interacts with the environment by making decisions or taking actions in pursuit of a specific goal, based on observations or states. The agent learns and adapts its strategy over time to maximize cumulative rewards through trial and error.

AI Agent: An autonomous entity in artificial intelligence that perceives its environment, makes decisions, and takes actions to achieve specific goals. AI agents can range from simple programs that respond to basic inputs to complex systems that interact with the world, learn from their experiences, and adapt their behavior over time.

Algorithm: A set of rules or instructions given to a machine to help it learn from data and make predictions or decisions.

Algorithmic Bias: A phenomenon where AI algorithms produce unfair or biased outcomes due to historical data that reflect human biases. This can lead to discriminatory practices if not addressed, particularly in financial decision-making.

Algorithmic Risk: The risk associated with the use of algorithms in financial decisions, where model errors or biases can lead to significant financial losses or systemic risks.

Algorithmic Trading: The use of computer algorithms to automatically execute trades in financial markets, based on predefined rules and real-time data. It allows for high-speed and high-frequency trading, optimizing trade execution far beyond human capabilities.

Anomaly Detection: AI techniques used to identify unusual patterns or behaviors in data that deviate from expected norms, often applied in fraud detection, compliance monitoring, and risk management.

Anti-Money Laundering (AML): Regulatory and compliance measures to detect, report, and prevent money laundering activities within financial institutions. AI enhances AML by analyzing transaction patterns and customer behaviors to identify suspicious activities.

Artificial General Intelligence (AGI): A theoretical form of AI that would have the ability to perform any intellectual task that a human can, exhibiting broad, adaptable intelligence. Unlike Artificial Narrow Intelligence (ANI), AGI would be capable of reasoning, planning, problem-solving, and learning across various domains, mimicking the cognitive abilities of the human mind.

Artificial Intelligence (AI): A branch of computer science aimed at creating machines capable of performing tasks that typically require human intelligence. AI systems can learn from data, recognize patterns, make decisions, and adapt to new inputs, performing tasks like image recognition, natural language processing, and decision-making.

Artificial Narrow Intelligence (ANI): Also known as Weak AI, this refers to AI systems designed to perform specific tasks within a narrow scope, such as voice recognition or image classification. ANI is the current state of AI technology, capable of high efficiency and accuracy within its specialized domain but lacking general intelligence and adaptability.

Artificial Neural Network (ANN): A computational model inspired by the human brain, consisting of layers of interconnected nodes (neurons) that process input data to produce an output.

Artificial Super Intelligence (ASI): A hypothetical level of AI that would surpass human cognitive abilities in virtually every domain. ASI would not only replicate human intelligence but vastly exceed it, potentially leading to significant technological advancements and posing existential risks if not properly controlled.

Attention Mechanism: A neural network mechanism that selectively focuses on specific parts of the input data, enhancing the model's ability to capture relevant dependencies and relationships. It is particularly used in Graph Attention Networks (GATs) to weigh the importance of different nodes in a graph.

AutoML (Automated Machine Learning): The process of automating the end-to-end process of applying machine learning to real-world problems, making it easier for finance professionals to build models without deep technical expertise.

Autoregressive Model: A type of generative model that generates data one step at a time, with each step conditioned on the previous steps, commonly used in language models like GPT.

Backpropagation: An algorithm used for training neural networks, where the error is calculated at the output and propagated backward through the network to update the weights.

Batch Normalization: A technique to improve the training of deep neural networks by normalizing the input of each layer to have zero mean and unit variance, stabilizing and accelerating the training process.

Bayesian Inference: A statistical method in AI that updates the probability for a hypothesis as more evidence or information becomes available, commonly used in risk assessment and decision-making in finance.

Behavioral Analytics: The use of AI to analyze decision-making patterns and behaviors, helping to identify and mitigate biases in investment decisions. Behavioral analytics aim to enhance objectivity in processes traditionally influenced by human intuition.

Bias: A parameter added to the output of a neuron before applying the activation function, allowing the model to better fit the training data by shifting the activation function.

Bias-Variance Tradeoff: The balance between a model's ability to generalize (variance) and its simplicity (bias), where high bias leads to underfitting, and high variance leads to overfitting.

Big Data: Large and complex datasets that are generated at high volume and velocity, often requiring advanced tools and algorithms, such as AI, to process, analyze, and derive insights from them. AI systems can quickly identify patterns, correlations, and anomalies within big data that would be difficult or impossible for humans to discern.

Biometric Authentication: The use of AI to verify identities through biometric data such as facial recognition, voice recognition, or fingerprints, ensuring secure and accurate customer authentication.

Black Box Problem: A challenge in AI and machine learning where the internal workings of an algorithm are not easily interpretable or understandable by humans, making it difficult to explain how decisions are made.

Blockchain: A decentralized digital ledger technology that records transactions across multiple computers, ensuring security and transparency. AI is often integrated with blockchain for enhanced fraud detection and contract automation in finance.

Capital Asset Pricing Model (CAPM): A financial model used to determine the expected return of an asset based on its risk, represented by its sensitivity to market movements (beta), and the risk-free rate of return.

Chatbot: An AI-powered software application designed to simulate human conversation. Chatbots interact with users via text or voice, handling tasks like answering questions, providing customer support, or facilitating transactions. They use natural language processing (NLP) and machine learning to understand and respond to user inputs, often improving over time through continuous learning.

Classification: A type of supervised learning where the goal is to categorize input data into predefined labels or classes, such as determining whether a transaction is fraudulent or not.

Clustering: An unsupervised learning technique used to group similar data points together based on their features.

Collaborative Intelligence: The combination of human expertise and AI capabilities to enhance decision-making. In investment banking, venture capital, and private equity, this approach leverages the strengths of both human judgment and machine learning.

Computer Vision: A field of AI that enables computers to interpret and process visual information from the world, such as images and videos, often used in financial applications like document processing and economic forecasting.

Conditional Generative Model: A generative model that generates data conditioned on a specific input, such as an image caption conditioned on an image or text generated based on a prompt.

Convolutional Neural Network (CNN): A type of deep neural network specifically designed for processing structured grid data, such as images, by using convolutional layers to automatically detect spatial hierarchies of features.

Cross-Validation: A technique for evaluating the generalization ability of a model by splitting the data into several subsets, training on some, and validating on others.

Data Augmentation: Techniques used to increase the diversity of data available for training models by generating new data points from existing data, often used in machine learning to improve model performance.

Data Governance: The framework of policies and procedures to ensure the accuracy, completeness, and security of data used in AI models, critical for maintaining data integrity and regulatory compliance.

Data Imputation: The process of replacing missing data with substituted values in a dataset, often used in financial data preparation to ensure the accuracy and completeness of models.

Data Preprocessing: The process of preparing raw data for analysis by cleaning, normalizing, transforming, and organizing it, essential for ensuring the quality and accuracy of machine learning models.

Decision Trees: A tree-like model used for both classification and regression in supervised learning.

Deep Learning: A subset of machine learning that involves neural networks with many layers (hence "deep"), allowing the model to learn hierarchical representations of data.

Deepfake: Synthetic media, often video or audio, generated using AI to convincingly mimic real people, typically using generative adversarial networks (GANs) or other generative models.

Deep Reinforcement Learning: A subfield of reinforcement learning that combines deep learning with reinforcement learning principles. It involves training deep neural networks to approximate the policy or value functions that guide an agent's actions in an environment.

Decentralized Finance (DeFi): A blockchain-based form of finance that does not rely on central financial intermediaries like banks, instead using smart contracts on blockchains like Ethereum to offer financial services such as lending, borrowing, and trading.

Diffusion Model: A type of generative model that starts with noise and iteratively refines it to generate realistic data, often used in image and audio generation.

Dimensionality: The number of features or variables in a dataset. High dimensionality can make a dataset more complex and harder to analyze, often leading to the "curse of dimensionality," where the volume of the feature space increases, making it difficult for the model to find meaningful patterns.

Dimensionality Reduction: Techniques used to reduce the number of features in a dataset while retaining the most important information (e.g., Principal Component Analysis).

Discriminator: In generative adversarial networks (GANs), the model that tries to distinguish between real data and data generated by the generator, guiding the generator to produce more realistic outputs.

Dropout: A regularization technique in neural networks where random neurons are ignored during training, reducing the chance of overfitting by preventing the model from relying too heavily on any single neuron.

Environment: The world in which an agent interacts in reinforcement learning.

Epoch: A single pass through the entire training dataset. Multiple epochs are typically used during the training process to iteratively adjust the network's weights.

Ethical AI: The field of study focused on ensuring that AI systems are developed and deployed in a manner that is fair, transparent, and respects privacy, particularly important in financial applications where decisions can significantly impact individuals' lives.

Evaluation Metrics: Quantitative measures used to assess the performance of a machine learning model, including accuracy, precision, recall, F1 score, mean squared error, and root mean squared error.

Explainable AI (XAI): Techniques and methods used to make AI models more transparent and understandable, allowing stakeholders to see the factors influencing AI-driven decisions, enhancing trust and regulatory compliance.

F1 Score: The harmonic mean of precision and recall, used as an evaluation metric in classification tasks.

Feature: An individual measurable property or characteristic of the data being used for learning (input variables).

Feature Engineering: The process of selecting, modifying, or creating new features from raw data to improve the performance of machine learning models, often involving domain knowledge and creativity.

Feature Selection: The process of selecting a subset of relevant features for use in model training, which can help reduce dimensionality, improve model performance, and reduce overfitting.

Federated Learning: A machine learning approach that allows models to be trained on data distributed across multiple devices or locations without needing to centralize the data, preserving privacy and security.

Feedforward Neural Network: The simplest type of neural network where information moves in one direction—from input to output—without cycles or loops.

Fully Connected Layer: A layer in which every neuron is connected to every neuron in the previous layer, typically used in the final layers of a neural network.

Generative Adversarial Network (GAN): A type of generative model consisting of two neural networks, a generator that creates data and a discriminator that evaluates it, trained together in a process of adversarial learning.

Generative AI: A branch of AI that focuses on generating new content, such as text, images, or data, based on learned patterns from training data, widely used in chatbots and creative applications.

Generative Model: A type of AI model that learns the distribution of a dataset to generate new, similar data, such as images, text, or audio.

Global Minimum: A global minimum is the point where a function's value is the lowest among all possible points. In machine learning, reaching the global minimum of the loss function means the model has found the best possible solution across the entire parameter space, yielding the lowest error.

Gradient: In machine learning, a gradient is a vector that represents the direction and rate of the steepest increase or decrease of a function. It's used in optimization algorithms like gradient descent to adjust model parameters, guiding the model towards minimizing the error by moving in the direction that reduces the loss function most rapidly.

Gradient Descent: An optimization algorithm used to minimize the loss function by iteratively adjusting the network's weights in the direction of the steepest descent of the gradient.

Graph: A data structure consisting of nodes (or vertices) and edges (connections between nodes), used to model pairwise relationships between entities. In machine learning, graphs are used to represent and analyze complex structures such as social networks, transportation systems, and financial transaction networks, enabling the application of algorithms like Graph Neural Networks (GNNs) to learn from the interconnected data.

Graph Attention Network (GAT): A type of Graph Neural Network (GNN) that uses attention mechanisms to adaptively weigh the contributions of different neighbors when updating node representations in a graph.

Graph Convolutional Network (GCN): A type of Graph Neural Network (GNN) that extends the concept of convolution from grid-structured data (like images) to graph-structured data, enabling the model to incorporate local context into node representations.

Graph Neural Network (GNN): A class of neural networks designed to process and learn from data structured as graphs, where nodes represent entities and edges represent relationships. GNNs are particularly useful for tasks involving complex interconnections, such as fraud detection and risk assessment in finance.

High-Frequency Trading (HFT): A form of algorithmic trading where large numbers of orders are executed in fractions of a second to capitalize on small price discrepancies, typically involving advanced technology to minimize latency.

Hyperparameter: Configuration settings used to tune the machine learning model that are set before the learning process begins (e.g., learning rate, number of layers in a neural network).

Integrated Risk Management: An AI-driven approach to managing different types of risk (market, credit, liquidity) as a unified whole, rather than in silos, by analyzing diverse data sources and identifying correlations across risks.

Intrinsic Interpretability: The quality of some AI models that allows them to be inherently understandable by humans, with clear and straightforward relationships between inputs and outputs.

K-Means Clustering: An algorithm used to partition data into K distinct clusters in unsupervised learning.

Know Your Customer (KYC): A regulatory process where financial institutions verify the identity and assess the risks associated with customers. AI enhances KYC by automating identity verification and continuous risk monitoring.

Label: The output variable or target value that the model is trying to predict, especially in supervised learning tasks.

Language Model: A type of generative AI model that predicts and generates text, trained on large datasets of text to learn the probability distribution of sequences of words.

Latent Space: A high-dimensional space where generative models like GANs or VAEs map input data during training, enabling the model to generate new data by sampling from this space.

Latent Vector: A point in the latent space used to generate data in models like GANs, representing compressed information that the model uses to reconstruct or generate new instances.

Learning Algorithm: A method or procedure used by a machine learning model to learn patterns from data, adjusting its parameters to improve its performance over time.

Learning Rate: A hyperparameter that controls the size of the steps taken during gradient descent. A small learning rate means the model learns slowly, while a large one may cause the model to converge too quickly to a suboptimal solution.

Linear Regression: A supervised learning algorithm used for predicting continuous values.

Local Interpretable Model-Agnostic Explanations (LIME): A technique used in explainable AI to provide insights into complex machine learning models by approximating the model's behavior with a simpler, interpretable model for a specific prediction.

Local Minimum: In optimization, a local minimum is a point where a function's value is lower than at any nearby points but not necessarily the lowest overall. In machine learning, it refers to a solution where the model's loss function is minimized within a small region, but there might be other regions with even lower values.

Logistic Regression: A supervised learning algorithm used for binary classification tasks.

Long Short-Term Memory (LSTM): A type of recurrent neural network (RNN) architecture designed to remember long-term dependencies and sequences, often used in tasks like language modeling and time series forecasting.

Loss Function: A function that measures the difference between the predicted output of a model and the actual output, guiding the optimization process during training.

Machine Learning (ML): A branch of AI where algorithms learn from data to make predictions or decisions without being explicitly programmed, widely used in risk management, fraud detection, and customer service.

Markowitz Modern Portfolio Theory (MPT): A foundational finance theory that guides the construction of investment portfolios to maximize return for a given risk level or minimize risk for a given return. It emphasizes diversification to reduce overall portfolio risk.

Mean Squared Error (MSE): The average of the squared differences between predicted and actual values, used as an evaluation metric in regression tasks.

Model: A mathematical representation of a process, trained using data, to make predictions or decisions.

Model Interpretability: The degree to which a human can understand the cause of a decision made by a machine learning model, crucial for ensuring transparency and trust in AI systems.

Monte Carlo Simulation: A computational technique that uses random sampling to estimate the probability distribution of possible outcomes, widely used in finance for risk assessment and portfolio optimization.

Named Entity Recognition (NER): A technique in natural language processing that identifies and classifies proper nouns (such as names of people, companies, or locations) in text, often used in financial document analysis.

Natural Language Generation (NLG): AI technology that automatically generates human-like text from structured data, used to draft financial reports, compliance documentation, and other textual outputs.

Natural Language Processing (NLP): A subfield of AI focused on the interaction between computers and human language, enabling AI systems to analyze and understand financial documents, news, and reports.

Neural Network: A computational model composed of layers of neurons that process input data through weights and activation functions to generate predictions or decisions.

Neuron: The basic unit in a neural network, receiving inputs, applying a weighted sum, adding a bias, and passing the result through an activation function.

News Analytics: The process of analyzing news articles, press releases, and other text-based sources to extract actionable insights, often using NLP and machine learning to inform trading strategies or investment decisions.

Noise: Unwanted or random variations in data that can obscure the underlying patterns the model is trying to learn. Noise can lead to overfitting, where the model learns to capture these random variations instead of the true signal, reducing its ability to generalize to new data.

Non-Linear Relationships: Complex interactions between variables that cannot be captured by simple linear models. AI techniques, particularly deep learning, excel at modeling these relationships, improving predictions and analyses in finance.

Open-Source: Software or tools that are freely available to the public, allowing users to view, modify, and distribute the source code. In the context of AI and machine learning, open-source platforms, libraries, and frameworks (such as TensorFlow, PyTorch, and Scikit-learn) enable widespread collaboration and innovation by providing access to advanced tools and resources for developing and deploying machine learning models.

Optical Character Recognition (OCR): A technology that converts different types of documents, such as scanned paper documents or PDFs, into editable and searchable data by recognizing the characters in the images.

Optimizer: In machine learning, an optimizer is an algorithm or method used to adjust the parameters of a model to minimize the loss function. It guides the model's learning process by determining how to update the weights and biases during training to improve the model's performance. Common optimizers include Stochastic Gradient Descent (SGD), Adam, and RMSprop.

Overfitting: A modeling error that occurs when a neural network learns the training data too well, including its noise and outliers, leading to poor generalization to new data.

Parameter: A variable in a machine learning model that is learned from the data during training, such as weights in a neural network, which determines how the model makes predictions or decisions.

Pattern Recognition: The ability of AI systems to identify patterns in data and use them to make predictions or decisions. Pattern recognition is fundamental to many AI applications, including image recognition, speech recognition, and predictive modeling.

Policy: The strategy that the agent follows to choose actions in reinforcement learning.

Pooling Layer: A layer in a convolutional neural network that reduces the spatial dimensions of the input, typically using operations like max pooling or average pooling, helping to reduce the computational load and prevent overfitting.

Portfolio Optimization: The process of selecting the best portfolio (asset distribution) to maximize returns for a given level of risk, often enhanced by AI techniques to analyze vast amounts of financial data.

Post-hoc Interpretability: Techniques used to explain the behavior of a machine learning model after it has been trained, helping to clarify how decisions are made by otherwise opaque models.

Precision: The proportion of true positive predictions out of all positive predictions, used as an evaluation metric in classification tasks.

Predictive Analytics: The use of AI and machine learning to analyze current and historical data to make predictions about future events, often used in fraud detection, risk assessment, and personalized financial services.

Principal Component Analysis (PCA): A dimensionality reduction technique that simplifies datasets by reducing the number of variables while retaining most of the original information.

Prompt Engineering: The process of designing and refining prompts to guide the output of generative AI models, particularly in natural language processing tasks like text generation.

Quantum Computing: A type of computing that uses quantum bits (qubits) to perform calculations exponentially faster than classical computers. Quantum computing leverages principles of quantum mechanics, such as superposition and entanglement, to solve complex problems, including optimization and cryptography, which are crucial in finance.

Quantum Machine Learning (QML): An emerging field that combines quantum computing with machine learning algorithms. QML aims to enhance the performance of machine learning tasks, such as data classification, clustering, and regression, by using quantum algorithms to process large datasets more efficiently than classical approaches.

Qubit: The fundamental unit of quantum information, analogous to the bit in classical computing. Unlike a classical bit, which can be either 0 or 1, a qubit can exist in a state of 0, 1, or both simultaneously (superposition), enabling quantum computers to perform many calculations at once.

Quantum Entanglement: A phenomenon where two or more qubits become interconnected such that the state of one qubit directly influences the state of the other, no matter the distance between them. Entanglement is a key resource in quantum computing, allowing for faster information processing and more complex computations.

Quantum Supremacy: The point at which a quantum computer can perform a calculation that is practically impossible for even the most powerful classical supercomputers to achieve. Reaching quantum supremacy has significant implications for fields like cryptography, optimization, and complex simulations in finance.

Random Forest: An ensemble learning method used for classification and regression tasks that operates by constructing multiple decision trees during training. Each tree in the forest is built on a random subset of the data, and the final prediction is made by averaging the predictions of all the trees (for regression) or by taking a majority vote (for classification). This approach improves accuracy and reduces the risk of overfitting compared to individual decision trees.

Recall: The proportion of true positive predictions out of all actual positives, used as an evaluation metric in classification tasks.

Rectified Linear Unit (ReLU): A popular activation function in neural networks that outputs the input directly if it is positive, otherwise, it outputs zero, helping to mitigate the vanishing gradient problem.

Recurrent Neural Network (RNN): A type of neural network designed to handle sequential data, where connections between nodes form directed cycles, allowing the network to maintain a memory of previous inputs.

Regression: A type of supervised learning where the goal is to predict a continuous output value, such as forecasting stock prices or estimating credit risk.

Regularization: Techniques used to prevent overfitting by adding additional information or constraints during training, such as L1/L2 regularization, dropout, or data augmentation.

Reinforcement Learning (RL): A type of machine learning where an agent learns to make decisions by taking actions in an environment to maximize cumulative rewards, commonly used in areas like trading and robotics.

Relation Extraction: A technique in NLP that identifies and categorizes the relationships between entities mentioned in text, such as "company A acquired company B," used to understand connections and interactions in financial data.

Reward Function: A component of reinforcement learning that defines the goal of the agent by assigning a reward to actions based on their outcomes, guiding the agent toward optimal behavior.

Robo-Advisors: AI-powered platforms that automate the investment process, providing personalized investment strategies based on algorithms and machine learning, democratizing access to financial advice.

Robotic Process Automation (RPA): The use of AI to automate repetitive, rule-based tasks such as data entry, report generation, and compliance checks, improving efficiency and accuracy.

Root Mean Squared Error (RMSE): The square root of the mean squared error, providing error in the same units as the output variable, used as an evaluation metric in regression tasks.

Sampling: The process of generating data from a generative model by drawing samples from the learned distribution or latent space, often used in the context of GANs, VAEs, or autoregressive models.

Self-Attention: A specific type of attention mechanism where the model focuses on different parts of the same input sequence. It enables the model to weigh the importance of each element in relation to every other element within the same sequence, making it particularly effective in tasks like text processing and sequence modeling.

Sentiment Analysis: A technique in NLP that assesses the emotional tone or sentiment of text data, categorizing it as positive, negative, or neutral, often used in market analysis to gauge investor sentiment.

SHapley Additive exPlanations (SHAP): A method used in explainable AI to provide consistent and interpretable explanations of machine learning model predictions by assigning each feature a contribution to the final decision.

Smart Contracts: Self-executing contracts with the terms of the agreement directly written into code, often deployed on blockchain platforms. AI can enhance smart contracts by automating and optimizing contractual conditions.

Softmax: An activation function typically used in the output layer of a neural network for multi-class classification problems, converting logits into probabilities.

State: The current situation of the agent in the environment in reinforcement learning.

State Representation: In reinforcement learning, the process of defining the state of the environment based on relevant features and variables that the agent uses to make decisions.

Supervised Learning: A type of machine learning where the algorithm is trained on labeled data (input-output pairs) to learn a mapping function that predicts outputs for new inputs.

Support Vector Machine (SVM): A supervised learning algorithm used for classification tasks that finds the optimal boundary between classes.

Systemic Risk: The risk of collapse in an entire financial system or market, as opposed to the risk associated with any individual entity. GNNs can model the interconnections in financial systems to assess and mitigate systemic risk.

Tensor: A multi-dimensional array used to represent data in deep learning, generalizing matrices to higher dimensions.

Testing: The phase where a trained model is evaluated using new data (testing data) to assess how well it generalizes to unseen data.

Text-to-Image Generation: A generative AI task where a model generates images based on text descriptions, typically using models like DALL-E or similar frameworks.

Time Series Data: Data points collected or recorded at specific time intervals, often used in financial analysis to track variables like stock prices, interest rates, or economic indicators over time.

Tokenization: The process of converting ownership rights of an asset into a digital token on a blockchain, often facilitated by AI to manage and trade tokenized assets efficiently.

Training: The process of feeding data into a machine learning algorithm to help it learn patterns and relationships in the data.

Transaction Networks: Networks formed by financial transactions between entities, where nodes represent entities (e.g., individuals, companies) and edges represent transactions (e.g., money flows, ownership). GNNs are used to detect fraud and assess risk in such networks.

Transfer Learning: A machine learning technique where a model developed for a particular task is reused as the starting point for a model on a different but related task, reducing the need for large amounts of data.

Transformer Model: A type of neural network architecture widely used in generative AI, particularly for natural language processing tasks, characterized by its ability to process sequences of data in parallel and capture long-range dependencies.

Underfitting: When a model is too simple to capture the underlying patterns in the data, resulting in poor performance on both the training and new data.

Unsupervised Learning: A type of machine learning where the model identifies patterns and relationships in data without labeled outcomes, often used for anomaly detection and customer segmentation.

Vanishing Gradient Problem: A challenge in training deep neural networks where gradients become extremely small, causing the network to stop learning or learn very slowly, often addressed by using ReLU or LSTM units.

Variational Autoencoder (VAE): A type of generative model that encodes input data into a probabilistic latent space and then decodes it to generate new data, balancing data reconstruction accuracy and regularization.

Virtual Assistants: AI-powered tools similar to chatbots but more advanced, capable of handling more complex tasks, understanding context, and providing personalized, proactive support.

Voice Recognition: A technology that allows AI systems to recognize and interpret human speech, enabling voice-activated commands and interactions, often used in AI-powered virtual assistants and customer service.

Weight: A parameter in a neural network that is learned during training, representing the strength of the connection between neurons and determining how input data is transformed as it passes through the network.

Weight Initialization: The process of setting the initial weights of a neural network before training begins, which can significantly impact the network's ability to learn. Common methods include random initialization and Xavier initialization.

Zero-Shot Generation: The ability of a generative model to generate data for tasks or categories it was not explicitly trained on, leveraging its understanding of the underlying data distribution.

ACKNOWLEDGMENTS

First and foremost, I want to thank my wife, Kerith, without whose unconditional love and support this book and most other things I've done in my life would not have been possible. Words cannot express how much she means to me.

In a maybe not-so-close second are Gerry and Sylvia Anderson, the creators of the 1970s sci-fi series "Space 1999," episodes of which ran on loop in the background as I wrote these pages. Thanks, too, to Commander Koenig for pulling me through.

And I'd especially like to thank my editor and friend, Andy Burt, who came in and helped me clean up this pedantic mess, transforming it into the hefty, but legible tome it is today.

Oh ... and Dall-E for creating most of the images in this book ... save for the cover, which my good friend Tom Martin (www.tommartindesign.com) designed, and for the ones I cobbled together in PowerPoint, and the ones I cajoled Kerith into creating. And also, Grammarly and the small army of AI-powered chatbots that got me through several patches of writer's block and editing when I'd written myself into a corner and "rewrite for clarity" became my favorite prompt.

And I'd like to thank my readers and students and anyone who's made it this far. If you're reading the acknowledgements in a textbook about AI and finance, you've gone above and beyond, and I salute you.

All glory to the Flying Spaghetti Monster!

Later, nerds!

ABOUT THE AUTHOR

Glenn Hopper is an author, speaker, and lecturer on the intersection of artificial intelligence and corporate finance. His best-selling book, *Deep Finance: Corporate Finance in the Information Age*, explores how technology is reshaping financial processes. Glenn's work emphasizes the transformative role of AI and automation in enhancing financial operations, improving accuracy, and driving data-driven decision-making.

Glenn is the Head of AI Research and Development at Eventus Advisory Group, where he spearheads the creation of AI-powered solutions tailored to the finance and accounting industries. His insights and expertise are regularly featured in publications such as Fortune Magazine and Forbes, and he contributes to platforms including the AI Journal and the Forbes Finance Council.

With more than two decades of experience as a CFO in private equity-backed companies, Glenn has led initiatives in finance automation, M&A, and operational efficiency. He has a proven track record of modernizing finance departments by integrating data and automation to achieve better business intelligence, faster reporting, and improved operational performance.

In addition to his professional work, Glenn is an instructor at Duke University's Executive Education program, the Corporate Finance Institute, AICPA/CIMA, and LinkedIn Learning, where he teaches financial leaders how to leverage AI in their strategic planning – making advanced AI concepts accessible to finance professionals worldwide.

Glenn holds a Master of Liberal Arts (ALM) in Extension Studies in Finance from Harvard University, where he also completed the Harvard Business Analytics Program; and an MBA from Regis University in Denver, CO.

He is an avid runner and cyclist and can frequently be found running along the Mississippi River near his home in Memphis, where he lives with his wife, Kerith, and is frequently visited by his grown children, Katherine, North, and Abigail.